THE CAMBRIDGE
THAT NEVER WAS

F. A. Reeve

The Oleander Press
of Cambridge

The Oleander Press
17 Stansgate Avenue
Cambridge CB2 2QZ

©1976 F. A. Reeve and The Oleander Press

ISBN 0 902675 72 9

Printed by
John G Eccles Printers Ltd, Inverness

THE CAMBRIDGE THAT NEVER WAS

Introduction

Had some of the early proposals been carried out, Cambridge today would have been a very different city. There could have been a railway station opposite Christ's Pieces in Emmanuel Road; Downing College might have been built on Parker's Piece; all of the old buildings of Corpus Christi College, including the picturesque Old Court, might have been swept away; the Fitzwilliam Museum might have resembled the Parthenon and be situated in front of King's College, or on the site of Caius College, which was to be removed to the Backs, or on various other sites. Instead of the famous "Bridge of Sighs" we might have had a suspension bridge or an iron bridge, and at one time it was intended that Gibbs' Fellows' Building at King's College should be "Gothicised."

In recent times there have been grandiose plans for the redevelopment of the Lion Yard and of the Fitzroy/Burleigh areas on a much larger scale than those now executed or contemplated. There have been numerous proposals for new roads to attempt to ease traffic congestion, beginning with Holford's scheme of 1950 for a "Spine Relief Road," no part of which has been built. This would have taken part of Jesus Green and Christ's Pieces. Later, a road across the "Kite" area from the Four Lamps to Gonville Place was said to be essential, although traffic experts concluded later that it was "not worth while."

Another scheme was for an underground road capable of taking double-decker buses, to run from Emmanuel Road, under the gardens of Emmanuel College and beneath the Lion Yard, to emerge at Jesus Lane. Gordon Logie, who produced this plan, also proposed that when a new road from Chaucer Road to Barton Road had been built, Fen Causeway and its bridges should be demolished. Schemes for a "Main Town Road" and one along the "Railway Route" have been dropped, as has the bold scheme of Professor Parry Lewis for a second large shopping and residential centre.

From the Fifteenth Century to 1950

King Henry VI's revised plans for his college envisaged magnificent buildings. The Chapel was designed to form one side of a splendid court. The east range towards the High Street (now King's Parade) would have had rooms in three storeys, with a handsome Gate-tower in the centre. Other ranges would have contained a Hall, Library, Lecture Rooms and more chambers. A smaller court west of the Hall was planned for a kitchen, bakehouse, brewhouse and stables. Between the Chapel and the river, the scheme envisaged a cloistered cemetery with a lofty bell-tower.

The only part of this grandiose plan to be carried out was the Chapel. In view of the intention to join it to the projected east range, the window in the southeast corner had glass only in the upper half, and it was not until 1841 that the stone filling the lower half was removed.

*   *   *

Sir Christopher Wren's first design for Trinity College Library, made when the south and north ranges of Nevile's Court were only about two-thirds of their present length, was for a free-standing circular building, rising from a square plinth, and surmounted by a dome and cupola. It was to have been about 90 feet high and 65 feet wide, with a double staircase on the east side, leading to a portico of semi-engaged columns supporting a pediment. In the interior, there were to be stone seats with stone tables round the walls, and three galleries with a staircase in each of the four angles. It would be lighted by the cupola and through semi-circular openings in the drum of the dome.

After his second design for the existing rectangular building had been adopted, the south and north ranges of the court were extended to join the ends of the Library. The side of the building towards the river was designed in a plainer manner because it was supposed that it would not often be seen, but later, after the grounds had been landscaped, the Library was of course seen equally frequently from both sides.

5

St Catharine's College began to rebuild in 1674, and the range facing Milne Street (now Queens' Lane) was finished by 1687. Loggan's view of 1688 depicts a complete quadrangle, but he was anticipating something that was never carried out. An inscription on his view says that it depicts, not "the remains and ruins of the old College buildings (a sight too ugly to appear as a picture among the other Colleges of this University), but only the buildings recently set up, as well as those which, today only planned, in a short time will be actually constructed." Loggan was unduly optimistic, as the east range was never built.

It is fortunate that the original plan to close the Court by building a Library or chambers was abandoned, because the height would have been too great for the area of ground enclosed. Viewed from the street, the college has retained a dignified, spacious look which drew the admiration of John Ruskin. The lawn once had a flower garden in the centre, still in existence in 1814, and described as "a small but pretty spot, and kept very neat, and on a Pedestal in the Centre stood a Statue of Charity, with a child at her breast, and two more by her side," and until 1921 there was a grove of elms in the forecourt.

In 1913 an anonymous benefactor offered to pay for a Library and chambers to be built in the forecourt, but when the Fellows eventually learned the name of the donor, they decided to reject his offer.

*   *   *

In 1714 Nicholas Hawksmoor, a pupil and later a collaborator of Sir Christopher Wren, was invited to submit designs for new buildings at King's. He proposed to erect a monumental gateway, a Hall to the south, a cloister with a bell-tower, and a new court west of the old fifteenth century court. He made two models of a Fellows' Building.

His plans were not adopted, and in 1723 James Gibbs, the most important architect of the first half of the eighteenth century, was appointed to design new buildings. He proposed to erect detached ranges on three sides to form, with the Chapel, a complete quadrangle, but only the west range, the Fellows' Building, was erected. It was intended that this building would be adorned with statuary, but this was not carried out, probably through lack of funds. When it was finished in 1729, no more building took place for almost a century.

*   *   *

It was probably while Hawksmoor was working on his plans for new buildings at King's that he conceived a bold scheme entitled *The Town of Cambridge as it ought to be reformed*. On a smaller scale, this plan resembled Wren's plan for the area of London devastated by the Great Fire.

He planned to demolish the south side of Petty Cury and to construct a wide street leading from the entrance of Christ's College to King's College Chapel. Between Great St Mary's and St Edward's Passage there would be a "Forum" or covered market. St Edward's would be pulled

St Catharine's College as it might have been if the Library (last range, foot of drawing) had not been abandoned on the advice of James Essex in the mid-18th century

7

Looking towards Trinity College, from a projected Forum.
Part of Hawksmoor's plan for Cambridge "as it ought to be reformed."

down to provide a site for a new University Church, leaving Great St Mary's to be used exclusively by the townsfolk. A Senate House beside the new University Church would be linked to it by a colonnade.

Trinity Street would be made straight, and St John's Street widened, and a new street would be made between Trinity and Sidney Sussex Colleges. Beyond the Great Bridge, he planned two squares.

Hawksmoor's plan was probably the most visionary scheme ever made for an English provincial town, but no-one had asked him to prepare it, no-one championed it, and no part of the plan was executed. Had it been carried out, the commercial buildings on the east side of the High Street would have been replaced by the new "Forum," University Church, and

8

Senate House. The King's Parade of today would have been a more grandiose thoroughfare, though we would have lost the features that enhance its charm, the small-scale shops and houses which contrast with the magnificent Chapel on the other side.

*   *   *

For centuries prior to 1730 the University had lacked a large building in which important ceremonies could take place. A Senate House was contemplated in 1640, but was not begun until 82 years later. Sir James Burrough, Master of Caius 1754-64, a distinguished amateur architect who designed several college buildings, proposed a scheme which was adapted by James Gibbs.

This plan envisaged a Senate House in its present position, with an identical building opposite to accommodate the University Registry and Printing House, the two wings to be linked by a new University Library. While the Senate House was being built (1722-30), many people violently opposed the projected south building. One of these was the Master of Caius, who said that it was "a Scheme for which I do in my Conscience believe the whole World will condemn Us; a Scheme that will so effectively shut out all View of that noble Fabrick King's-Chapell, that I wonder how the University or that College can bear it; and a Scheme so injurious to Caius College, that I am fully resolv'd not to bear it."

Proposals for a building to match the Senate House were revived again when plans were being made to enlarge the Library. The beautiful east front of the Old Schools was begun in 1755 to the plans of Burrough, though Stephen Wright was responsible for the elevations and supervised the construction. There was still much opposition to the plan for a building which would have partially obscured the view of King's College Chapel, and it was again abandoned.

The plan was revived once more in 1783, and in 1792 a design by Sir John Soane for a building comprising a museum, lecture room and music room was rejected.

*   *   *

At Peterhouse, Burrough, who designed the Fellows' Building in a Palladian style in 1738-42, and ashlared the Principal Court in 1728, intended to pull down the building of 1633 which has a pleasing oriel towards Trumpington Street, but it was spared.

*   *   *

In 1741 Essex proposed that the ground in King's west of the river should be planted with trees in regular lines around a rectangular lake or basin communicating with the Cam, and that a circular temple with a dome should be erected on a central mound west of this lake.

*   *   *

At Queens', a building of clunch and stone erected in 1564 beside Silver Street was replaced in 1756 by a brick range designed by Essex,

9

The West front of the new Building at Queen's Coll

Plan by Essex for a riverside building at Queens' College, 1756

but this is only one wing of what was intended to be a much larger range. The college planned to demolish all of the attractive red brick buildings beside the river, including the Lodge, and build another identical wing, with a central block surmounted by a pediment. A tall classical doorway, with a smaller pediment, would have given access to the bridge. The *Cambridge Guide* (1796) has an illustration showing what was planned but never executed.

* * *

In 1773 James Essex published a plan for rebuilding Corpus Christi College in the Italian style, with a single quadrangle left open on the Trumpington Street side. He proposed to demolish all of the old buildings, including the picturesque Old Court, the first court of any Cambridge college to be completed.

* * *

Mr Lancelot Brown, the celebrated landscape gardener, was presented with a piece of plate in 1778 for his work in improving the grounds of St John's. He is probably the same Mr Brown mentioned by Dyer who made a plan to improve the Backs. He proposed that the river from Newnham should be removed to a greater distance from the colleges, and pass between St Peter's Church and Magdalene College, and that all of the houses near the bridge should be removed.

* * *

At a meeting of the nobility, gentry, and freeholders of Hertfordshire,

10

Essex, Cambridgeshire, Huntingdonshire and the Isle of Ely held in 1788, resolutions supporting a scheme promoted by the Navigation Committee of the City of London for a canal from the Stort at Bishop's Stortford by way of Saffron Walden to the Cam at Cambridge were passed by a large majority. A Bill was introduced in Parliament in 1811, but was opposed and thrown out in committee.

* * *

Cambridge might have lost one of its most cherished open spaces, Parker's Piece. When Sir George Downing died in 1749, he left money to establish a new college, but legal complications delayed building for a very long time. In 1796 an agreement was made with the town that Parker's Piece would either be sold or leased for 999 years for the site. The town was also willing to sell ground at Pound Hill. These agreements were subject to the college obtaining a charter of incorporation within a year, but as this charter was not granted until 1800, the agreements became null and void.

In 1798 the town sold ground at Doll's Close in Maid's Causeway for £350, but in 1801 it was decided that a more convenient site would be the common called Pembroke Leys, and an Act of Parliament authorised this site. James Wyatt prepared two designs for buildings in 1804, but these were not approved and several other architects submitted plans. The designs of William Wilkins were chosen in 1806.

The large site that had been acquired extended from Lensfield Road to the south side of Downing Street, and there was a proposal for a new road to run in a straight line from the end of Jesus Lane, along the east side of the Market Place and Corn Exchange Street to St Andrew's Hill, with the new college forming an impressive termination to a long vista, but the scheme was not adopted.

* * *

In 1815 there was a proposal to enclose Coe Fen, Coldham's Common and Christ's Pieces, but fortunately the Corporation refused its assent.

* * *

When, in 1816, Richard, seventh Viscount Fitzwilliam, bequeathed to the University the interest on £100,000 and his important collection of paintings, engravings, illuminated manuscripts and books, a site had to be found for a building to house the collection. The University was anxious to find one near the Senate House, and King's College was asked to sell the property it owned along King's Parade in front of the college. Understandably, King's was unwilling. The next choice was the Bull Inn, but St Catharine's would not sell. The third suggestion was ground in the Backs opposite Clare Hall Piece, which was said to be large enough for the Museum, a new Botanical Garden, and an Observatory.

Other suggested sites were the south side of the old Botanic Garden

The Fitzwilliam Museum as it might have been. A rejected design of 1835 by Rickman and Hussey. Courtesy: British Architectural Library (RIBA), London

fronting on Downing Street; behind Pembroke College; the north side of the grounds of Downing College; Senate House Yard; the area between King's Parade, Bene't Street, Peas Hill and St Mary's Passage; and the area between Great St Mary's and St Michael's. Another scheme was to remove Caius College to a site in Trumpington Street beyond Peterhouse and leased to Mr Pemberton, and to build a Museum which would be an exact replica of the Parthenon in Athens, but without the sculpture.

Caius, on a cramped site, seemed willing to move, but Mr Pemberton refused to surrender his lease. Finally, the present site in Trumpington Street was chosen in 1821.

Apart from the location, the building itself might well have been in a completely different style, because twenty-seven architects submitted a total of thirty-six designs. Rickman and Hussey submitted a design in the Gothic style, very similar to the New Court of St John's College. The most extraordinary feature of this design was a very tall tower which would appear to be most unsuitable to form part of a Museum.

* * *

By 1822 King's College had sufficient funds to complete their quadrangle. Gibbs' design was abandoned, and after a competition, the plans of William Wilkins, amended by a committee of architects, were chosen.

As it was executed, the plan differed in several significant ways from the original proposals. Wilkins had intended to have a cloister behind the Screen, and that it would be separated by gateways from the Chapel to the north and the Hall range to the south. He also intended to have a second Fellows' Garden between Trumpington Street and King's Lane, to build the Library at right angles to the Hall, and separate the Provost's Lodge from the remainder of the range by a cloister on the site of the present Library.

The old King's Lane entered Trumpington Street about 70 feet north of its present position. Mr Cory, the owner of a house on the corner, required an exorbitant price for it, so the court was made 22 feet narrower than had been intended.

The most surprising part of the scheme was: "Agreed that when the above Contract shall be completely executed, the Provost be hereby authorized to enter into another Contract with any person or persons he may think fit to Gothicise Gibbs' Building, according to the plan originally proposed by Mr Wilkins."

* * *

When, in 1825, St John's decided to build New Court, the college intended that it should be of brick and in "as nearly as may be the style of the present Second Court." Rickman and Hutchinson were appointed to prepare the designs, and in January 1827 it was still intended that the exterior should be of red bricks with stone dressings. The building was, however, executed in white brick faced with stone on all sides except the north, and the style is Perpendicular Gothic, quite unlike that of Second Court.

The famous enclosed bridge, commonly called the Bridge of Sighs, might have been very different, as the architects originally intended it to be a suspension bridge. A second plan was for an iron bridge, but finally a stone bridge was built when it was found that it would cost less than had been expected.

* * *

King's College sold their old buildings behind the Old Schools to the University in 1829, and it was intended to erect a new large University Library on the site. The designs of C.R. Cockerell envisaged the removal of all the old buildings to make way for a completely new quadrangle, but only one range, bordering Senate House Passage, was constructed.

* * *

When the Eastern Counties' Railway reached Cambridge in 1845, the station was situated a considerable distance from the centre of the town at the insistence of the University. There were many proposals for lines and for stations much closer to the centre, and had they been carried out, several would have caused a serious loss of amenity.

A proposal of 1836 for a railway from London to York, passing through Cambridge, envisaged a station at the east end of Jesus Green, which meant that the lines would have passed near the Backs. Another proposal was for a station near the farmhouse at the end of what is now Latham Road.

The Great Northern Railway was also anxious to reach Cambridge, and at a shareholders' meeting in 1851 the Chairman said: "The Eastern Counties . . . say to us you shall not come to Cambridge . . . Now, if there be any Eastern Counties shareholders here I will tell them with perfect respect that my duty will be to go to Cambridge. I will do it in the most amicable and harmonious way possible, if they will permit me, but go I must and undoubtedly I shall."

The Great Northern promoted several Bills, one for a station adjoining the south side of the Botanic Garden, and another for a station on Coe Fen at the rear of the Museum of Classical Archaeology, with a branch line to join the Eastern Counties Railway near Hills Road bridge. This scheme was rejected when the University complained that the line would pass "under the windows of St Peter's College and at the back of the University."

In 1862 the Eastern Counties became the Great Eastern Railway, and in 1864 the Great Northern promoted a Bill for either an independent line or for running powers over the G.E.R. to a station between Orchard Street and Emmanuel Road, the line to run in a cutting with bridges at Brooklands Avenue, Hills Road, and Mill Road, or over the G.E.R. line to Mill Road, and then a new line between the Workhouse (now the Maternity Hospital) and the cemetery to Emmanuel Road.

The latter scheme was supported by the Borough Council, but opposed by the Master of Christ's College, who said that a goods and coal depot in Emmanuel Road would "render Christ's and Emmanuel Colleges almost uninhabitable owing to the continued howling and whistling of engines." While the Bill was being considered, the two companies came to terms, and the Great Northern secured running powers over a portion of the G.E.R. lines, and a separate platform at the existing station.

*   *   *

It was not until 1963 that Cambridge obtained an indoor swimming pool, but there have been several earlier schemes to provide one. In 1857 the New Music Hall and Public Rooms Company, Cambridge, Ltd., supported by some of the College Masters and leading citizens of the town and county, was formed to carry out an ambitious scheme. The company secured the site of the Hoop Hotel in Bridge Street, near the corner of Jesus Lane, and prepared plans for a large building.

The scheme envisaged a concert hall for about 2,000 persons, with an organ and a stage for orchestras, on the first floor, above a second-class swimming bath to be entered from Park Street, and a first-class bath to be entered from Jesus Lane. The main entrance in Jesus Lane was to have a glazed arcade 30 feet long, and a grand staircase leading to a promenade, with supper-, refreshment- and card-rooms.

The plans included a hotel with an entrance in Bridge Street, with a large clubroom, billiard tables and three lecture rooms. Although many people welcomed the proposals, there was some opposition, and in May 1858 it was announced that the scheme had been abandoned.

*   *   *

Following the fire of 1849 which destroyed eight buildings of a block on the west side of the market, it was considered that it was a good occasion to enlarge and improve market facilities. The Corporation obtained a Bill authorising it to borrow £40,000 for making improvements. "The Mayor, Aldermen, and Burgesses may enlarge and improve the Market-Place, and take by compulsion certain specified property situate in the Parishes of St Mary the Great and St Edward, and any other lands which they may purchase by agreement, and may enlarge or rebuild the Guildhall, or erect a new one on a more eligible site."

In 1859 the Town Council invited architects to submit plans for entirely new municipal offices. It was intended to build, first of all, an Assembly Room, Free Library and Reading Room, Town Clerk's office, Committee Rooms, Telegraph Office and a School of Art, but the designs were also to include a Corn Exchange, Post Office, Inland Revenue Office, Council Chamber, Magistrates' Court, and so on, to be erected later. Only parts of this ambitious scheme were carried out, and the large Assembly Room, with a Public Library below it, was opened in 1865.

The Corn Exchange built in 1842 at the Downing Street end of Slaughter House Lane (now Corn Exchange Street) soon became too

15

small, and as part of the 1859 scheme for new municipal buildings it was intended that a new Exchange would be built between the Assembly Hall and Peas Hill. Instead, in 1870, the present site to the south of Wheeler Street was selected.

Alderman Peed said that money could be raised by building on the commons, 20 houses on part of Coe Fen, 15 between Parker's Piece and East Road, 5 near Zion Chapel and 17 on Midsummer Common in Maid's Causeway. An income of £600 per annum might be obtained from Coldham's Common, £125 from Stourbridge Common and £70 from Sheep's Green by letting them for market gardens. The Council voted against this proposal.

The Vice-Chancellor and some ratepayers involved the Town Council in a law suit in an attempt to prevent any of the money borrowed to improve market facilities from being used for building a new Corn Exchange. They argued that the site in Wheeler Street was independent and not connected with the Market Place. When the case was heard, many people gave evidence in support of the Council's contention that Wheeler Street was used as an extension to the market.

It was said that Mr Wheeler put baskets on the roadway in front of his shop; Mr Johnson put out casks and tubs; Th. Smith of Saffron Walden laid hides in Wheeler Street; butchers had stalls against the Red Cow Inn; Mr Bleak, shoemaker, worked in an open stall on the pavement; chairs, tables and other furniture were placed in Parson's Court; and Mr Clayton exposed fish for sale opposite his shop and hung up hares and rabbits suspended from sticks or poles. A man employed to collect market tolls said that although Petty Cury and Market Street were not part of the market, he had collected tolls from butchers' stalls in the Cury and from stalls for suckers, tins and baskets in Market Street.

Judgement was given in favour of the Corporation, and the new Corn Exchange was completed in 1875.

* * *

The custom of holding a service at the summit of the tower of St John's Chapel could not have become established if the building had been constructed in accordance with the original design. Scott's first design of 1862 provided for a spire at the intersection of the chapel and antechapel, but in 1864 Henry Hoare, a former Scholar, suggested a tower, and offered to contribute £1,000 per annum until the work was completed, "subject to the condition of living so long." Scott altered his design to include a tower which cost an additional £6,100. Unfortunately for St John's, Mr Hoare died after being injured on the Great Eastern Railway in 1865 when he had contributed only £2,000, and the college had to meet the remainder of the cost.

* * *

After the death of Prince Albert, the University considered plans for a memorial. It was suggested that it might take the form of a Museum for Natural Science, or a bronze statue to be placed in Senate House Yard. Finally, it was decided to have a life-size marble statue. There were arguments about where it should be sited. The sculptor wanted it to be placed in the Fitzwilliam Museum, but a University Syndicate recommended that it be placed in the Senate House. This Report was rejected, and a fresh Syndicate decided to place it in the Museum, where it was set up in 1877.

*   *   *

It has already been stated that there were a number of proposals to put up another building to match the Senate House. When a new Divinity School was planned, Professor William Selwyn, who had given nearly £9,000 towards the cost, preferred this site and claimed that as the projected building would not be as large or as high as the Senate House, it would not spoil the view of King's College Chapel. The University also considered a plan to build in the Old Botanic Garden, now the site of the New Museums, but finally chose the site opposite St John's College on which the building was opened in 1879.

*   *   *

At Pembroke College, in 1879, there were plans to demolish one of the most interesting buildings, the Old Chapel licensed by the Pope in 1354, and the first of the college chapels in Cambridge, which has a beautiful plaster ceiling of 1690 by Henry Doogood of London, who worked in more than thirty of Wren's City churches. These plans were abandoned after strong protests by Sir G.G. Scott.

*   *   *

In 1897 the Town Council again considered plans for rebuilding the Guildhall, and appointed an architect, Mr Belcher, who reported that the existing buildings were so inadequate and defective that it would be impossible to preserve any of those between the Large Assembly Hall and the Market Square. He said that: "No town possesses a finer site for its Corporation buildings than Cambridge, and their importance should be emphasised in the new design."

Mr Belcher produced a design for an elaborate façade. Arcades with pillars supported the first floor, and the central entrance was surmounted by a baldachin with eight tall stone columns. The ends of the building were crowned with large stone balls.

He said of his design that: "By careful attention to proportion and scale, a broad and dignified effect has been obtained, thus avoiding the charge of unnecessary extravagance, and preserving the simplicity so characteristic of this style; and where ornament has been introduced it has been for the special purpose of emphasising the more important

17

Belcher's design for a new Guildhall, 1897

features of the building."

With its colonnade, pillars and pinnacles, and hardly a square foot left undecorated, it would be considered far from simple today. The estimated cost was £40,000, but some people thought that it might be as much as £60,000, and the scheme was dropped. A major project was not undertaken until about forty years later.

* * *

The Cam Bridges Act of 1889 authorised the Victoria Bridge built in 1890 and a second bridge to be constructed nearer to Chesterton. When the Chesterton Urban District was incorporated into the Borough in 1911, a promise was given to the residents that the second bridge would be built by 1917. Half a century was to elapse before this promise was honoured.

* * *

In 1895 there was a scheme for a road on a viaduct across Coe Fen so that the horse trams could go down Bateman Street and continue to the corner of Barton Road. A correspondent of the *Cambridge Chronicle* wrote that this road would attract "the people from the slums and alleys of our congested, unhealthy town into the green lanes and fair meadow land of the country where the wild violet blows and the daffodil dances in the breeze and the winter aconite hangs its golden bell." In spite of this lyrical prospect, nothing came of the scheme.

18

In 1896 the Borough Council agreed to erect a ladies' bathing place on Hell Meadow, with a bath 75 feet by 30 feet enclosed in a structure of wood and iron, but the scheme was abandoned when the miller of the King's Mill would not allow water from the bath to be discharged into Coe Fen Ditch.

*　　　*　　　*

When plans for the north court of Emmanuel College were being considered just before the First World War, there was a proposal that Emmanuel Street should be closed. Instead, a subway was built beneath it. One can imagine how the closure of this street would have complicated traffic problems today.

*　　　*　　　*

Before Fen Causeway was built, after much opposition, in 1924-26, a number of different lines for a road to relieve Silver Street were considered, notably in 1910. Among them was a proposal for a bridge at the west end of Mill Lane and a road across Laundress Green. Six different routes starting from the end of Coe Fen Lane were considered, and two which were more or less on the line of Chaucer Road to Barton Road.

*　　　*　　　*

The former White Horse Inn, an attractive building of 1423 now occupied by the Folk Museum, remains, but when it was purchased for £1,500 in 1933 by the Council, it was intended to demolish it to effect a road widening at that corner.

*　　　*　　　*

Christ's College, in 1935, invited Walter Gropius, one of the pioneers of modern architecture, who had come to England a few months previously, to submit designs for a building to face Hobson Street. His design set the building back from the street, and would have had a forecourt planted with trees. There were to be shops at ground level, with three floors of undergraduate rooms above. The college decided to reject the design, which would have greatly improved the appearance of Hobson Street, and instead we have, in King Street, the ugly rear of Denys Lasdun's building.

*　　　*　　　*

Plans for a palatial swimming stadium were announced in 1935. A site behind Parkside was secured, and the scheme envisaged a swimming pool 100 feet by 42 feet. There were to be seats for 400 spectators, with standing room for another 200. A tea room, 60 feet long, was planned for the front of the building, and there were to be 16 Zotofoam baths on the balcony floor, with massage rooms and rest rooms.

Two years later, two other syndicates announced that they intended to erect an indoor swimming bath, but all of these projects were abandoned.

* * *

In 1946, when the population of the town was about 80,000, the Council agreed with one dissentient to erect a larger Assembly Hall when circumstances should permit, but we still await the propitious moment. The councillor who opposed this said that the increased population of Cambridge was a floating population, here today and probably gone tomorrow, and that unless some serious steps were taken to encourage childbirth, the population of the country would decrease in fifty years by roughly 50%, and Cambridge would of course share in that position.

* * *

In 1956 the Council proposed to erect a Floral Hall to hold at least 2,000 persons, and a swimming bath, on Christ's Pieces, and the Borough Surveyor was instructed to prepare preliminary plans.

* * *

Before the Second World War, the main proposal for easing traffic congestion in the centre was a Ring Road. Parts of it were constructed, but the scheme was abandoned in 1947, to be reconsidered again in 1976.

Since the Holford Report of 1950
Roads and Shopping

For a quarter of a century, the "Spine Relief Road" was endlessly debated by the City and County Councils, the University authorities, and was the subject of hundreds of letters in the local press. It was the chief road proposal in a Report made to the County Council in 1950 by Sir William Holford and Professor Myles Wright.

The Report concluded that to relieve traffic congestion along the main route through the centre of the city, from Hills Road to Huntingdon Road, and also along Queen's Road, a relief road should be constructed from the corner of Histon Road, to cross the river by a new bridge near Jesus Lock, then beside Jesus Green to Jesus Lane and across Christ's Pieces to a widened Emmanuel Street.

On the opposite side of St Andrew's Street, a New Emmanuel Street would join a dual carriageway, New Guildhall Street, parallel with Corn Exchange Street, at a large road island. Three central car parks at Lion Yard, King Street and Park Street were suggested, and a new covered country bus station where Bradwell's Court has since been built.

20

The importance of constructing a new Chesterton Bridge and its approaches was emphasised. In West Cambridge, a New West Road would connect Huntingdon Road, Madingley Road and Barton Road, with a continuation across a new bridge to Chaucer Road and Trumpington Road.

The space overlooking the Pool at the foot of Mill Lane and adjacent to the Mill public house is often thronged by numerous students and tourists, a splendid spot where one can relax and watch boats on the river, but it might have been radically altered if one of Holford's suggestions had been adopted. When the Report was issued, the iron Silver Street Bridge was coming to the end of its life, and it was suggested that instead of rebuilding, it might be better to construct a new bridge at the bottom of a widened Mill Lane, to connect with Silver Street just east of Newham Grange. This would give a more direct route from Pembroke Street, and take traffic away from Queens' College. The Silver Street Bridge was, in fact, rebuilt in 1959.

Holford believed that, with a small extension, the historic centre could accommodate all large-scale shopping requirements. Additional shops could be built in the Lion Yard on both sides of the proposed New Guildhall Street; in Emmanuel Road and Parker Street; in King Street; and off Bridge Street, just beyond the Round Church. The Report recommended that a large area of West Cambridge should be reserved for the future needs of the University and Colleges.

The Development Plan submitted to the Minister by the County Council in 1952 was basically the Holford Proposals, but with reservations about the Spine Relief Road and the deletion of the section of the New West Road between Madingley Road and Huntingdon Road. Instead of new shops in Emmanuel Road, the County wished to develop a number of small centres for shopping in the outer suburbs.

The University lodged a formal objection to parts of the Development Plan, including the development of the Lion Yard area for commerce and car parking. They suggested that there was a substantial pressure for an expansion of shopping which could best be sited in the "New Square-Fitzroy Street neighbourhood." Due to its shape, this became known as the Kite area. The University was opposed to the Spine Relief Road.

The Minister's decision of 1954, following a Public Enquiry, gave approval to most of the Development Plan, but said that the Lion Yard shopping centre should be a pedestrian precinct. A Joint Advisory Committee with representatives of the City, County and University was set up, but during their deliberations the University continued to oppose additional shops in the central area.

*   *   *

In 1955-6 Sir William Holford prepared designs for new Assize Courts to be built to face Castle Street on the lawn and car park of the Shire

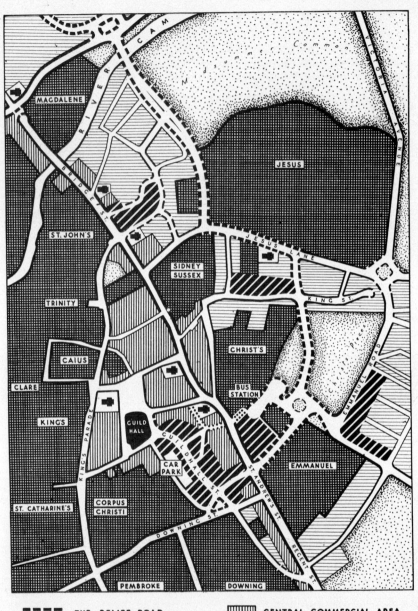

MAGDALENE
JESUS
ST. JOHN'S
SIDNEY SUSSEX
TRINITY
KING ST.
CHRIST'S
CAIUS
CLARE
BUS STATION
KING'S
GUILD HALL
EMMANUEL
CAR PARK
ST. CATHARINE'S
CORPUS CHRISTI
PEMBROKE
DOWNING

RIVER CAM
BRIDGE ST.
KINGS PARADE
JESUS LANE
EMMANUEL ROAD
ST. ANDREWS ST.
DOWNING ST.
REGENT ST.
GUILDHALL ST.

==== THE RELIEF ROAD   ⛛⛛⛛ CENTRAL COMMERCIAL AREA
▨▨▨ PROPOSED NEW SHOPS   ▦▦▦ UNIVERSITY AND COLLEGES

Holford's proposals for Central Cambridge, 1950

22

Hall, i.e. where the former Courts had stood. After a delay of twenty years, it has been decided that Courts will eventually be built on top of the Lion Yard Car Park.

*   *   *

King's College, in 1957, considered a plan to demolish property on a site bounded by St Mary's Passage, Peas Hill, St Edward's Passage, and a new lane beginning at David's bookshop. Sir Leslie Martin and Colin St John Wilson prepared a plan for two levels of step-backed terraces above ground floor shops. The scheme would have destroyed some attractive old buildings and the mediocre St Mary's Chambers, and the college decided not to proceed with it. Some features of the design were later realised in Sir Leslie's Harvey Court, built for Caius College in West Road.

*   *   *

In 1958, the City and County agreed on a scheme for the Lion Yard, and property companies were invited to submit detailed plans. At this time it was proposed to develop the whole area between Petty Cury, St Andrew's Street, Downing Street and Corn Exchange Street, except Great St Andrew's Church and the Post Office.

A scheme by Edgar Investments Ltd. was approved in principle. This envisaged the rebuilding of the entire area, with a four-storey frontage in Petty Cury and a three-storey pedestrian precinct at right angles to the Cury, incorporating two twelve-storey office blocks. There would be a new Central Library, a twelve-storey hotel near Downing Street, and an underground park for 730 cars.

At a Public Enquiry held in 1959 the University called evidence to show that there was no need for additional shopping facilities in Cambridge, but accepted the possibility of limited commercial development in the Lion Yard, together with University, civic and residential uses.

The Minister's decision of 1960 rejected the proposals as submitted, and concluded that the authorities had not made a case for shopping expansion. In the same year, the University proposed that an area of 65 acres bounded by Newmarket Road, East Road, Parkside and Emmanuel Road should be redeveloped for a large regional shopping centre, a car park for at least 10,000 cars, and some residential accommodation. It was envisaged that this would become the principal shopping centre for the city, and that some form of compulsion should be used if necessary to move the larger shops from the existing centre. This proposal was a complete reversal of the evidence given on behalf of the University at the 1959 Enquiry to show that no additional provision for shopping was needed.

The First Review of the Cambridge Town Map was submitted by the

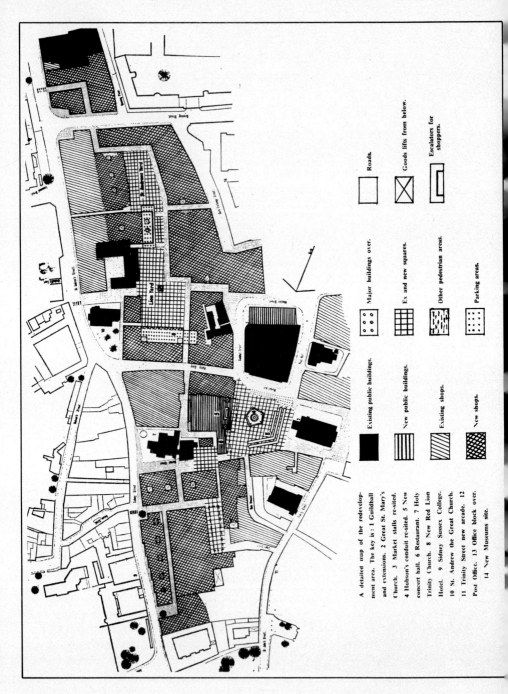

A detailed map of the redevelopment area. The key is : 1 Guildhall and extensions. 2 Great St. Mary's Church. 3 Market stalls re-sited. 4 Hobson's conduit re-sited. 5 New concert hall. 6 Restaurant. 7 Holy Trinity Church. 8 New Red Lion Hotel. 9 Sidney Sussex College. 10 St. Andrew the Great Church. 11 Trinity Street new arcade. 12 Post Office. 13 Office block over. 14 New Museums site.

Roads.

Goods lifts from below.

Escalators for shoppers.

Major buildings over.

Ex and new squares.

Other pedestrian areas.

Parking areas.

Existing public buildings.

New public buildings.

Existing shops.

New shops.

Logie's plan, 1963

24

County Council to the Minister in 1961. This included revised plans for the Lion Yard, expansion of shopping in the Fitzroy-Burleigh Street area, the Chesterton Bridge scheme, and an Inner Relief Road, the latter being Holford's Spine Relief Road but sited east of Christ's Pieces.

In the same year, the University published *The Shape of Cambridge. A Plan*, and mounted an exhibition in the Corn Exchange, suggesting that the expansion of shopping should be in the Kite area on a site of 60 acres, with parking for 7,000 - 10,000 cars. By rebuilding, residential accommodation could be increased even when space had been found for other uses. This plan said that the Lion Yard should be used for a civic centre, with a large, multi-purpose hall, library, arts centre, hotels and restaurants.

At a Public Enquiry in 1962 the University changed their arguments. They no longer proposed the development of the whole of the Kite area as a major regional shopping centre, but put forward a reduced scheme for shops on 12-14 acres. They continued to oppose any increase in the number of shops in the historic centre.

In 1963, Gordon Logie, the city architect and planning officer,

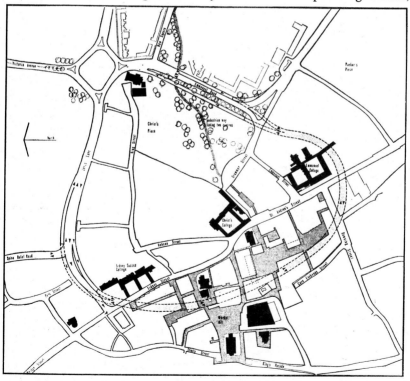

The underground road proposed by Logie, 1963

25

announced a grandiose scheme for large pedestrian precincts, new shops and a concert hall, and an underground road from Emmanuel Road, passing under the gardens of Emmanuel College, at the backs of shops in St Andrew's Street and the Lion Yard, then east of Market Hill, to emerge near the corner of Jesus Lane. This loop road, accommodating buses, vans servicing the shops, and cars, would have parking for 1,500 cars on three underground decks.

This scheme envisaged the replacement of all existing property in Sidney Street between Whewell's Court and Market Street. A large concert hall and a restaurant would replace property on the east side of the Market Square. In the centre of the Lion Yard there would be an open space extending almost to Downing Street, with the major block of shops along Corn Exchange Street.

The Guildhall would be extended at the rear. A pedestrian precinct would include Petty Cury, Market Square, Market Street, and the area between Great St Mary's and the Senate House. No through traffic would be allowed in King's Parade and Trinity Street.

Logie said that the work could be spread over 10-15 years. He had no idea what the actual cost would be, but thought that if the redevelopment were sufficiently profitable, the developers would be willing to provide the underground road and car parks without cost to the Council.

The Town Clerk said that the scheme was Mr Logie's "pipe-dream and Shangri-La" and the Civic Society said that the plan envisaged more rebuilding than was necessary or desirable. The Divisional Road Engineer of the Ministry of Transport considered that one definite weakness of the scheme was that all traffic entering the proposed underground road from any direction would have to traverse the Four Lamps roundabout, which would be grossly overloaded, and it would probably have to be converted into a multi-level flyover.

The Minister's decision on the Lion Yard proposals was given in 1964. He was not convinced that it was necessary to pursue a drastic policy for the removal of the regional shopping facilities from inside the ring of the colleges, but it was nevertheless clear that there was an intolerable congestion both of people and of vehicles within the existing ring. He was not satisfied that the proposals would be adequate if the whole of the city's shopping facilities were kept there.

He pointed out that the current movement towards the establishment of really large supermarkets had hardly yet reached Cambridge, but it was growing in other regional centres, and there was no reason to think that it would pass Cambridge by. The resulting increase in traffic could not be contained within the central area, and provision should be made elsewhere, on land to the east of Emmanuel Road and north of Parker Street.

He was prepared to authorise an increase of 30,000 square feet of shopping floor-space in the Lion Yard (the City and County had suggested

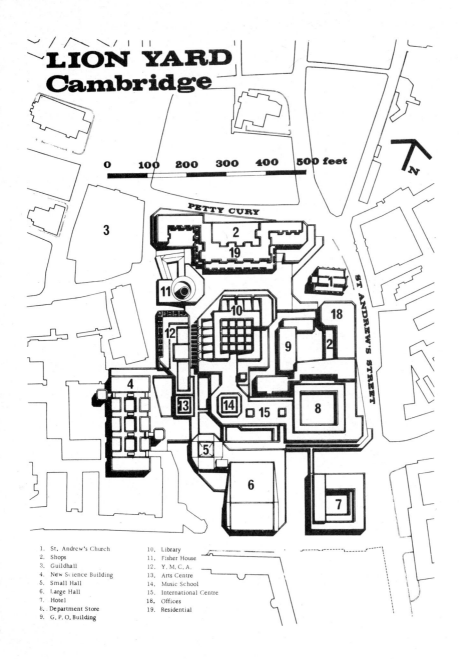

LION YARD
Cambridge

0   100   200   300   400   500 feet

N

PETTY CURY

ST ANDREW'S STREET

3

2

19

1

11

10

18

12

9

2

4

13

14

15

8

5

6

7

1. St. Andrew's Church
2. Shops
3. Guildhall
4. New Science Building
5. Small Hall
6. Large Hall
7. Hotel
8. Department Store
9. G. P. O. Building

10. Library
11. Fisher House
12. Y. M. C. A.
13. Arts Centre
14. Music School
15. International Centre
18. Offices
19. Residential

90,000 square feet), and he asked the Council to prepare a scheme for the Lion Yard concurrently with proposals for an extension of central shopping to the east of Emmanuel Road and north of Parker Street. The Minister rejected the proposals for a car park in King Street and for New Emmanuel Street.

A Report on traffic prepared by R. Travers Morgan and Partners in 1964 suggested routing the Inner Relief Road east of the proposed shopping in the Kite area.

Logie's second plan for the Lion Yard, announced in 1965, proposed that pedestrians and traffic should be separated by building a 12 feet high podium above a servicing and parking area, with the main access along Emmanuel Street. Petty Cury, Wheeler Street and Market Hill would be pedestrian precincts. A new Central Library would be near the centre of the Lion Yard, with a new University Music School and Y.M.C.A., and a large hall and a hotel could be built near Downing Street.

In 1966 Logie revealed yet another new plan for the development of the Lion Yard. In order to ensure the best chance of success for an extension of shopping either in the Fitzroy-Burleigh area or at the Emmanuel Street-Parker Street corner, it was now considered essential to reduce the number of shops in the Lion Yard. He therefore proposed that new shops should be placed along Petty Cury and to the west of St Andrew's Church, some to be grouped round a square, with a new concert hall in the centre. The new central library would be built above shops.

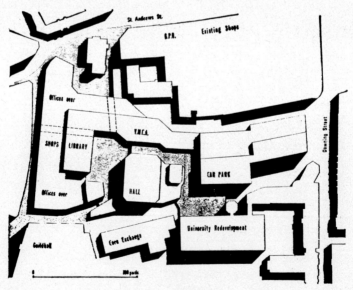

Logie's third plan for the Lion Yard, 1966

28

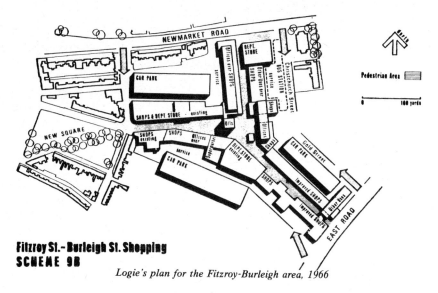

Fitzroy St.- Burleigh St. Shopping
SCHEME 9B

Logie's plan for the Fitzroy-Burleigh area, 1966

The City and County agreed to consider locating regional shopping facilities in the Fitzroy-Burleigh Street area, and Logie's new scheme assumed that it would be possible for the existing shops there to be enlarged so that in the course of time it could be transformed into a regional shopping centre. He proposed three pedestrian shopping streets — Fitzroy Street, Burleigh Street, and a new street from the junction of these to Newmarket Road. Three car parks would provide a space for a total of 1,800 cars.

*   *   *

In March 1966, Gordon Logie, at the request of the Joint Committee of the City, County and University, prepared a Report, *The Future Shape of Cambridge.* This suggested that new housing should be along linear tongues on existing main roads leading out of the city. He proposed a "Main Town Road" from Trumpington Road to Huntingdon Road, via Brooklands Avenue, Tenison Road, Gwydir Street, to link up with the proposed New Chesterton Bridge, then by Chesterton Road and Section One of the Inner Relief Road to Huntingdon Road.

From Trumpington Road he proposed a "Botanic Garden Road," via Chaucer Road and a bridge, to Barton Road. He said that if this road were constructed "the loss of amenity it would cause to Sheep's Green and the open country to the south should be made good by closing Fen Causeway and demolishing the road and bridge. The whole of Sheep's Green would be returned to its former rustic calm and it would be possible to direct the great weight of motor traffic away from the Backs and to close Queen's Road and Grange Road to cross traffic."

29

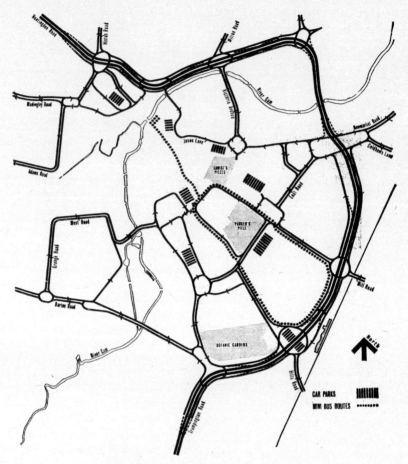

Logie's plan for a Main Town Road, 1966

In June 1966, the City Council accepted by 29 votes to 12 a recommendation that detailed drawings of Stages One and Two of the Inner Relief Road, i.e. from Huntingdon Road to Jesus Lane, should be submitted to the Minister and to the County Council.

For months during the latter part of 1966 the controversy about the Inner Relief Road raged, and numerous letters, for and against the scheme, appeared in the *Cambridge News*. In December, the City Council decided by 26 votes to 23 to reject Stage Two, but to ask the Minister to construct Stage One. The plan to create a regional shopping centre in the Fitzroy-Burleigh area and to develop the Lion Yard primarily as a civic centre was approved.

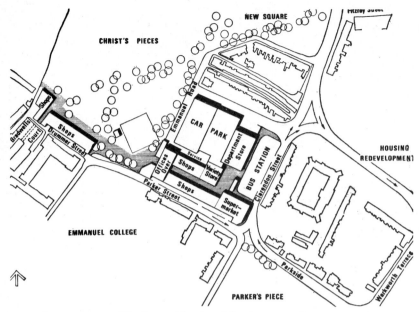

The County Planning Officer's plan, 1966

A Report submitted by economic consultants estimated that the city needed an additional 150,000 square feet of shopping space, but emphasised that new developments must be closely linked with the existing centre. Logie thereupon prepared six alternative schemes. The plan favoured was to develop the southern part of Christ's Pieces, and to extend the park towards Jesus Lane to compensate for the lost open space. Car parking would be on the opposite side of Emmanuel Road.

Describing this plan, Logie said: "The various groups of shops would be large pavilions set in open space. The general effect would be light and airy, more reminiscent of an exhibition than of a normal shopping centre." There was understandably much opposition to this scheme to place shops on Christ's Pieces, and a compromise plan of December 1966 by the County Planning Officer was for shops on the site of the bus station in Drummer Street, which would be replaced by a new station in Clarendon Street; shops along Parker Street, a car park in Emmanuel Road, and a department store between them.

*   *   *

In March 1967, Travers Morgan and Partners were appointed to carry out a Cambridge Transportation Study. When their Report was presented in 1972, it had cost £150,000.

In the same year, the City Surveyor issued a Report on *Cambridge*

31

Roads, Traffic and Car Parking. At this time, there were already schemes for Section One of the Inner Relief Road, Chesterton Bridge and its approaches, dual carriageways along East Road, Gonville Place and Lensfield Road, and the New West Road. It had been decided to build a car park at Queen Anne Terrace, and as part of this scheme it was proposed to take a small part of Parker's Piece for an entrance to an underground means of approach, so that traffic entering the car park from the direction of Hyde Park Corner would not have to make a right-hand turn across the stream of traffic. This was deleted after many protests. It was intended that another car park would form part of a comprehensive development scheme for Castle Hill.

The Report emphasised the need for outer bypasses and a Main Town Road from a widened Brooklands Avenue to the new Chesterton Bridge. It did not give high priority to the Outer Ring Road, but said that "it might be considered as an expensive refinement to the city's road system," pointing out that to travel by it from south to north would involve a journey of about nine miles, against six miles by the present inner ring. It would carry a relatively small flow of traffic and give insignificant relief to the central area.

There would have to be a link road between Four Lamps and Gonville Place, and he said that: "This involves the most important decision on roads which the City Council will be called upon to resolve for many years to come and is equal in importance to the Northern Access Road in relation to the closure of the 'spine'." Further, "There is no doubt whatsoever that if the city centre is ever to be closed to through traffic . . . then some link between Four Lamps and Gonville Place will have to be provided."

Eight draft layouts for this road were prepared, and three were selected for further consideration:—

Scheme 2(b) was to widen Emmanuel Road, Parker Street and Parkside. This would have destroyed the whole or part of four or five streets.

Scheme 6 was for a new 40 feet-wide road across the Kite area, from the northeastern corner of New Square to Gonville Place, with a gyratory system round Short Street, Maid's Causeway, Fair Street, and the north side of New Square or Willow Walk, and another gyratory system round the Police and Fire Stations. This scheme was excellent from a planning point of view, but the new road would go over three streets, destroy twenty houses, and have serious aesthetic drawbacks.

Scheme 8 was to widen Maid's Causeway and Newmarket Road, dual East Road, and have a gyratory system round the Police and Fire Stations. Much property would have to be taken in Maid's Causeway and Newmarket Road.

Travers Morgan and Partners, asked to report on these alternatives, recommended Scheme 6 without reservation, and the City Council subsequently decided in principle to construct this road.

32

In 1968 there was a Public Enquiry into Section Two of the Inner Relief Road, and in 1969 the Minister decided that a comprehensive review of the whole scheme should be included in the Transportation Study.

*　　　*　　　*

There was much opposition when in 1969 the City Council resolved to move all of the Market Square stalls to one end, and use the remainder as a car park. This plan was dropped, and today, stalls occupy the whole of the space.

*　　　*　　　*

Draft proposals for the Kite area, by Llewelyn-Davies, Weeks, Forestier-Walker and Bor, were released in February 1969. Their Report stated that the City Council had decided in principle to construct a Four Lamps/Gonville Place link road, and many alternative routes had been explored by the Town Centre Working Party. The consultants preferred a road which would join East Road near the Drill Hall, and suggested that it should go under New Square in a tunnel. New Square could then be returned to grass, and the pedestrian route between Christ's Pieces and Fitzroy-Burleigh would not be impeded. The road would displace about thirty-five houses. The Report suggested three multi-storey car parks to provide 2,000 parking spaces, and that the country bus terminus should be relocated in the northeast corner. The main shopping streets should be pedestrian precincts.

Redevelopment of the Lion Yard area finally began in 1970, and Elizabeth Way and Bridge were opened in 1971.

Draft proposals for the Fitzroy-Burleigh area were prepared in 1971 by a joint consortium of Samuel Properties Ltd. and Jesus College, in association with the City Council. Taking the Llewelyn-Davies Report as a basis, they made more detailed development proposals. Fitzroy Street and Burleigh Street would be retained as the main pedestrian routes, with the former enclosed by a high-level translucent covering.

The premises of the Co-op, Laurie & McConnal, and some other modern buildings would remain, but other properties would be re-developed to give an increase of approximately 340,000 square feet of shopping over the existing amount of approximately 303,000 square feet. The new buildings could provide a major department store, two multiple stores, two supermarkets, three medium-sized stores, and fifty-seven unit shops.

Parking for 1,500 cars could be provided above the shops on both sides of Fitzroy Street, and another 500-1,000 cars could be accommodated at the end of Burleigh Street. From the roof car parks, shoppers would reach the shopping mall by lifts or escalators. It was claimed that this plan made the optimum use of the land and reduced the site area.

A country bus station would be sited in an improved Napier Street, and there would be a one-way system round the Kite area, with a pedestrian link with the city centre below Emmanuel Road. A high-level restaurant was suggested above Burleigh Street at the junction with Fitzroy Street.

*　　*　　*

The Transportation Plan of Travers Morgan, issued in 1972, concluded that Section One of the Northern Access Road should be constructed and Victoria Road reserved for local traffic. It rejected proposals for a Kite link road between Four Lamps and Gonville Place: "Major development of the Inner Relief Road incorporating the Kite Link area between Four Lamps and Donkey's Common is not worthwhile." It did not favour the dualling of Gonville Place and Lensfield Road, and it also rejected the suggested Main Town Road and advocated instead the construction of a new road, the "Railway Route," from Trumpington to Milton Road. It took its name from the fact that for a large part of its route it would run beside the railway. As part of the New West Road, a route from Long Road was preferred to one using Chaucer Road. The Eastern Relief Road was said to be too far out to relieve effectively the inner areas of the city.

After about a year's examination of the Railway Route, both the City and the County Councils decided that it would be too expensive and too destructive of property. It would destroy nearly 100 houses, displace some business firms, and the cost of more than £10 millions would absorb all the funds available for roads for the next fifteen years.

As an alternative, the City Council has recommended that the Outer Ring Road scheme, partly built over forty years ago and then abandoned, should be revived. It is claimed that it could be completed in much less time and at half the cost. Only twelve houses would have to be demolished. If fully completed, it would link Histon Road with Milton Road via the Arbury peripheral road and King's Hedges Road. From there it would use part of Green End Road and Cam Causeway, cross the river on a new bridge to link with Wadlows Road and Barnwell Road. A link across Coldham's Lane with Brooks Road would eventually reach Trumpington Road via Perne Road, Mowbray Road and Long Road. On the western side, a road between Trumpington Road, Barton Road, Madingley Road and Huntingdon Road had already been proposed and partly agreed.

The most controversial part of the scheme is the link between Trumpington Road and Barton Road. The original proposal for a road between Chaucer Road and Barton Road aroused much opposition because it would run beside the Lammas Land and increase traffic along the residential portion of Barton Road. The route from Long Road and across Grantchester Meadows has been still more fiercely opposed.

34

A thorough survey, which took two years to complete, of the sub-region with Cambridge at its centre, was made by a team led by Professor Parry Lewis of Manchester University. His Report of 1973 concluded that although the population of the city has been controlled, the growth of the sub-regional population, increased mobility and tourism exert an ever-growing commercial pressure on the historic centre.

The population of the South Cambridgeshire area increased by 27% in the 'sixties, and it was estimated that the population of the city would increase by about 38,000 as a result of natural growth in the next twenty years.

His main proposal was that a second major centre should be built, preferably in the Trumpington area, to become comparable with the existing centre in about twenty years, and that then the population of Cambridge could rise from about 100,000, as now, to about 185,000. He insisted that this plan would not be viable if the Fitzroy-Burleigh scheme were implemented.

The City and County planning authorities concluded that his proposals could not be accepted. His bold scheme would be extremely costly, and even if it were thought to be desirable, lack of resources would make it impossible to carry it out within the time-scale contemplated.

*   *   *

In April 1976, the City Council decided to reject the scheme for a major regional shopping development in the Fitzroy-Burleigh area. It had been hoped that it could be carried out jointly by a development company, Samuel Properties Ltd.; Jesus College, the largest landowners in the district; and the Council. It was reported that the total cost would be about £30 million, and the proportion to be paid by the City Council would be about £13 million.

The Council's return on this investment would be only £150,000 a year, and it would have cost the ratepayers 4p in the pound for fifteen years, and probably a further 2p in the pound for the next fifteen years. The Council decided that this would place an intolerable burden upon the ratepayers.

Thus, after discussions extending over almost twenty years, the problem remains. Many people oppose a major scheme and believe that the area should be gradually renewed. Others are convinced that Cambridge needs this additional centre for regional shopping, and that although this scheme had to be rejected on financial grounds, some form of comprehensive development must eventually take place.

The University and the Colleges
Since 1950

In the meantime, the University was making plans for future developments. It is intended, in due course, to erect new buildings on the site vacated by the University Press, and on the Old Addenbrooke's Hospital site when it becomes available. Three other possible sites were suggested:—

1. The New Town area between Lensfield Road, Hills Road and Trumpington Road. This was one of the few sites close to the centre which had been scheduled for residential development, and any attempt by the University to acquire it would have been vigorously opposed.

2. The Leys School. Even if the school were willing to move, rebuilding on a new site would be very costly.

3. The Botanic Garden. Moving it far from the city centre would have caused a serious loss of amenity.

In *The Shape of Cambridge — A Plan*, the University had said that: "With regard to teaching and research, the University has stressed the importance of retaining as much of this as possible on its central sites," and "There are solid grounds for the view that by progressive redevelopment of its central sites (and the new buildings at Sidgwick Avenue), the University could adequately accommodate any population increase in the foreseeable future."

It was clear that if all of the science departments were to be retained within the centre, high density development would be necessary. A survey made in 1963 concluded that an additional 1,000,000 square feet of floor space could possibly be obtained by developing the New Museums, Downing and Old Addenbrooke's sites at a higher density.

In 1961, Denys Lasdun produced a bold plan for the New Museums site which included three tower buildings, two of them over 200 feet and one 150 feet high. The two highest towers would have been a third higher than the tower of the University Library, and two-and-a-third times its bulk. The third tower would have been about the same height as that of the Library, but one-and-three-quarter times as bulky. Thus, within a few hundred yards of King's College Chapel, there would have been two buildings three times as high and another twice as high as the Chapel.

Balloons were put up to indicate the height of the towers, and showed that they would have been visible from many parts of the city. Above all, the famous view of King's College Chapel, the Gibbs' Building and Clare College, seen from the Backs, would have been fundamentally altered, since the towers would have disastrously reduced the scale of the existing buildings.

The plan was abandoned by the University when it became clear that it was opposed by the City Council, the County Council planning authority, the Preservation Society and numerous individuals.

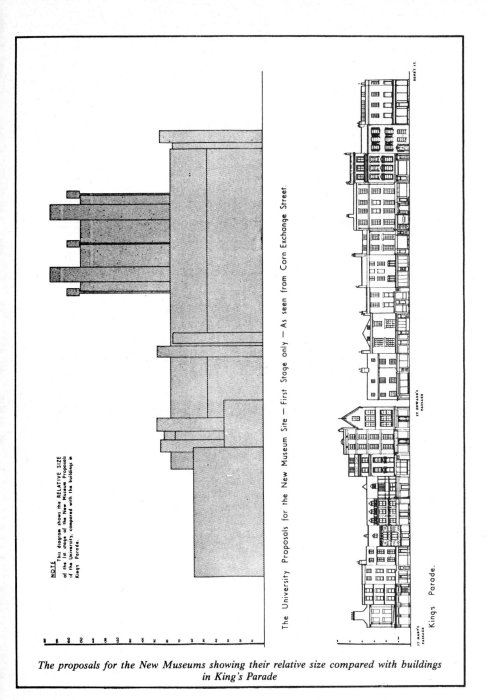

The University Proposals for the New Museum Site — First Stage only — As seen from Corn Exchange Street.

King's Parade.

The proposals for the New Museums showing their relative size compared with buildings in King's Parade

37

How the towers of the New Museums proposals would have been seen from the Backs.

A revised plan was made in 1962 for buildings of four and five storeys, with a single tower of thirteen storeys, 151 feet high. When planning permission was still refused, a third scheme was put forward in 1964. In the meantime, the physicists had pointed out that towers were unsuitable for delicate experiments, and it had been decided that the Cavendish Laboratory would go elsewhere. In this plan, towers remained, but reduced to a height of 95 feet and 110 feet. The County Council still opposed the scheme, Denys Lasdun retired, and Philip Dowson took over. His first buildings for Zoology, Mathematics and Metallurgy were approved and have now been constructed.

Hitherto, the University had considered redevelopment on central sites, but the Deer Report of 1965 came to the conclusion that these could not provide sufficient space for future needs. "Only the development of a new science site on open land will provide the room for planning and development which is urgently necessary if the progress of science in Cambridge is not to be unreasonably held up."

The Committee recommended a policy of locating many new buildings on land on both sides of Madingley Road. This West Cambridge site contains approximately 140 acres for building. An idea of its size may be obtained by imagining that if it were superimposed over the central area of the city, it would stretch from Lensfield Road to Magdalene College, and from the river to Regent Street.

The Deer Report was accepted by the University and a West Cambridge Development Plan was prepared. Since the adoption of this policy, huge additional buildings for the Cavendish Laboratory have been built there. Critics of this policy pointed out that it would be better to build on a number of college playing fields which were little used and were much nearer to the centre, moving the playing fields to Madingley Road. Others referred to the poor route for cyclists from the city centre. They would have to travel by Garret Hostel Lane and Burrell's Walk, which were only ten feet wide. It was suggested that a new route could be made from King's Parade, along the north side of King's College Chapel, continuing by a new bridge to King's Meadow and Queen's Road. King's is already invaded by thousands of tourists, and this additional influx would have been disastrous.

*　　*　　*

Holford had suggested sites in Huntingdon Road and Storey's Way for new colleges, and Churchill, Fitzwilliam and New Hall have been built there. The sites were adjacent, and there was an opportunity for a comprehensive plan to form a fine new precinct. When plans for Fitzwilliam College were being made in 1958, Chamberlain, Powell and Bon, who had been appointed to design New Hall, said that: "It would seem unimaginative not to make the most of this coincidence of three new colleges by designing a group of buildings which would match the majestic scale of the great periods of architecture."

Fitzwilliam did not agree with this suggestion, and appointed Denys Lasdun & Partners. Chamberlain, Powell and Bon proposed to resite New Hall on St John's kitchen garden, opposite Churchill, but it was decided to build on the smaller Huntingdon Road site presented by the Darwin family. The opportunity to group the three new colleges in a comprehensive scheme was thus lost.

In 1960 Selwyn College prepared a development plan, but most of it was abandoned because of the cost and because some of the buildings would have been too close to those on the Sidgwick site. In 1964 the college proposed to build new accommodation at the corner of Grange Road and Cranmer Road, incorporating two ten-storey towers and a three-storey range, but the scheme was not approved by the planning authorities and the Royal Fine Art Commission, and a different building arose in 1966-8.

Conclusion

Discussing planning in Oxford, P.E.P. said in 1960: "Events . . . leave the impression of a succession of plans without planning, discussions without decisions, and words without end."

We have noted some of the major schemes which, since the Holford

Report, have been endlessly discussed and finally abandoned. Sections of the Spine Relief Road were progressively deleted, and no part of it is now contemplated. The Main Town Road, the Railway Route, the Kite Link Road, and an underground road from Emmanuel Road to Jesus Lane were the subject of exhaustive studies, but were not approved.

For the Lion Yard there were the Edgar Investments Ltd scheme of 1958, Logie's plans of 1963, 1965 and 1966, but here at least a scheme was eventually carried out. Plans for the Kite area are still in the melting pot.

The Transportation Study cost £150,000. Who could compute the total cost of preparing all the abortive schemes, the number of hours during which councillors discussed them, and the millions of words written about them? There have certainly been "discussions without decisions," and more certainly still, "words without end."

SELECT BIBLIOGRAPHY

(i) General

Atkinson, T.D. *and* Clark, J.W., *Cambridge described and illustrated* (1897)

Booth, P. *and* Taylor, N., *Cambridge new architecture* (1970)

Sharp, T., *Dreaming spires and teeming towers: the character of Cambridge* (1963)

Willis, R. *and* Clark, J.W., *The architectural history of the university of Cambridge* (1886)

(ii) Official Plans

Holford, W. *and* Wright, H. Myles, *Cambridge Planning Proposals* (1950)

Cambridge University, *A Statement of Principles and Policy for the Future Planning of the City of Cambridge* (1960) *The Shape of Cambridge* (1962)

Cambridgeshire County Planning Department, *Report on Modifications to the Plan proposed by the Minister of Housing and Local Government* (1964)

Cambridge City Architect, *The Future Shape of Cambridge* (1966)

Cambridge City Surveyor, *Cambridge Roads: Traffic and Car Parking* (1967)

Travers Morgan and Partners, *Travel in Cambridge* (1969)

Llewelyn-Davies, Weeks, Forestier-Walker and Bor, *Fitzroy Burleigh* (1969)

Arup Associates, *Lion Yard* (1970)

Cambridge City Surveyor, *The Road System in the Central Area* (1970)

Piano and Rogers, *Fitzroy Burleigh Redevelopment* (1971)

Cambridgeshire County Planning Department, *Fitzroy Burleigh* (1972)

Travers Morgan and Partners, *Cambridge Transportation Plan* (1972)

Lewis, Parry, *Cambridge Sub-Regional Study* (1973)

Getaw...

Rou...
& Overberg

Brent Naudé-Moseley & Steve Moseley

SUNBIRD
PUBLISHERS

First published in 2009

A division of Jonathan Ball Publishers (Pty) Ltd
Sunbird Publishers (Pty) Ltd
www.sunbirdpublishers.co.za

Registration number: 1984/003543/07

Edited by Sean Fraser
Designed and typeset by Megan Knox
Cartography by John Hall

Reproduction by Resolution, Cape Town
Printed by Star Standard (Pte), Singapore

ISBN 978 1 919938 91 2

While every effort has been made to check that the information in this guide is correct
at the time of going to press, the publisher and its agents will not be held liable for any
damages incurred through any inaccuracies.

In putting together a book like this, we have been assisted by hundreds of people, and although we can't thank all of them individually, we are sincerely grateful for their willingness to help. Special thanks go to Glenda of Gansbaai Tourism; Janine and Stephanie of Stanford Tourism; Surene and Theronda of the Route 62 tourism office and website; Anton of Assegaaibosch Country Lodge; Hilde Uyttenhove-van-Damme of Robertson Tourism and Ballinderry Guest House; Leoné Rouillard, Greyton Tourism Manager; Lizette Kok, Tourism Manager of Overberg Tourism; and Adin and Sharon Greaves in Swellendam for going out of their way to ensure we had everything we needed before and during our visit to the area. Thanks also to Percy, of Percy's Tours in Hermanus, and the cellar staff of Fraai Uitzicht, Weltevrede, Wolvendrift and Joubert-Tradauw for sharing their knowledge of terroir, viticulture, viniculture and everything else there was to learn about wine production and enjoyment. As always, we'd also like to thank the great team at Sunbird Publishers!

Brent Naudé-Moseley & Steve Moseley

Contents

MAP KEY

▬▬▬ National route	➕ Medical centre / hospital	▣ Restaurant / bar
gravel tar Main route	𝚰 Memorial / statue	═══ Road, main route
‑‑‑‑‑ Secondary route	🏛 Monument building	▭ Swimming pool
▪▪▪▪▪ Trail	🅿 Parking	▦ Shops
🏠 Lodge / accommodation	✳ Place of interest	📖 Library
⛺ Camping	Ⓦ Place of worship	ⓘ Information
🍷 Wine farm	✺ Police station	🛏 Accommodation
✈ Airport / airfield	⓫ Bus terminus	‑//‑● Train station

The old harbour in Hermanus.

Baboons are a common sight in nature reserves and even some towns throughout the Overberg.

HOW TO USE THIS BOOK

This book is designed to assist independent travellers, but is by no means a comprehensive guide. We've chosen to focus on the smaller, lesser-known places covered by Route 62 (including the Winelands, Little Karoo, and the Langkloof) and the region known as the Overberg. Some may wonder at how we managed to come up with the idea of combining a predominantly coastal region with a semidesert inland route not usually associated with each other. The reason is that the regions flow into each other – and, individually, offer a variety of attractions – and together they make up an uninterrupted chunk of the Southern Cape in which to plan a new holiday experience. In the first three chapters, we provide some background and practical travel information on aspects of the region most relevant to visitors, as well as a brief look at the plants, animals and landscapes of the area's national parks and reserves. Finally, we offer an overview of what travellers might expect to encounter here.

Chapters 4 to 9 cover Route 62, in a west-to-east direction, starting with the Winelands region, through the Little Karoo, and then into the Langkloof. These chapters cover the main towns in each respective region, offering useful information on where to sleep, eat and drink, and some of what there is to see and do. Chapters 10 and 11 cover the Overberg region, and provide useful information on what can be expected in terms of activities and accommodation. These chapters also showcase the region's main attractions and activities, as well as the many individual destinations listed.

For easy reference this volume lists alphabetically the towns and stopovers within the individual regions, which makes these destinations readily accessible and easy to navigate – and investigate! If you would like to venture beyond our suggested routes and stopovers, contact the relevant tourist information.

Introduction

Route 62, the Little Karoo – also popularly known by its Afrikaans name, the Klein Karoo – and the Overberg all have their unique and diverse attractions and activities and all continue to draw visitors on an ever-increasing scale. From a tourist's point of view, Route 62 provides an alternative means of getting between Cape Town and Port Elizabeth, taking the traveller through towns and scenery very different to those seen on the usual N2 coastal highway. For the purposes of this book, we have concentrated on the smaller towns along the way rather than the cities and bigger urban centres at either end. Route 62 is known for its vineyards and wine cellars and is dubbed the 'longest wine route' in the world. It's so long (around 500 kilometres west to east) that, for convenience, we have broken it down into 3 sections, namely the main wine-producing region in the west, the semidesert Little Karoo in the centre, and the fruit-producing Langkloof in the east.

The Overberg, on the other hand, is a compact region of small rural and coastal towns scattered among rolling farmlands and indigenous fynbos barely an hour's drive from Cape Town. Not to be out done in the wine-producing stakes, the Overberg has pockets of vineyards and some very good cellars. This region abuts Route 62 in the southwest and both are easily accessible from each other, providing an area of diverse landscapes, spectacular scenery and fascinating towns in which to plan a holiday.

The area covered in this book has 2 distinct seasons: high (September to April) and low (May to August). During the high season, places to stay, restaurants and attractions are abuzz with activity and it's advisable to book beforehand, while in the low season things are a lot quieter – so quiet, in fact, that business hours are reduced and many places even close for a couple of months (mostly June and July) while the owners escape for a little R&R of their own. So don't be surprised if, during the low season, you drop in on a place and there's a sign on the door saying, 'Gone fishing!' However, with a wide choice of facilities in most towns, you will almost certainly find a wholesome meal and a bed for the night.

Remember, too, however, that change in the tourism industry is constant. New places open, existing places close their doors (possibly even while this edition is on sale), reputations of places fluctuate, and management and staff change, so it's possible that some of the descriptions here may differ to the reality at the time of your visit – we hope not by too much, though, and you're welcome to send us updated information for the next edition by e-mailing info@karooimages.co.za.

When all is said and done, in order to provide a good cross section of what you will need to plan your journey, we have taken a sip of interesting facts, a tot of humour, a glug of highlights, a slurp of good places to stay and eat, a decanter of attractions, and a barrel of contacts, and created what we hope will go a long way to helping you have a great holiday.
Cheers and Bon Voyage!

While whales are the 'biggest' attraction in the Overberg, there are many creatures at the opposite end of the scale, like this dung beetle, that are just as fascinating.

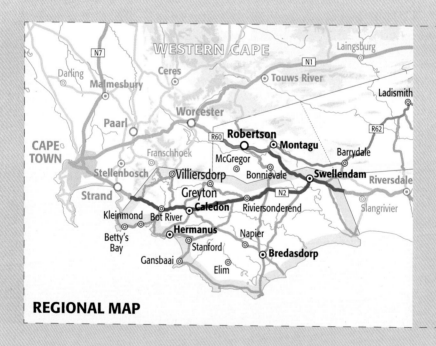

REGIONAL MAP

Facts, figures & highlights

1

Route 62 and the Overberg are two areas that are making a name for themselves in tourist circles. The former runs west to east through a semiarid region of diverse landscapes and sublime beauty lying in the rain shadow of coastal mountains. The latter traverses an undulating landscape to a coastline of white sands and azure seas washed by the Atlantic and Indian oceans.

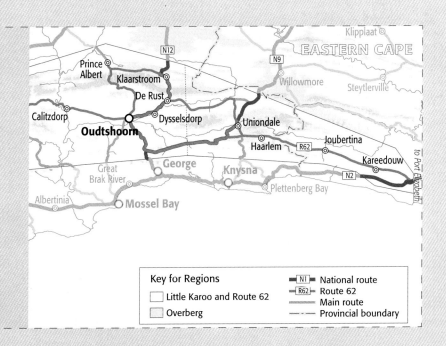

Key for Regions

☐ Little Karoo and Route 62

☐ Overberg

━N1━ National route
━R62━ Route 62
〜〜〜 Main route
—·—·— Provincial boundary

Size

As a tourist attraction, Route 62 provides an alternative road between Cape Town and Port Elizabeth. However, for the purposes of this book, we have opted to leave out the cities and large, better-known centres about which so much has already been written. Here we cover meanderings through the Little Karoo at the heart of Route 62, the vineyards of the Winelands in the west, and the Langkloof in the east. It's a journey of 500 kilometres, mostly across a narrow plain (seldom more than 20 kilometres wide) and through valleys flanked by ranges of the Cape fold mountains. South of the winelands in the west, on the other side of the Riviersonderend mountains, the low-lying landscape of the Overberg pushes towards the sea and the most southerly point of the African continent. This Overberg region is roughly 200 kilometres from west to east at its broadest point and 100 kilometres from north to south.

Topography

From start to finish, Route 62 is flanked on both sides by mountains. From west to east, its southern boundary is made up of the Riviersonderend, Langeberg, Outeniqua and Tsitsikamma ranges, and to the north the Warmwaterberg, Klein and Groot Swartberg and Kouga. The highest peaks in the Western Cape occur in the Klein Swartberg, with a number towering above 2 200 metres, and Seweweekspoort Peak the kingpin at 2 325 metres. Much of the region falls in the rain shadow of the southern mountains so the landscape is semiarid, with a mix of Karoo scrub, succulents and fynbos on the mountain slopes. In the winelands the vineyards are irrigated by the waters of the Breede River, while further east orchards rely on mountain water captured in irrigation dams.

Most of the Overberg comprises a landscape that stretches from the base of the Hottentots-Holland mountain range in the west and the Riviersonderend and Langeberg mountains in the north. These ranges have peaks in excess of 1 500 metres. The western half of the region is characterised by isolated ridges ranging from 500 metres to 1 000 metres, while the east flattens out considerably and lies at lower altitudes. The majority of the landscape is a patchwork of cultivated fields interspersed with fynbos thickets, while trees dot the river courses. In the south, the Indian and Atlantic oceans unload onto a shoreline of sandy beaches and rock promontories, with the eastern border formed by the Breede River, the sixth largest in South Africa.

Climate

The weather all along Route 62 varies. Generally, the climate in the west is Mediterranean, with mild winters and hot summers; in the Little Karoo it becomes more extreme, with frost possible on winter mornings and summer daytime temperatures of over 40° Celsius; and in the east the Langkloof experiences crisp winters and hot summers. Along the entire route at least some rainfall is possible at almost any time of year, but generally falls in winter in the west, becoming

Spring flowers add colour to the rocky shore of the Overberg.

more frequent when the seasons change the further east you go, with thunderstorms occurring in the summer months. Snow can fall on the mountain peaks in winter.

The Overberg has a predominantly Mediterranean climate. Minimum temperatures seldom drop dramatically, with the lowest average of 9° Celsius occurring in the traditionally coldest month of July. Winter days are generally mild, while average summer maximums hover in the upper 20s and low 30s from October through to March. Rain can be expected throughout the year, with the wettest months being in autumn and late winter. The mountain peaks bordering the north can see snow with the passing of cold fronts in winter.

Cities and towns

There are no designated cities along Route 62 or in the Overberg. Generally, the regions covered in this book are dotted with small laid-back towns that provide basic services to local, mostly rural, communities. There are, however, a few major towns, such as Hermanus in the Overberg, and – along Route 62 – Robertson in the Winelands and Oudtshoorn in the Little Karoo.

Population

None of the regions covered here can be considered densely populated. The urban centres are relatively small and population numbers range from around 85 000 at the top end to just a few hundred in the tiny rural villages. The only town where you'll experience anything close to rush hour at the start or end of a working day is Hermanus. Otherwise, the towns and rural roads are quiet, instilling a great sense of freedom in those used to that proverbial rodent dash.

Language

Throughout the region, the main languages are English and Afrikaans. In the bigger centres, especially those well frequented by overseas and local tourists, English is widely spoken, while in the smaller rural towns Afrikaans is usually the dominant language. Again, in the bigger centres, isiXhosa may also be spoken.

Tourist highlights

Each region has, in its own right, enough highlights to keep visitors entertained for at least a couple of annual leave-from-work quotas. Not only is there a feast of things to see and do, but there is sure to be something that'll tickle your fancy, whether you're into hedonistic, gastronomic, scenic, adrenalin or just plain soporific pastimes.

The road through Seweweekspoort meanders below cliffs of twisted orange rock.

For connoisseurs of fine wines – and those who don't care whether its vintage or just plain plonk – the Winelands region has, as its name suggests, a pleasing profusion of wines from around 50 producers in the Breede River Valley. In fact, wines are produced in a number of locations along Route 62, making it the longest wine route in the world.

The highlight capital of the Little Karoo is undoubtedly Oudtshoorn, where there is at least a week's worth of memory-making attractions and activities, including the only crocodile cage-dive in the world, the fascinating formations in the world-famous Cango Caves, a few privileged hours of being part of a family of meerkats, hot-air ballooning at sunrise, ostrich show farms, and a day trip over the spectacular Swartberg Pass to the historic town of Prince Albert. That's quite an itinerary but there's more in the Little Karoo: taste port in Calitzdorp, the 'Port Capital of South Africa'; scale the Western Cape's highest mountain peaks at Ladismith; and be held in awe by the twisted rock formations in the natural mountain gateways of Meiringspoort and Seweweekspoort.

The Overberg, too, has its fair share of highlights. Let's start with those long sandy coastal stretches that include not only the longest beach in the southern hemisphere – curving 14 kilometres along the coast at Struisbaai – but also those that have achieved Blue Flag status for their excellence. These include Grotto Beach in Hermanus, the beach at nearby Hawston, as well as that at Kleinmond. Then there's the southernmost tip of Africa at L'Agulhas, which is also the official meeting point of the Indian and Atlantic oceans (and no, you can't actually see the line where they meet). Then there's the world's shark-cage-diving mecca at Gansbaai, and the best land-based whale watching in the world, not only in Hermanus but also a short distance along the coast at De Kelders. Moving from the coast, there's the historic town of Swellendam, great national parks, such as the Bontebok, and nature reserves such as that at De Hoop. And, oh, let's not forget there are also very good wines produced in the Overberg.

Nature reserves 2

The Little Karoo and Overberg are not known for their abundance and diversity of big game, but when it comes to scenery and flora they are up there with the best. Mountains feature big throughout – in fact, Route 62 is sometimes referred to as the Mountain Route – and wherever there're mountains there's great scenery.

The Kogelberg Biosphere Reserve forms part of the Fynbos World Heritage Site, which contains more species per 10 000km² than anywhere else on earth.

Big, bold scenery aside, there are lots of little things that make a visit here interesting, not least of which is the wealth of plant species. The Little Karoo falls into the Succulent Karoo biome – a world biodiversity hotspot – and takes a healthy third place in the succulent diversity rankings in South Africa. Then there's that wealth of floral splendour, fynbos, which thrives on the mountain slopes throughout and in isolated pockets among the cultivated fields of the Overberg. Last but not least there's the avifauna and, with the diversity of habitats, bird lists surpass 250 species in some areas.

The fauna and flora of the regions covered here are protected within the boundaries of 2 national parks and 12 nature reserves. Visitors are able to view South Africa's national bird (the blue crane), the national animal (the springbok) and the national flower (the king protea). The reserves also protect endangered species, such as bontebok and Cape mountain zebra, and pockets

---

Here we briefly

outline the national parks, and reserves controlled by CapeNature. There are other reserves run by botanical societies and munici-palities, but these are dealt with under the relevant towns.

To find out more about the national parks, visit the website of **South African National Parks** (SANParks) at www.sanparks.org. For more on the nature reserves, see the website of **CapeNature** at www.capenature.co.za.

---

of fynbos. The coastline in De Hoop Nature Reserve is also a great place for whale spotting between July and November when these giants of the deep breed in the stiller waters.

Agulhas National Park

Situated adjacent to Africa's southernmost town, L'Agulhas (see page 120), this recently proclaimed park is in its developmental stages and at the time of writing there were still no proper facilities – although there may well be by the time you read this. Plans include the plotting of several hiking trails, the building of an environmental education centre, and a museum and interpretive centre. There is also a 60-bed accommodation facility that should be up and running sometime during 2009.

Bontebok National Park

The original park was situated near Bredasdorp and was proclaimed in 1931 to protect the bontebok whose numbers had been reduced to just 30 through hunting and habitat loss. However, it was moved in 1961 to where it now lies against the backdrop of the Langeberg mountains just a few kilometres from the historic town of Swellendam (see page 205) on the main N2 highway. The smallest of South Africa's national parks, it protects not only the fauna within its boundaries but also endangered flora in the fynbos biome. In addition to the bontebok, the park is also home to Cape mountain zebra, red hartebeest, grey rhebuck and Cape grysbok, as well as some 200 bird species. Activities here include

The rugged Overberg coastline has claimed many ships and lives during the centuries since seafarers passed these shores.

3 hiking trails, mountain biking, fishing, swimming in the river and, for those with their own equipment, canoeing. The accommodation and campsite are situated at Lang Elsie's Kraal among a riverine thicket of trees and aloes near the banks of the Breede River. Facilities consist of 10 self-catering chalets with wheelchair access, and caravan and camping sites, some of which have electrical points. There are also picnic spots with braai and ablution facilities for day visitors, and a shop with basic supplies at the park's reception.

Vrolijkheid Nature Reserve

This small reserve is located in the Breede River Valley, just 5 kilometres from the beautiful little town of McGregor (see page 34). It is characterised by rugged scenery and succulent vegetation dotted with guarri and karee trees, with sweet-thorn along the seasonal watercourses. It's a great park for hiking or just strolling. Springbok, klipspringer, grey rhebok and grysbok are fairly common. For twitchers, the bird list is impressive, with 175 species, and there are hides at two dams, both of which can be reached via an easy 3-kilometre hike. A second trail in the park is for the serious hiker, covering 18 kilometres and taking 7–8 hours to complete. A creature to look out for is the tiny Robertson dwarf chameleon. For those who want to spend a night, there is a self-catering guesthouse that sleeps 6.

> **FACT FINDER**
> ♦ **Agulhas National Park** (central reservations) 021 428 9111
> ♦ **Bontebok National Park** 028 514 2735, (central reservations) 021 428 9111
> ♦ **Vrolijkheid Nature Reserve** (Bredasdorp) 028 425 5020

Cape mountain zebra occur throughout the Overberg. Beyond are the dunes of De Hoop.

De Hoop Nature Reserve

Each year between June and November whales return to the rugged coastline of this 34 000-hectare reserve near Bredasdorp (see page 131) to breed. During this time the marine reserve supports 40% of the world's southern right whale population. Although these may be the drawcard for many visitors there is much more in the line of nature-based activities for the visitor. Lowland fynbos is the dominant vegetation throughout the reserve and this supports bontebok, Cape mountain zebra, grey rhebuck, eland and baboon, as well as many smaller mammals. It's a great destination for twitchers with the De Hoop vlei attracting a large number of water birds and pushing the recorded species to an impressive total of 260. Besides being able to walk anywhere in the reserve there are several day hikes and the popular 5-day Whale Trail. Mountain bikers have the use of roads within the park as well as the De Hoop Mountain Bike Trail, and, being on the warm Indian Ocean side of where the two oceans meet, snorkelling in the rock pools of the protected coast is rewarding. Day visitors are welcome but it's worth spending a night or more. For those wanting to stay over, the big news is that the accommodation has recently been upgraded and it now falls under the De Hoop Collection. The options are varied from cottages and rondawels to restored houses and neat camping and caravan sites amongst the milkwood trees. Most accommodation is around what is known as Die Opstal in the vicinity of the fresh water vlei and park reception. There is also a restaurant serving breakfasts, lunches and refreshments, and a shop.

Salmonsdam Nature Reserve

This small reserve lies in the Perdeberg mountains about 20 kilometres east of Stanford (see page 197). The area is inhabited by small antelope and other mammals, as well as 120 species of birds. Various short hiking trails, ranging from 2 to 4 kilometres wind through fynbos and forest in the kloofs, leading to waterfalls and viewpoints. Basic accommodation is in 3 rustic self-catering cabins sleeping 2 to 6, or you can pitch your tent on the large grassed site.

Kogelberg Biosphere Reserve

This 100 000-hectare (70 000 hectares terrestrial and 30 000 marine) reserve near Betty's Bay (see page 127) was the first biosphere to be designated by UNESCO in southern Africa and is a great outdoors venue of mountain landscapes, exceptional fynbos and a pristine coastline. It lies within the southern stretch of the Hottentots-Holland mountain range, and includes the local communities of the Hangklip-Kleinmond area. The area is remarkably unspoilt and the core of the reserve is the pristine 18 000-hectare **Kogelberg Nature Reserve**, which is a component of the Cape Floral Kingdom World Heritage Site, the world's richest, with 6 000 plant species over 10 000 square kilometres (the next richest is the Amazon rainforest with just 420 species). The reserve is signposted on the R44 east of Betty's Bay and open June–September. At reception, about 3 kilometres along the gravel road, you can either book into accommodation or get permits to spend the day. For those visitors with plenty of endurance, there's a 26-kilometre mountain-bike ride through the **Kogelberg Biosphere Reserve**, but there are also various hiking trails, meandering along the Palmiet River or through mountainous forests and valleys, as well as river rafting for the adventurous. Boasting some 1 850 botanical species, a new species of fynbos can be seen at almost every step within the reserve. This biodiversity hotspot is home, for example, to the rare marsh rose (*Orothamnus zeyheri*), once almost extinct but now occurring on isolated peaks in an area smaller than the average residential plot. The forest is home to yellowwood and other indigenous trees, and fauna includes small antelope, baboons, Cape clawless otter and other small mammals. The modestly furnished self-catering accommodation has great views and comprises 4 rustic cabins, each sleeping 6. Take your own braai wood and towels.

Walker Bay Nature Reserve

Walker Bay Nature Reserve curves around the coast for approximately 17 kilometres from the mouth of the Klein River east of Hermanus (see page 164) to De Kelders near Gansbaai. There are several day hikes along the coast and swimming, angling and picnicking are allowed. The reserve is open 07h00–19h00 daily and the entrances can be reached from either Stanford or De Kelders. Entry permits are required, but these are readily available at the entrance gates or from the Walker Bay Nature Reserve office in Voelklip, Hermanus, 08h00–16h00 Monday–Friday. The Walker Bay Fishing Trail is a 4x4 route that allows anglers easy access to spots along Die Plaat, a popular stretch of beach for fishing. Entrance to the trail is via Stanford. There are no overnight facilities in the reserve.

FACT FINDER

◆ **De Hoop Nature Reserve** and **Salmonsdam Nature Reserve** (Bredasdorp reservations office) 028 425 5020

◆ **Kogelberg Biosphere Reserve** 028 271 5138, (Cape Town reservations) 021 659 3500

◆ **Walker Bay Nature Reserve** 028 314 0062

De Mond Nature Reserve

This picturesque reserve is located on the coast between Struisbaai and Arniston (see page 124) at the mouth of the Heuningnes River. There are no roads in the reserve but a swing bridge across the river leads to walks that stretch down to the coast, with its towering sand dunes. Small animals can be spotted in the reserve and it provides excellent bird watching – it's an important breeding ground for the threatened Damara and Caspian terns. There's also a 7-kilometre circular hiking trail that takes in fynbos and milkwood thickets, or you can walk to Arniston along the coast. Fly-fishing is good during summer. The reserve is open 07h00–16h00 daily, but the only accommodation is a small self-catering cottage, near the entrance gate, that sleeps 6.

Tortoise alert!

At De Mond Nature Reserve, be sure to check for tortoises under your car before driving off! There may well be one sheltering there.

Marloth Nature Reserve

The Marloth reserve conserves a huge chunk of the Langeberg mountains behind the town of Swellendam (see page 205). Vegetation is predominantly mountain fynbos, with small patches of afromontane forest in the kloofs, and state pine forest on the slopes. Wild animals are mostly small and hard to spot, but bird species number 114, including 4 woodpecker species.

If you're lucky, you may catch a glimpse of the Cape vulture and Narina trogon. Besides the scenery, the big attractions of the reserve are the various hiking and mountain-biking trails. Hikes vary from easy 5-kilometre walks to strenuous ascents to the peaks of Tienuurkop and Twaalfuurkop. The 6-day, 80-kilometre Swellendam Hiking Trail is a good challenge. Accommodation in the reserve is limited to 2 self-catering units, one sleeping 8 and the other 5, not far from the entrance. They are fully equipped, with braai facilities and indoor fireplaces for winter. There are rustic overnight huts on the multi-day trails. Day visitors are welcome.

Gamkaberg Nature Reserve

Located south of Route 62 between Calitzdorp (see page 69) and Oudtshoorn (see page 84), this reserve, which encompasses the isolated Gamkaberg mountains, was established primarily to conserve the endangered Cape mountain zebra and its natural habitat. Other animals that can be seen here include grysbok, steenbok, duiker, klipspringer, grey rhebok, red hartebeest and eland. There's a 4x4 trail, good birding, a multi-day hiking trail and other, shorter options. Day visitors are welcome, but for those wanting to spend longer there's rustic accommodation at the reed-and-thatch Tierkloof Bushcamp or in converted stables, and tent sites at the foot of the Gamkaberg, or at Oukraal at the top of the mountain (the latter can only be reached in a 4x4 vehicle and has no facilities). The park is open daily from sunrise to sunset.

De Mond Nature Reserve, with its swing bridge over the Heuningnes River, is a beautiful place to stroll among the fynbos to the dunes along the coast.

Kammanassie Nature Reserve

This reserve starts at Uniondale (see page 112) and runs westward along the Kammanassie mountains towards the small settlement of Dysselsdorp. It conserves various veld types, the Cape mountain zebra, small antelope, and a variety of bird species. At present the reserve has no facilities and is closed to the public.

Swartberg Nature Reserve and Gamkaskloof

This nature reserve is a proclaimed World Heritage Site and runs along the Swartberg mountain range from De Rust (see page 74) in the east past Oudtshoorn (see page 84) and Calitzdorp (see page 69) towards Ladismith (see page 79). It covers more than 120 000 hectares and travellers traverse the reserve through the natural gateways of Meiringspoort and Seweweekspoort, and over the Swartberg Pass. One of the main attractions for visitors to the reserve is Gamkaskloof, also known as Die Hel.

> **FACT FINDER**
> ◆ **De Mond Nature Reserve** and **Marloth Nature Reserve** (Bredasdorp) 028 425 5020
> ◆ **Gamkaberg Nature Reserve,** **Swartberg Nature Reserve** and **Gamkaskloof** (George reservations) 044 802 5310
> ◆ **Kammanassie Nature Reserve** 044 752 1110

Sun-drying fruit the traditional way in Gamkaskloof, also known as Die Hel.

style bushcamp, and campsites, while other restored cottages and campsites are privately owned and run by a family descended from some of the original inhabitants of Gamkaskloof. The 20-kilometre long valley is surrounded by beautiful scenery, and mountain biking, walking, and fishing in the Gamka River are popular pastimes. The 6-kilometre Grootkloof Hiking Trail has 26 stops with information on natural and cultural aspects of the valley. Outside of Gamkaskloof, the longest trail in the reserve is the 5-day Swartberg Trail. For 4x4 enthusiasts a challenging trail follows a similar route to the hikers.

This was once dubbed South Africa's lost valley and was, until the latter half of the twentieth century, home to a community who had lived in isolation for more than 100 years. It is reached via a winding gravel road that turns off from the Swartberg Pass and culminates in a steep descent along the last few kilometres. The only accommodation in the entire reserve is here. Cape Nature runs fully equipped restored cottages of the original inhabitants, a dormitory

Anysberg Nature Reserve

Around 80 kilometres west of Ladismith (see page 79), this isolated reserve encompasses typical Karoo scenery of arid plains and Cape fold mountains. The vegetation varies from succulents to fynbos. Some 180 bird species can be spotted here, and mammals to look out for include Cape mountain zebra, gemsbok, red hartebeest and other small antelope. There are no laid-out hiking trails but visitors can make their own way through the veld. The 2-day horse trail is recommended. Accommodation is in 5 basic Karoo-style cottages – one is en-suite and the rest share ablutions – and basic camping sites.

FACT FINDER

♦ **Anysberg Nature Reserve**
023 551 1922, (Bredasdorp reservations) 028 425 5020

Practical information 3

When it comes to people, culture and a *platteland* ambience, Route 62 and the Overberg are much like most other rural areas of South Africa. Many towns and attractions have received well-deserved publicity and folk here are beginning to realise that they can make these areas a new and interesting destination. With these exciting possibilities, the whole area is becoming more tourist-friendly and even the smaller towns have most of the facilities a visitor would require.

Colourful fishing boats in Struisbaai harbour. On a calm day, big rays can be seen basking on the sandy seabed near the jetty.

Getting there and getting around

Getting to the region in your own vehicle is very easy and all the major routes are tarred and in excellent condition. From Cape Town to the start of Route 62, it is an easy 2-hour drive along the N1 via Worcester, or within an hour and a half along the N2 from Cape Town you'll be deep into the Overberg. From Port Elizabeth, in the east, the turnoff to Route 62 near Humansdorp is a little over an hour away along the N2, while the Overberg is a further 5-hour drive. Approaching from the main centres in the north, Route 62 is easily accessed via the N12 from Beaufort West on the N1. Alternatively, stay on the N1 to Worcester, then take the R43 to Villiersdorp and further into the western extremes of the Overberg.

The Overberg and Route 62 are also easily accessed from each other, most readily between Barrydale and Swellendam via the scenic Tradouw Pass or along the R317 between Robertson and Bredasdorp.

While visits to these areas are more suited to independent travellers with their own vehicle, coach companies pass through some of the towns on a regular basis. The Overberg towns along the N2 are visited daily by at least one of the major coach companies but getting any further into the region may prove more difficult. The only towns along Route 62 that can be reached via coach are Oudtshoorn and De Rust, and you have to first make your way to George or Mossel Bay from where the coaches depart.

To get to all other towns along Route 62 from Cape Town, the only option if you don't have your own car is the few taxi companies running a regular service. They pick up and drop off in all towns along Route 62 for around R200 one-way. Alternatively, hire a car from one of the established hire companies with branches in Cape Town, George and Port Elizabeth.

Money and banking

In most cases, banks are open 09h00–15h30 Monday–Friday, and 08h30–11h00 Saturdays. In small towns they may close between 13h00 and 14h00. In the main centres, most of the bigger banks (Absa, Standard, First National) will be represented, but not all will have

BY ROAD

Contact the following for up-to-date information on coaches, taxis and hire cars:
* **Greyhound** 083 915 9000, www.greyhound.co.za
* **Intercape** 0861 287 287, www.intercape.co.za
* **Translux** 0861 589 282, www.translux.co.za
* **Baz Bus** (hop-on-hop-off tickets for backpackers) 021 439 2323, www.bazbus.co.za
* **DD Steyn Taxis** (Oudtshoorn) 044 279 2176
* **Gysmen Transport** (Oudtshoorn) 044 272 0516, 083 946 8862
* **Avis Rent-a-Car** 0861 021 111
* **Budget Car Rental** 0861 016 622
* **Imperial Car Rental** 0861 131 000
* **Hertz Rent A Car** 0861 600 136

A flock of sheep is being moved from one pasture to another near Bredasdorp.

foreign-exchange facilities. Further off the beaten track, small towns may only have an ATM (cash machine), but there are a few really small towns that will have neither a bank nor an ATM. It is strongly advised that you carry sufficient cash when venturing away from the larger centres, as many establishments do not accept credit cards.

Safety

One of the greatest assets of the *platteland* is the very low crime rate, and the mostly safe environment the region offers tourists. That said, however, visitors should still take all the usual precautions: lock your doors, do not leave valuables lying around and, in larger towns, check with your hosts before wandering the streets at night (a pastime quite safe in most small towns!). Some of the more popular tourist centres, such as Hermanus, have instituted their own community police service, members of which maintain high visibility by patrolling tourist areas.

Spring flowers may be encountered along the hiking trails of the Overberg.

Fuel

In bigger centres, service stations are generally open 24/7, while in smaller towns they're often closed after business hours (usually open 08h00–18h00) and on weekends and public holidays. In fact, in really tiny towns, there may be no fuel available at all.

Health

Although the region is malaria free, be prepared to ward off those annoying, buzzing, biting mosquitoes during the summer months and make sure you have repellent with you. Outside the bigger centres chemists or pharmacies are also hard to come by so, if you are on regular medication, take enough with you and be sure to pack the basics, such

as painkillers, antihistamine, antiseptic and sunscreen, for example. To attend to more serious hazards to your health, the larger towns have doctors, dentists and hospitals but the smaller centres may have none. In a number of towns, locals love to share the fact that if you want to be pampered there are beauty treatments galore but for goodness sake don't run out of your blood pressure pills, get toothache, or need a doctor. Be aware that the climate can be extremely dry – especially in the Little Karoo – so always drink plenty of fluids, and wear sunscreen, hats and lip balm when you are out in the sun.

On the road

Tarred roads are generally in good condition with hard shoulders on some of the major routes, but there are also a great number of gravel roads, the state of which may vary throughout the year, depending on how much rain there's been recently and when the roads were last graded. Generally, though, bar a few corrugations, most of the roads that criss-cross the broader region are easily negotiated.

As a general rule, speed limits – unless indicated otherwise – are 60km/hour in urban areas, 100km/hour on rural

> For those not used to driving on gravel, it's best to reduce your speed, and dropping tyre pressure to around 1.8kpa will help your vehicle grip the road better and provide a smoother ride.

roads, and 120km/hour on the major routes. And do not get complacent because of the lack of traffic. Distances are long, with not a lot of action to keep your concentration sharp. Stop regularly and stretch your legs – oh, and enjoy the silence …

Where to stay

The towns along Route 62 and in and around the Overberg are well geared for tourists and most have well-established accommodation options ranging from hotels, guesthouses and B&Bs to self-catering units, caravan and camp sites and popular farmstays. So, unless you hit a town unannounced during a festival when accommodation is mostly booked out, you're unlikely to go without a bed for the night. Remember, however, that in the high season, and especially during the December/January school holidays and Easter weekend, prebooking is essential. Remember, too, that most establishments have great low season (winter) specials, with discounts of 40–50%. Also, low season is when many establishments close (usually sometime in June and July), so don't be surprised if you find a place closed at this time of year. It is highly unlikely, however, for the entire guesthouse fraternity of one town to take their holiday at the same time so you're sure to find a comfortable bed no matter when you arrive.

Photography

If you're a keen photographer, there are ample opportunities for some stunning shots to show those back home. Route 62 has an abundance of mountain

South Africa's national bird, the blue crane, is easily observed throughout the region during most of the year.

Painted ostrich eggs are probably the number one souvenir item on sale in Oudtshoorn.

scenery, with the twisted rocks in Meiringspoort near De Rust being among the most spectacular, while in winter the patchwork wheat and canola fields in the Overberg are photographic icons. Make sure you have everything you need, however, because only the big centres have photographic shops that stock accessories, batteries, film and memory sticks.

Shops and shopping

Generally, most shops are open 08h30–17h00 Monday–Friday and 09h00–13h00 Saturday. However, in the more popular centres shops specifically aimed at the tourist market may also open on Sundays. This is especially true in the high season – but never true of liquor outlets, which are all closed on Sundays.

A big feature on shopping lists for both regions are the wine estates, a large number of which are open for tasting and sales, and offer quality wines at very reasonable prices – so make sure you have plenty of available boot space.

On Route 62, ostrich products are the main theme and many places, especially in and around Oudtshoorn, sell items made with feathers, painted eggshells and fine ostrich-leather goods, including handbags, wallets, purses and belts.

For something a little different in the Overberg, try Gansbaai, which has the great white shark as its icon. On sale here is 'Shark' mineral water and, for those who have to try everything once, there's shark biltong.

Many towns have a market, usually on a Saturday morning, where you can purchase fresh produce, boutique cheeses, homemade soap, arts and crafts, second-hand books and the like. They're good places to go for an outdoor breakfast while mingling with the locals.

Welcome to the Winelands 4

The start of the tourist Route 62 doesn't necessarily follow from the regional R62 road, so if you can only find the R60 on the map, don't worry that you've lost your way. The change comes just west of Montagu en route to Ashton. And what lies ahead is a delight!

There are plenty of back roads throughout the Winelands region, and almost all will take you on a journey of discovery.

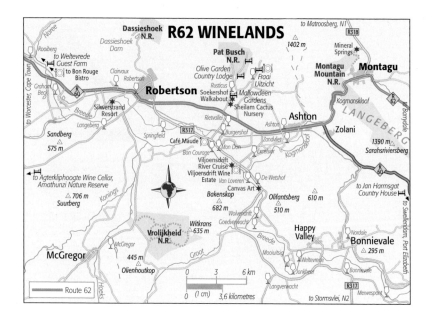

Strung out between the Langeberg mountains to the north and the Riviersonderend range to the south, this section of Route 62 falls into what is known as the Cape Winelands. More specifically it covers the Robertson Wine Valley through which the Breede River – the sixth largest river in South Africa – flows.

From its name, it's clear the region is big on wine production and, with around 50 wineries in the area, there's no disputing the fact. This profusion of wine estates is mainly due to the water of the Breede River, which is diverted to many of the vineyards via magnificently engineered irrigation schemes. Many cellars offer wine tasting and, because it's further from Cape Town than the Stellenbosch wine region, most don't charge for this very pleasant pastime. The Breede River is also the focus of water activities, ranging from canoeing and rafting to tranquil ferry trips while sipping a glass of your favourite cultivar.

In addition to wine, the valley is also known for its roses, which, alongside the vibrant hues of cannas and bougainvillaea, turn the road verges into a colour-fest during summer.

The Winelands is great country to drive around, following the minor roads until they fade into the fynbos at which point you turn around and enjoy the scenery all over again. The roads will take you into the valleys and gorges, past barns stacked with bales of lucerne, and paddocks with grazing sheep and lazing cows. Around farmsteads and cottages, chickens strut their stuff and pigs wallow in slushy heaven. Dams mirror the sky and hillsides, their reflection rippled by drifting water birds preening on the glide; and, from tractors tilling the land, labourers and farmers wave to every passer-by.

Route 62:
The Winelands

5

From Bonnievale and McGregor to Montagu, Ashton and Robertson, this is Wine Country. Abundantly green and blessed with hot, balmy summers, it offers some of the best farmland in the country. It is a place to relax, while breathing in the warm scented air and indulging in the finer things in life.

A rowing boat and ducks on a farm dam are a familiar rural sight in the Winelands region.

BONNIEVALE

You may be surprised to know that, despite the sweeping vineyards that surround the town, Bonnievale is more synonymous with dairy. The presence of the big Parmalat dairy factory next to the Bonnievale wine cellars attests to this, and nearby Mooivallei Dairy is another big cheese producer. However, with a mix of no fewer than 10 wine co-ops, estates and private cellars in the vicinity, people tend to refer to the town and the valley in which it lies, between the Langeberg and Riviersonderend mountains, as the 'Valley of Cheese and Wine'. Even with this interesting title, that would have pleased even the gods, tourists often miss the town because it requires a short detour off Route 62. But it's well worth the effort to get here, whether from Robertson along the R317 or from Swellendam and Ashton along the R60. The area and town are a mix of fields, paddocks, vineyards and fruit orchards, and its cultivated riches are thanks not only to the Breede River but also its irrigation scheme, which was constructed by Christopher Forrest Rigg. The undertaking was completed in 1914 and newspapers at the time described it as 'the greatest engineering project of its time in South Africa by one man'. The system as it is today is little changed from those times.

Out and about in Bonnievale

Timjan is a wonder juice made from the raw sap of the *Aloe ferox* and Port, which is said to cure many ailments from stomach complaints to diabetes and high blood pressure. The small factory is located in the same building

WHY VISIT?
Cheese and wine and a trip up the lazy Breede River.

WHAT'S WACKY?
Being brave enough to take a sip of raw aloe juice at Timjan.

WHAT'S WHAT?
Contact Surene and Theronda at the Route 62 info office in the main road near the junction with Church Street, tel: 023-616-3563 or visit www.route62.co.za.

as the tourist information office at the Swellendam end of Main Road. It's open for tasting (please note, we're not suggesting that you should taste … just that it is open for tasting) and a production explanation 08h00–13h00 Monday–Friday is conducted by Jan, of the Tim-and-Jan partnership that started the enterprise. Jan will also tell you about its medicinal uses, so call him for an appointment on tel: 082-774-4221. Next door is the **Parmalat** shop selling its range of dairy products at very reasonable prices.

If you enjoy life in the slow lane, book a ride with Kelvin Phillips and his *Breede River Goose* just 6 kilometres out of town. The boat travels just a little over 2.5 kilometres along the serene waters of the Breede River and a trip lasts 1.5–2 hours. There are bass rods on board for a bit of trawling and casting, the bird watching is great, and they stop for a swim on a hot day. You are welcome to take your own drinks

The Rigg Church in Bonnievale has a touching story to tell.

and snacks and you can even braai on the large grassed verge after the trip. Wine-tasting boat trips with Bonnievale Cellars can be arranged. The minimum number for a cruise is 6 or pay the full price for 6 at R60 per person (R30 for kids). Launching depends on weather and river conditions. To book, tel: 082-759-5727.

For wine lovers, Bonnievale has plenty of cellars along the Breede River offering good wines to taste and buy. Those with a penchant for Chardonnay, don't miss **Weltevrede Wine Estate**, not far from town (they also have a range of other wines). The estate still has 700 vines, planted in 1926, that have been declared a national heritage site and are still producing well. Open 08h30–17h00 Monday–Friday and 09h00–15h30 Saturday.

Another must-visit is the family-run **Wolvendrift Private Cellar**, which has a small range of good wines at affordable prices. The older Chardonnay is fabulous, and if we haven't bought their entire stock, then you'd better because it's just a matter of time before they're famous. Open 08h30–16h30 Monday–Friday and 10h00–13h00 Saturday.

To view cheese-making in progress, head to **Mooivallei Dairy** just outside town on the Ashton/Montagu road across from the golf course. The cheese-maker, Hendrik, has constructed a viewing deck behind glass, over the factory and maturing room, and, by the time you read this, will have information boards explaining the process. Visitors can observe the floor-to-ceiling cheese rounds (totalling around 200 tons) in the maturing room. The cheese is for sale in the factory shop.

The tiny **Rigg Church** isn't just another church built to serve another expanding community, but rather,

There are good restaurants aplenty in the winelands region of Route 62, and many, such as Friends @ Weltevrede, serve local wines.

it has a sad story attached. It was built in memory of Mary Myrtle Rigg, daughter of one of the town's forefathers, Christopher Forrest Rigg. Mary died from meningitis in 1911 at a mere 8 years of age. She was a deeply religious child and on her deathbed she requested that her father build her a church. To view, get directions and the keys from the tourist officer at the Wijngarten Wine Shop/Timjan.

The small (in fact, very small!) but immaculately kept **Bonnievale Museum** in Main Road is run by the very enthusiastic Cathy Joubert and well worth a visit. It displays the plans of the Rigg Church as well as a diverse collection of bits and pieces from all aspects of life and natural history. Check out the fish fossils and the Big Blunderbuss. It's open 09h00–17h00 Monday–Friday and 10h30–15h00

Saturday. It claims to be the smallest museum in the country, but that might depend on your definition of a museum. They also serve tea and coffee in The Museum Café and Gallery.

If you're into art, a visit to the **Route 62 Art Gallery** in Church Street is a must. Here Irena Coetzee displays her oils of portraits, landscapes and still-life. The multi-purpose **Outdoor Arena**, in Main Road on the edge of town before heading towards Robertson, is a good place for a day of fun in the sun. There are numerous dams on the property, all of which form part of a grass carp hatchery from where the fish are distributed throughout the country to control aquatic weeds. Interesting, *eh*? Tours of the hatchery can be arranged, and the dams also offer angling on a catch-and-release basis. You can hire a club or two and test your skills around their 9-hole Kap 'n Raps (chip-and-flick) golf course built around the water obstacles or just do a touch of bird watching. Otherwise, grab a drink from the bar and park off under a palm tree or umbrella on the deck. There is also a restaurant and accommodation.

For more things fishy, pay a visit to the nearby **Platinum Koi Farm** (get directions from Surene or Theronda at the R62 office). In the breeding season, they have up to 3 million young in the dams, and after grading might have 250 000 fish that they can pamper in readiness for export. The Andries sisters will give you a rundown on the breeding of these sought-after and expensive ornamental fish. Open 10h00–13h00 and 14h00–17h00 Monday–Friday, and on weekends by appointment by calling tel: 023-616-2083.

Vineyards flourish thanks to the Breede River and Rigg's irrigation system.

Overnight in Bonnievale

Get hold of the bubbly Theronda Bruwer to book your stay at **Amanzi Self-catering Cottage**, located on the Bruwer farm Shalom, across the Breede River a few kilometres from town. It's set among vineyards 200 metres from the riverbank. The cottage sleeps 6 and has a double and twin en suite, as well as a sleeper couch. The sitting area and kitchen is open plan, with a wooden deck and braai outside. It is very neat, compact, clean and well equipped. A second cottage was being built at the time of writing. Rates are R150–R250 per person sharing. For more info, tel: 082-871-9730.

At **A Place in Thyme B&B**, in Church Street just off Main Road, Theuns and Elana have 4 en-suite rooms with DStv and air conditioning. The rooms lead onto a courtyard, called the Kuiergat (visiting hole), with a braai and heated pool. A movable deck slides over the pool when a braai is in progress – the design a result of Theuns' architectural prowess. Prearranged dinners are enjoyed around a communal table with your hosts. Rates are R250 per person B&B – for details, tel: 082-478-7555.

Outdoor Arena has a range of options, including The Fishing Village with 3 wooden self-catering air-conditioned cottages, each sleeping 6, built over the trophy angling dam and linked by wooden walkways (fish from your deck); the self-catering Aan-die-drif Guesthouse, which can sleep 16 and has its own swimming pool, pool room and games room; and 2 suites, sleeping 4 on the top floor of the thatched lodge. Rates are R150–R300 per person. There's a restaurant on the premises. For details, tel: 023-616-2444 or click on www.outdoorarena.co.za

Happy campers can head to the **River Goose Campsite** adjacent to the spot from which the ferry of the same name departs. There's one large open grassed site and another smaller one under trees. There's a small ablution block but no electricity. Costs are R60 per person per day, so call Kelvin on tel: 082-759-5727.

Eating out in Bonnievale

The **Friends @ Weltevrede** restaurant is a great place for a leisurely meal. It's located at Weltevrede Wine Cellar not far from town en route to Robertson. The tasting room is just across the vine-draped courtyard with a tinkling fountain as centrepiece. You can eat, then taste; taste, then eat; or do the two together with the cellar matching their wines to the food you're ordering. The restaurant has a good, slightly different menu with unusual combinations put together by the cheerful Hanli, who's the owner and will most likely be your hostess. Open 09h00–16h00 Tuesday–Saturday for breakfast, lunch, drinks and light eats. Call them on tel: 023-616-3665.

Rigg's Restaurant, at Mooivallei Dairy on the outskirts of town, operates 10h00–17h00 (kitchen closes 15h00) Thursday–Monday. Monique, the cheese-maker's wife, conjures up her own gastronomic combinations in the restaurant's kitchen, from croissants to full lunches with starters, mains and desserts. The slow-roasted Greek lamb and fillet are recommended by the locals. The place is licensed to sell beer and wine.

The restaurant at **Outdoor Arena** is open 09h00–22h00, Monday–Saturday, and 09h00–15h00, Sunday. There is a comprehensive à la carte menu, a cosy atmosphere, and big windows affording a view across the lawns and fish dams. The adjoining bar is great for a drink inside or on the deck.

Into Africa is a coffee shop, restaurant and farmstall in Main Road and open 09h00–17h00 weekdays and 09h00–15h00 weekends. The menu includes breakfasts, teas and coffees, a loooong list of pizzas, veggie burgers, meaty burgers, salads, steaks, savoury pancakes, and much more. It's fully licensed. On a pleasant day, the back veranda that overlooks vineyards is the place to be.

MCGREGOR

When the town of McGregor was first laid out in the second half of the 1800s it was known as Lady Grey, but this caused untold confusion in the postal service because of another little village of the same name in the Eastern Cape. So, in 1904 the town was renamed McGregor after the much-loved pastor Reverend Andrew McGregor of the Dutch Reformed church in Robertson. Back in the late 1800s the town had a somewhat unusual claim to fame in the production of whipstocks used by drivers of horse carts, mule trains and ox wagons. The bamboo was grown around the town and in residents' gardens before being processed and exported as far afield as Germany. Today, the town is renowned for its well-preserved historic buildings, and as a place for weary city folk to escape

Tebaldi's Restaurant is just one of a number of pleasant eateries in McGregor.

WHY VISIT?

To experience an authentic mid-19th-century village with a slow pace of life long forgotten in the cities.

WHAT'S WACKY?

◆ The Overdraught Pub in McGregor Country House is both wacky and wonderful!
◆ The gardens at Temenos are food for the soul.

WHAT'S WHAT?

The tourism office is located in Voortrekker Street, diagonally across from the church. Open 09h00–13h00 and 14h00–16h30 Monday–Friday, 10h00–13h00 Saturday–Sunday. Tel: 023-625-1954, www.tourismmcgregor.co.za

the stress of daily life in the unhurried atmosphere. A single line on Siegfried's menu at The Highlander Restaurant (see page 38) says it all: 'If you came in a hurry, best you forget your hurry in a hurry.' Intertwined with the rural charm of a century ago, McGregor has an air of purity, acceptance, peace and serenity centred around the wonderful gardens of Temenos Country Retreat.

An anecdote that sums up what McGregor is all about comes from Carol of McGregor Country House. On her first visit with a friend who'd stopped at the police station to collect some keys, she was waiting in the car when she realised that the police station had no razor wire around it (it still doesn't), no guards patrolling, and it had a lovely little garden in front, and she thought,

'I'm in Noddy Land. Any minute now, Mr Plod's going to come waddling through the front door.'

Out and about in McGregor

McGregor Wine Cellars is on the left about 3 kilometres before entering McGregor from Robertson and can't be missed. The cellars are open 08h00–17h00 Monday–Friday and 10h00–15h00 Saturday for tasting and sales. There are a number of boutique cellars in the vicinity but most are by appointment only so ask tourism to arrange a visit.

Across the road from McGregor Wine Cellars is **Eseltjiesrus Donkey Sanctuary**, which provides safe beds and square meals for abused, neglected and elderly donkeys. The sanctuary is run by Johan van Zyl, who will introduce you to Eeyore, who's quite famous in the area. The sanctuary survives on donations, so please be nice and put some money in the box attached to the fence. To find out more, tel: 023-625-1593.

As has become expected of small towns, many artists reside and work here, contributing much to the vibe and character of McGregor. **Mulberry Studio Art Gallery** on the corner of Tindell and Voortrekker streets has become known as 'The Home of McGregor Artists', exhibiting pieces by local talents as well as those of owner Anne Binos, who works in various media. There is also an Internet café. In Voortrekker Street, pay a visit to Edna Fourie's **Gallery Edan**, where her soulful works are displayed. It's open 09h00–17h00 on weekends or by appointment, so call on tel: 083-302-5538. Those with a love of pottery should take a walk down Bree Street to **Millstone Pottery** where Paul and Nina produce and sell their exquisite pieces. While there, ask Paul

If it's total relaxation you want, then Temenos in McGregor is the place to head for. 'The Well' is just one of many peaceful places in the gardens where visitors come to clear the mind.

Feeding time at the Eseltjiesrus Donkey Sanctuary near McGregor.

about his ancient wood-firing technique, the unpredictability of which creates some unique items. It's fascinating and his explanation is spoken like a true artist delving into the deepest recesses of creativity, full of expression and meaning. Mostly open daily, but if you're making a special trip give them a call first on tel: 023-625-1599. At the bottom end of Voortrekker Street, take time to browse in **The Villagers Art Café and Restaurant** where Engela will serve you with typical country friendliness. The shop has a bit of everything but specialises in olive products from the nearby Rhebokskraal Olive Estate. This includes some really innovative stuff, like olive chocolate (R20 for 2 sticks), which is rich and sweet with a slightly salty aftertaste that goes down a treat with a glass of red wine.

For an hour or two of total relaxation pop in at **Temenos Country Retreat** on the corner of Voortrekker and Bree and ask to spend some time in the gardens. You will be welcomed – unless there is a retreat in progress. Wander in a garden of ponds, fountains and cascading water, through mini forests and thickly planted flowerbeds, and across neat lawns. There are walled-off gardens within gardens and arches of bougainvillaea where little Cape White-eyes sit at arm's length. Dotted around the grounds are serene angel statues, small shrines and temples from numerous religions; the Hindu god Ganesh sits on a lotus flower looking out of a small shrine towards the rising sun while prayer flags of red, yellow, blue and green flutter in the breeze around a 6-foot cross-legged Buddha. A pathway shaded by trees and flanked by plumbago and ivy spirals to a central point, and nearby is the Zen Garden, itself a little away from a small Christian chapel. The Well is an idyllic meditation room with a bubbling central water feature, candles and a relaxing sense of tranquillity. All over the gardens are benches and chairs in nooks where visitors can clear the mind and cleanse the soul. The office is open mid-morning to late afternoon, or tel: 023-625-1871.

Hikers have plenty to keep themselves busy along various local trails. For short rambles nearby head to the **Krans Nature Reserve**, which adjoins the town and is accessed via stiles at the end of some of the side streets. The tourist information office has a brochure outlining the trails and a few interesting aspects of the reserve. Also on the edge of town is the 2-hour **Kleinberg Trail** offering good views across McGregor and leading to what is known as Badge Hill where the McGregor crest lies. About 5 kilometres out of town towards Robertson, the **Vrolijkheid Nature Reserve** (see page 15) has 2 trails, one an easy 1-hour 3-kilometre walk; the other a strenuous day hike of about 18 kilometres. Then there's the **Boesmanskloof Hiking Trail**, which starts 14 kilometres south of McGregor and meanders through the Riviersonderend conservation area to Greyton, a distance of 14 kilometres. It's a good full day's hike and you must first obtain a permit from Nature Conservation. Tourism has further info, and will also provide details on the mountain-biking spots on the area (they rent out bikes too).

Overnight in McGregor

There are four establishments spread out along Voortrekker Street. The first is the 3-star Victorian-style **McGregor Country House**, laid-back and comfortable and a place to really feel at home. Add to this the proprietor Carol, who's a delight and loves to tell a story in an interesting and humorous way, and you have a memorable experience in the making. Carol has 2 en-suite double rooms and 1 family suite, and there's a guest lounge with TV. B&B rates are R275–300 per person. To book, tel: 023-625-1656.

Green Gables Country Inn is located in an old trading store, the original part of which was built in 1878. It offers 6 en-suite rooms and a self-catering house set among lovely gardens. The original barn where the whipstocks were bundled now makes up one of the units. B&B rates are R275 per person sharing. Call the Inn on tel: 023-625-1626 or visit www.mcgregor.co.za/greengables.htm.

If you want to get to the heart of peace and tranquillity, then Temenos Country Retreat is just the place you've been looking for. There are various accommodation options, including Cape cottages, suites and hermitages – mostly twins and doubles, with showers rather than baths, and a little kitchenette. These are set in amazing gardens (see page 37). Self-catering rates are around R700 per double per night (discounts for longer stays) and singles R420. On offer are wellness weeks, therapies and retreats. Treat yourself and call them on tel: 023-625-1871 or visit www.temenos.org.za.

For a good budget option, contact Johann and Linda of **The Jack & Grape**, who have 3-star rooms above their restaurant. They have 1 en-suite room at R150 per person sharing; and a double, twin and a backpacker room with 2 bunks that share a full bathroom at a cost of R120 per person (bed only). For more info, tel: 023-625-1257 or 072-423-8378.

If you are drawn to McGregor because of its Scottish connection, stay at **The Trossachs**, a short drive from town. This 4-star establishment is built of rock and thatch and resembles a modern version of a medieval Scottish Highland village, complete with chapel flying the Scottish flag atop its towering spire. There are great views across surrounding hills and valley. Chalets all have fireplaces and Scottish tartan linen. B&B costs R425–R675 per person. For a wee bit more info, tel: 023-625-1881 or visit www.trossachs.co.za.

Eating out in McGregor

Out of town, **The Highlander Restaurant** at The Trossachs is run by

Breakfast time on the stoep at the Green Gables Country Inn on McGregor's main street.

Siegfried, who makes more money from composing music for TV programmes but just loves to cook and will get your taste buds doing the Highland fling. Siegfried's added a humorous personal story to each dish on the menu to keep you entertained, and emphasis is on slow food using fresh ingredients only. In winter, a fire in the huge hearth enhances the medieval theme. Open for dinner from 19h00 Tuesday–Sunday, but booking is preferable in the low season. Licensed. To book, tel: 082-448-9534.

Closer to town, alongside the donkey sanctuary, is **Eseltjiesrus Country Kitchen** where Debbie and Jimmy serve country meals and refreshments 10h00–17h00 Thursday–Sunday. You can choose a table under a thorn tree

and watch chickens and geese scratch for food, or sit under an umbrella on the patio. If the weather is foul, there are tables inside. It's a popular place with the locals for leisurely Sunday lunches (they also sell wines of the region). In the old McGregor Hotel at the bottom end of Voortrekker Street, Johann and Linda cook up a storm at **The Jack & Grape**, serving dinner from 18h00 Tuesday–Sunday and lunches over weekends. They have a reasonably priced à la carte menu and their ribs and steak are highly recommended. Depending on the weather, you can eat inside or out and the bar is a good place for sundowners and a chat with the locals.

A little further up Voortrekker Street, at **Green Gables Country Inn**, a daytime coffee shop, evening restaurant and bar fulfil all the expectations of an inn. **The Gables Coffee Shop** is a great place for hearty breakfasts on the front stoep while watching sedate country life amble by. Try their Men's Canadian Breakfast (2 waffles, 2 bacon, 2 eggs) cooked and served by Clinton and Greta. They also do light lunches – the potted pie is good. Open 09h00–16h30. Dinners are in the **Green Gables Restaurant**, and the cook, Tiger, has a reputation for excellent roasts (particularly roast potatoes!) The kitchen's open 19h30–21h30, and the bar is open from 10h00 until evening … depending on patronage.

Continuing up Voortrekker, past the church, **Tebaldi's at Temenos** is open 08h30–16h30 Tuesday–Sunday for breakfast, lunch and refreshments, and 19h00 until closing Thursday–Saturday

– for something a little different they often conjure up theme evenings. Here Kurt and André put together a host of dishes, each with something special, and take pride in the fact that they don't use any MSG, artificial colorants or flavourants, and strive to use organic produce where possible. Meals are enjoyed in a cool and tranquil ambience, either inside, on the front patio, or out back looking onto the peaceful gardens of the retreat. We can recommend the eggs 'Benedict-ish' with either salmon or bacon to start your day or the bacon and Gorgonzola burger for lunch. They also cater for vegetarians.

Before you leave McGregor, you have to have a drink at the **Overdraught Pub** in McGregor Country House. While sipping your beverage, ask Carol about the photo of Nicolas Cage who had a drink there during the filming of *Lord of War*, some scenes of which were shot in the vicinity. The pub is open Monday, Wednesday, Friday and Saturday from 18h00 until around 20h30 unless a party really gets going! There have been times when 42 people have squeezed into what must surely be one of the smallest pubs in the country – if not the world. The atmosphere is enhanced by the fact that the only lighting is from a string of fairy lights and a few candles flickering on the old wooden counter (ask Carol what happened to the centre light). In winter, they light the wood-burning stove.

MONTAGU

Montagu is situated on top of a huge natural source of underground water, in a natural basin surrounded by mountains. Above ground, two rivers – the Keisie and Kingna – embrace three sides of the town before joining and flowing through Kogmanskloof (also fairly commonly known by its English name, Cogman's Kloof) and finally linking up with the Breede River. Kogmanskloof itself is a natural gateway through the Langeberg mountains and is a declared national monument. Through this, Route 62 passes before entering the town from the west.

Montagu is a very picturesque town, not only with regards to it's setting, but also because of it's well-maintained houses and gardens that line the streets. As with many towns along Route 62, there's a diverse range of architectural styles; but here there seems to be more of a tendency towards art deco, which other towns don't have. In Bath Street there are a number of art deco buildings, and the style can also be seen in the interiors of some accommodation establishments, most notably the Montagu Country Hotel.

From spring to autumn local tourists are joined by those from overseas and the guest houses and restaurants bubble with the chatter of those who've come to enjoy the plethora of activities and attractions in the area, or just to relax in the charming ambience of the town. From the healing powers of the hot mineral springs, to the lusty palate of the locally produced wines, Montagu has that enigmatic something that makes it a special place to visit.

Out and about in Montagu

For a good view over the town, take a drive up **Kanonkop**, which looks

Travellers may pass through this tunnel in Kogmanskloof through the Langeberg mountains.

The combination of fresh air, good restaurants, great lodgings, the healing power of the hot springs, and stunning scenery.

WHAT'S WACKY?

◆ A guided tour of the area in Gert Lubbe's 1956 Cadillac.
◆ Watching old classics of the big screen in the coffee and liqueur lounge of the charming Montagu Country Hotel.

WHAT'S WHAT?

The office at 24 Bath Street is just across the road from the big church and operates 08h30–17h30 Monday–Friday, 09h00–17h00 Saturday and 09h30–17h00 Sunday. Tel: 023-614-2471, www.montagu-ashton.info.

down on the Keisie River and across to the Langeberg. Joubert Museum in Long Street is open 09h30–17h00 weekdays and 10h00–12h00 Saturday. For a nominal entrance fee of R5.00, you get a guided tour and explanation of some interesting aspects of life in the early days in Montagu and some historical facts surrounding the building. Then you're free to wander around the indigenous medicinal herb garden.

Staying with Montagu's past, pick up a brochure from your guesthouse or the tourism office, don a pair of comfortable shoes and do the **Montagu Historical Walk**, which takes in some of the town's architectural treasures. For longer hikes, there's a brochure with a sketched map, also available from tourist info. All hikes start at the old mill

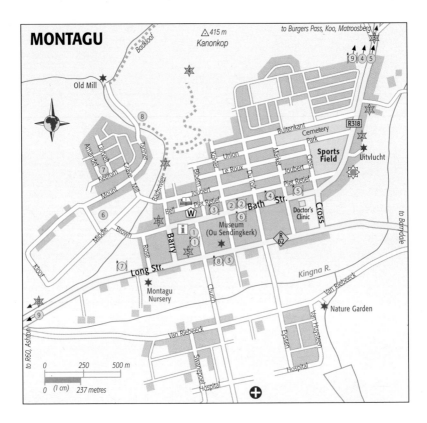

MONTAGU

△415 m
Kanonkop

to Burgers Pass, Koo, Matroosberg

Old Mill

Buitenkant
Cemetery Park

R318

Sports Field

Uitvlucht

to Barrydale

Union
Le Roux
Joubert
Piet Retief

Joubert
Bell
Piet Retief
Bath Str.

Doctor's Clinic

Museum
(Ou Sendingkerk)

Long Str.

Montagu Nursery

Kingna R.

Nature Garden

to R60, Ashton

0   250   500 m

0 (1 cm) 237 metres

Van Riebeeck

Hospital

Places to stay

1. Mimosa Lodge
2. Montagu Country Hotel
3. Four Oaks Guesthouse
4. Avalon Springs Spa Resort
5. Montagu Springs Resort
6. Montagu Caravan Park
7. The Little Gem
8. Rainbow Glen
9. Jan Harmsgat Country House

Places to eat

1. Mimosa Lodge
2. Montagu Country Hotel
3. Preston's
4. Jessica's
5. Pappardeli
6. Village Deli
7. Die Kloof Padstal
8. Templeton's Restaurant
9. Avalon Springs Hotel

Places of interest

1. Montagu Co-op Wine Cellar
2. Montagu Dried Fruit
3. Hot Springs
4. Viewpoint at Kanonkop
5. Joubert House Museum
6. Bird watching on Leidam
7. Lover's Walk, hiking trails, rock climbing
8. Kogmanskloof

and a popular stroll is **Lover's Walk**, through the gorge where the Keisie River flows, to the hot springs. For a day in the mountains, try the **Bloupunt** and **Kogmanskloof** routes, 15.6 kilometres and 12.1 kilometres respectively.

Bird watchers can follow their favourite pastime right in town at the **Leiwater Dam** on the corner of Bath and Barry streets. Built in the 1850s, the water from this dam is directed along channels to flood-irrigate plots in the town. With the smell of guano in the air, you can get close to 18 breeding species and 50-plus visiting species, and you can't miss the huge flock of sacred ibis. The tourism office has bird lists. If your pursuits in the great outdoors include rock climbing, there are a number of graded sites in the vicinity (again, check with the tourism office).

Staying with energetic activities in the fresh country air, mountain bikers won't feel left out as there are several trails from 12 to 40 kilometres suitable for the novice through to the experienced rider. For updated info, bike hire, and maps, call Petro on tel: 023-614-1932. To complete the feel-good factor, take yourself off to the hot springs for a leisurely dip in the 43 °C thermal waters (see page 45).

There are a couple of options for tractor rides: on one you chug around the town streets with a glass of Muscadel in hand, while the other – 30 kilometres from town on a protea farm – is apparently world renowned and

Do yourself a favour – give yourself more time than you think you need in Montagu. You do not want to rush your visit here.

takes you up the Langeberg mountains. Both have set days, times and costs. Bookings can be made through the tourism information office.

For a unique chauffeured sightseeing trip, call Gert Lubbe at the Montagu Country Hotel and he'll escort you in a 1956 blue-and-white Cadillac. It costs around R300 an hour (depending on the fuel price, of course!) and he takes a maximum of 5 passengers. Book by calling him on tel: 023-614-3125.

Stock up on *padkos* and snacks at **Montagu Dried Fruit** in Bath Street on the eastern edge of town. Its farmstall is a treasure trove that'll make you feel like a kid in a candy store. Varieties include diced papaya cubes, delectable fruit-and-nut mixes, cake mixes, virtually every dried fruit, nut, and mixture of the two that's conceivable, fruit rolls, seeds, candy-coated nuts and seeds, roasted, plain and salted nuts, and a Japanese rice mix consisting of all shapes, sizes and colours. The wine boutique across the parking area sells wines from a range of cellars along Route 62.

A number of wine cellars offer tastings, including **Montagu Cellar** on the corner of Bath Street and the appropriately named Muscadel Street. They're open 08h00–12h30 and 13h30–17h00 Monday–Friday, and 09h00–12h00 Saturday, and are known for their Chenin Blanc and Muscadel.

In Montagu, Mimosa Lodge is a comfortable and long-standing favourite.

Overnight in Montagu

A long-standing favourite overnight stop is the historic 4-star **Mimosa Lodge** in Church Street. The building has changed a lot over the years but, during its colourful past, once served as a school boarding house, old-age home and brothel – at different times, of course. Today it continues to change and expand under the ownership of Bernhard and Fida Hess, who offer a range of accommodation and scrumptious meals in the restaurant. Accommodation is in 9 en-suite bedrooms and 7 garden suites, each with its own patio. All units are well furnished and luxurious. Tea and coffee are just a phone call away and available throughout the day, and waiters will deliver your drinks to whichever nook in the gardens you're relaxing in, be it the croquet lawn, boule court or swimming pool. B&B rates for bedrooms are from R495 per person, and garden suites from R700 per person. There's also the Orchard Suite, with its own private champagne pool at R875–R1 200 per person. A 4-course dinner in the restaurant costs R195 a head. Winter discounts of up to 40% apply, so call on tel: 023-614-2351 or visit the website www.mimosa.co.za.

Montagu Country Hotel will take you back to the era of art deco not only with its façade – it's apparently the only authentic art deco hotel in South Africa – but also furniture and other touches in the interior. According to the proprietor, Gert Lubbe, he's selling his guests a time warp. It has day and night restaurants, a pub, and the coffee and liqueur lounge is where old movies such as *Casablanca* and *Breakfast at Tiffany's* are screened. The hotel has 33 en-suite 3- and 4-star rooms, each with TV, air conditioning and a tea/coffee tray. In the grounds, the Carrington Villa wellness centre offers various

Quiet side streets, colourful gardens and mountain scenery are a trademark of picturesque Montagu.

treatments, as well as hot mineral-water baths and steam showers. For a cooler dip, there are swimming pools in the gardens. B&B rates for Classic rooms are R380–R480 per person, and Luxury rooms R480–R640 per person. Single supplements apply. The hotel is pet-friendly and has some great winter specials. For details, tel: 023-614-3125 or click on www.montagucountryhotel.co.za for more information.

The 4-star **Four Oaks** in Long Street has 4 rooms (2 doubles, 1 single and 1 family unit) leading off a courtyard, and costs from R275 per person. For further information, tel: 023-614-2778.

Located at the mineral springs, the size and grandeur of the **Avalon Springs Spa Resort**, with its multistorey hotel tucked into the base of the rocky hills, almost takes you by surprise. It offers 2- to 5-star accommodation, has 3 bars, 2 restaurants and a 24/7 café, and besides the 43 °C thermal springs there are cold pools, a health spa, Supertube, entertainment park and a variety of water fowl on the river. Day visitors are welcome, so it can get very busy on weekends and during public and school holidays. If you're after a relaxing stay, choose your timing carefully. Accommodation costs R470–R800 per person sharing B&B, and R600–R950 for a single. Day visitors pay R30–R50 in low/high season. Springs are open 08h00–23h00. For more info, tel: 023-614-1150 or visit www.avalonsprings.co.za.

Bordering the resort is **Montagu Springs**, which is an entirely separate operation. It's more of a budget establishment, with various options (from Plettenbergs to villas sleeping 4) and rates of R500–R900 per unit Sunday–Thursday – and much higher over weekends and holidays. They're also very busy at these times. For details, tel: 023-614-1050 or click on www.montagusprings.co.za.

Rainbow Glen in Tanner Street, Montagu West, has self-catering cottages, lots of space for kids to run around and a swimming pool. The smaller units sleep 2–4 people, have their own kitchenette and braai areas, and also the use of the TV in The Cabin, while the biggest unit is fully equipped, sleeps 6–8, has a braai area and its own DStv. Rates per unit per night are R350–R450 for 2–4 people, and R1 200 for the bigger unit. For details, tel: 023-614-1294 or visit www.rainbowglen.co.za.

Also in Montagu West is **The Little Gem** in Keerom Street, which offers 4-star luxury self-catering Karoo cottages. They have fireplaces, DStv, tea/coffee facilities, a braai area and off-street parking. Pets are welcome on request. Rates are from R650 for 2 to R1 200 for 4, with discounts for stays of 2 nights or more. For more info, tel: 072-482-6576 or visit www.littlegem.co.za.

Montagu Caravan Park is a 3-star spot and offers grassed camp/caravan sites, wooden cabins (which use the campsite's ablution facilities) and en-suite chalets. Pets are welcome in the camping area and there's a large dam, which offers pedal boats, good bird watching and fishing. There's also a swimming pool. Campsites cost R120–R140 for 2 people, wood cabins and chalets from R280–R750 per unit, and backpackers' accommodation at R180–R260 for 2–4 people. For details, tel: 023-614-3034 or 082-876-2242 during business hours.

Near Montagu, on the R60 to Swellendam, is the popular **Jan Harmsgat Guest Farm** (see 'Overnight in Swellendam' on page 210).

Eating out in Montagu

The restaurant at **Mimosa Lodge** (see page 44) is open to the public, but lodge guests get preference so it's best to book in season. They serve 4- to 5-course table d'hôte dinners – the menu is posted on the notice board at the front door each day – so guests are requested to arrive for dinner around 19h00–19h30. They're licensed and have an excellent wine list. To book, tel: 023-614-2351.

There are plenty of eateries in Bath Street, so starting closest to the church and moving east, here goes … Alongside the post office, **Preston's** is best for a lunchtime or evening drink. It has a relaxed English pub atmosphere and is kept cosy in winter with a log fire. They have a small pub menu and an à la carte menu in the adjoining restaurant, which has seating inside or out. Open daily 10h30–14h30 and 17h30 until late.

In the next block, the **Garden Terrace @ Montagu Hotel** serves light lunches, teas and refreshments throughout the day. In the evenings the hotel's main

restaurant, **The Wild Apricot** serves traditional cuisine usually accompanied by tunes played on a baby grand piano. There's also a small bar, **The Dog & Trumpet**, for patrons to enjoy pre- or after-dinner drinks. They do an excellent Sunday buffet for R85 a head. It's often full in season so book your table on tel: 023-614-3125.

Further along, **Jessica's** offers fine dining in an old house at 47 Bath Street and opens for dinner from 18h30. During October–November and January–February they open 7 days a week but in December and out of season are closed on Tuesdays. Booking is advisable as they take a maximum of 30 people, so call Adele on tel: 023-614-1805 or 072-122-8163. Fully licensed. No children under 10 years.

Further still, **Pappardeli Wine Bar and Ristorante** is owned by the same folk who provide classy accommodation and delectable cuisine at Mimosa Lodge. Here, though, they serve up osso bucco and other Italian specialities.

If you just want something to munch while walking the streets, **Village Deli** – diagonally across the road from the posh-looking Vic Hotel – sells pies, cakes, and savouries. In Long Street, which is also the R62 that runs through the bottom end of town, try **Die Kloof Padstal** just before you leave town heading towards Ashton. They do breakfasts, light lunches, drinks and cakes, and are licensed to sell beer and wine. There's a diverse, reasonably priced menu, seating inside or out, and a kids' playground out back. The front section is a deli-cum-curio shop selling healthy, wholesome, sweet and

---

The town of Ashton
falls under Montagu Tourism so if you require more information give them a call on tel: 023-614-2471.

savoury snacks and goodies. Open 08h00–17h00 Monday–Saturday and 09h30–17h00 Sunday.

Then, half way along Long Street, on the corner of Kohler Street, **Templeton's Restaurant** at Four Oaks Guesthouse is a fine-dining experience with dishes served from a small but distinguished menu. Open 12h30–14h30 Monday–Saturday for lunch, 19h00–22h00 for dinner, and for Sunday lunch in season only. It's fully licensed and has a small wine bar. Booking is essential, so call on tel: 023-614-2778.

Avalon Springs Hotel is also pleasant if you just want a drink, but if you're not a resident you have to pay the resort's entry fee.

Near Montagu

Ashton lies on the other side of Kogmanskloof, about 10 kilometres along the R62 southwest of Montagu. Like many other towns in the region, it's surrounded by vineyards and extensive fruit orchards, and the two large canning factories lend it something of an industrial atmosphere. Other than that, trainspotters might want to check out the Class 14CRB steam locomotive next to the municipality in Main Road. Ashton forms part of the Robertson Wine Route, and the **Ashton Wine Cellar** – on the R62 towards Robertson – is open for tasting 08h00–17h00 Monday–Friday and 09h00–12h30 Saturday, and stocks a good range of wines. There's also **The Wine Boutique** at the Total garage in Main Road, which sells wine from just about every cellar in the region at cellar prices. Open 09h00–17h00 Monday–Saturday.

ROBERTSON

The section of the Breede River Valley in which Robertson slumbers – between the Langeberg and Riviersonderend mountains – has for years been fondly referred to as the Valley of Wine and Roses. On a drive along the R317 to Bonnievale, the reason is evident in the hedges of rose bushes bordering the patchwork vineyards. Add the red and yellow of cannas and the effervescent colours of bougainvillaea, and the region is a veritable rainbow. Recently, horses have been added – and with good reason, too, when you consider not only the number of horse studs in the area but that wine estates, such as Zandvliet, have for years been striving to produce excellent horses alongside distinguished wines. There's something about sipping a good Shiraz while watching young

In springtime the fruit orchards of the winelands burst into blossom.

This happy strawbale family welcomes visitors to the Affie Plaas Farm Stall alongside the R60.

thoroughbreds cantering around a paddock that makes you think, wow, life is good. First and foremost, though, it is the juice of the vine that makes a visit to this town so memorable. There are no fewer than 50 wine cellars in the greater area of Robertston, Bonnievale, Ashton and McGregor, so the selection of whites and reds is vast – something to tickle every palate, and of *coursssh* while you're *sschhearching* you get to *tastessh lotssh* of *winessh*, hic. Remember to appoint a non-tasting driver.

The town itself has streets lined with old jacaranda and oak trees, and the pace here alternates between frenetic and laid-back. There are lots of great places to spend a night or more, but during summer many of the top-end establishments are fully booked by overseas visitors wanting to soak up the sun, the atmosphere and the good life. In the surrounding area, with the mountains and Breede River as

WHY VISIT?

For the excellent range of wines available in the region.

WHAT'S WACKY?

◆ The gracious hosts, the concept, and the stories at Soekershof Walkabout.
◆ The Wacky Wine Weekend.

WHAT'S WHAT?

On the corner of Voortrekker and Reitz Street the tourist office carries a comprehensive range of brochures on the area. Open 08h00–17h00 Monday–Friday, 09h00–14h00 Saturday and 10h00–14h00 Sunday.
Tel: 023-626-4437 or 023-626-6248, www.robertsonr62.com.

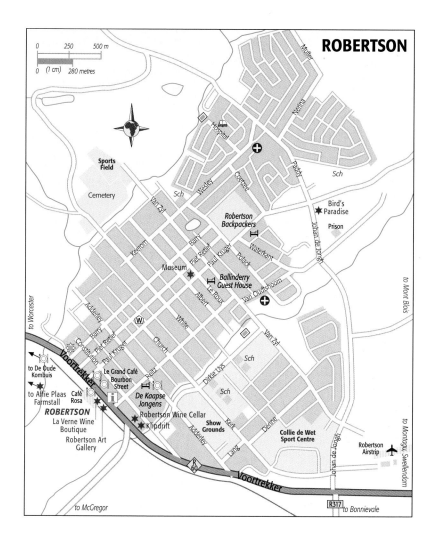

ROBERTSON

0   250   500 m

0 (1 cm) 280 metres

Sports Field

Cemetery

Hospital

Robertson Backpackers

Bird's Paradise

Prison

Museum

Ballinderry Guest House

to Worcester

Le Grand Café Bourbon Street

De Kaapse Jongens

ROBERTSON
La Verne Wine Boutique

Robertson Art Gallery

to De Oude Kombuis

to Affie Plaas Farmstall

Café Rosa

Robertson Wine Cellar

Klipdrift

Show Grounds

Collie de Wet Sport Centre

Robertson Airstrip

to McGregor

R317 to Bonnievale

to Mont Blois

to Montagu, Swellendam

playgrounds, there are plenty of out-door activities as well as scenic drives to fill idle moments.

Out and about in Robertson

If you are a lover of wine, then Robertson is the right place to base yourself for a few days as you taste your way through wineries to the east, west and south. *Sssshluvvly …*

Voortrekker Street runs along the southern edge of town from the circle where the R60 and R317 meet on the eastern outskirts until it again becomes the R60 as it leaves town to the west. Along this street there are a number of places that shouldn't be missed. First up on the right is **The Home of Klipdrift**, producers of a favourite South African brandy. Here you can get an idea of the brandy-making process on tours that take place 10h00, 12h00 and 14h30 Monday–Friday, and 10h00, 12h00 and 14h00 Saturday. The tour costs R20 per person plus R15 for tasting, and lasts about 1 hour – but how long it takes to leave after that is entirely up to you (as long as you drink responsibly). If you don't want to know how brandy is made, but want a dop, visit 08h00–21h00 weekdays and 09h00–16h00 Saturdays. There's a lounge/bar with big-screen TV, and a restaurant serving dishes such as the Klipdrift Burger to fill a grumbling tummy. As the slogan says, *'Maak jouself maar tuis'* (Make yourself at home). There's also a novelty shop.

Next along are the Robertson and Roodezandt wine cellars, which are both open for tasting and sales. The next block is what could be called Robertson's 'trendy strip'. If you don't have the time to visit the wine cellars in the area, then **La Verne Wine Boutique** is a one-stop wine experience showcasing the produce of around 40 cellars. It's open from 09h00 Monday–Saturday, offering wine tastings and wines at cellar prices! Art lovers should stop at **Robertson Art Gallery**, which has several rooms hung with works by well-known artists from around the country. There are also good eating establishments in the vicinity, including **Bourbon Street**, **Café Rosa** and **Le Grand Café** (see 'Eating out in Robertson' on pages 54–56).

Leaving the strip and town on the R60 towards Worcester, look out for the smiley family made of lucerne bales on the right. These have been a landmark here for a good few years and photos of them appear in many books and magazines. Turning in here will bring you to **Affie Plaas Farmstall**, a shop crammed with jams, condiments, nuts, dried fruit, fresh fruit and veg, cheese from the region, sweets, teas, coffees, rusks, biscuits and fresh waterblommetjies for those traditional bredies. The place is a real shopping treat and on many days there's a steady stream of vehicles through the gates. Open 08h00–16h00 Sunday–Friday.

As with most towns, the best way to get acquainted with Robertson is to take a stroll along its atmospheric tree-lined streets. To add interest, pick up a *Heritage Walkabout* brochure from the tourism office. This outlines 3 routes of about half an hour each, which take in some of the older buildings in town. The **Robertson Museum** in Paul Kruger Street is worth a visit (usually open mornings only Monday–Saturday), but if you're into something more exciting, such as a guided river-rafting trip on the Breede River, contact **Rafting Route 62** on tel: 023-626-1280.

Bird's Paradise is great for the kids or those who enjoy marvelling at the colours, sizes and shapes of exotic bird species while listening to the cacophony of shrieks and whistles. The venue has 85 species in 200 cages, with a few strange-looking primate species lurking in between, beneath a canopy of palm trees. There's a swimming pool, playground and outdoor enclosures with waterfowl, farm animals and crocodiles, as well as a coffee and curio shop. Open 7 days a week. For more info, tel: 023-626-3926.

Klaasvoogds West is a suburb at the base of the Langeberg about 8 kilometres along the R60 towards Ashton. It is an area of smallholdings and vineyards with some great accommodation, wine cellars and things to see.

After you've turned left off the R60, **Sheilam Cactus and Succulent Garden** is the first place you come to on the right. The garden was established in the 1950s and today its 3.5 hectares is covered by over 2 000 species of cacti, succulents and cycads. It's an operating nursery selling mostly waterwise plants but even if you wouldn't like these as part of your garden it's worth spending some time observing the fantastic array of shapes and sizes. Entrance fee is R10 per person, which is refunded with purchases of R200 and more. The gardens are open 08h00–17h00 Monday–Saturday.

Just a little further along is **Soekershof Walkabout**, which markets itself as the 'primary unusual destination'. It's run – and very strictly at that – by Herman, who has quite an imagination and a passion for what they've created here. Amongst other curiosities, there's the oldest cactus in South Africa (planted in 1910), 2 467 succulent species, reputedly the largest planted hedge maze in the world, and a labyrinth. Herman reckons an average visit should last 4–5 hours to fully appreciate the concept of the attractions and what the place is about, but you might get by in 2 hours. Open 08h00–16h00 Wednesday–Sunday to look and buy at the nursery but – and here's the tricky bit – to experience the 'Maze Quest' you have to be there 10 minutes before the 11h00 tour.

The sun rises on another day at Klaasvoogds West near Robertson. There's a whole host of things to do but perhaps today relaxing round the pool at Mallowdeen Gardens will suffice.

Don't be late or you'll have to come back tomorrow. Free-range walks and exploring are not allowed. Picnics can be taken along or prearranged with Soekershof so you don't go weak with hunger during your half-day visit. You'll also get to meet Joey, who does wonderful wire art. Entrance to the nursery is free and the tour costs R60 for adults and R40 for kids under 12. To find out more, call Herman or Yvonne on tel: 023-626-4134.

Further still is **Rusticus**, a wine cellar open 10h00–16h00 Tuesday–Saturday for tasting and sales. The cellar is a working museum during harvest season, when the antique equipment on display for the rest of the year is used in the wine-making process.

Along the R317 towards Bonnievale is where you'll find a number of well-known wine cellars, including Springfield, De Wetshof and Van Loveren. Besides tasting wines, set aside an hour for a lunch with a difference on a **Viljoensdrift River Cruise**. From their deli you select a range of mouth-watering snacks, choose a bottle from their range of wines, and step aboard the ferry for a relaxing cruise on the Breede River. On a still day, with the sky and trees reflected on the mirror waters, there's no place we'd rather be. The boat leaves at 12h00 Wednesday–Saturday. If the boat is not your thing, the cellar does offer wine tasting or you can picnic on the grassed banks of the river.

Also on the R317, just east of the Kogmanskloof River, is **Canvas Art**, displaying local artworks and décor items for sale. Open 10h00–17h00 weekdays and 10h00–14h00 Saturdays.

Colourful blooms like these sunny cannas line the road around Robertson.

Overnight in Robertson

The 4-star **Ballinderry Guesthouse** is one of our favourite places to stay. Luc and Hilde, the Belgian owners of this big double-storey guesthouse fronted by huge oak trees, will spoil you, and the 2 000-square-metre verdant garden offers several secluded spots to chill out in. Accommodation is in 7 elegant en-suite units, either double/twin rooms, or garden suites, each stylish and individually decorated. Hilde has earned her chef's hat, and breakfasts that come with a glass of champagne are really special. Make a point of preordering dinner too. It's 3 courses and always excellent. Luc, who likens himself to Manuel of Fawlty Towers fame, is your waiter. This is wine country and Luc's knowledge allows him to recommend the best cellars for specific tastes and arrange tours. B&B rates are R365–R525 per person sharing (with dinner an optional extra). For details, tel: 023-626-5365 or click on www.ballinderryguesthouse.com.

De Kaapse Jongens guesthouse on the corner of Adderley and Reitz streets has nicely furnished rooms for R450 per double B&B and R250 single, but rooms are not en suite. There's a pub on the premises so you need not go far for a drink. Call Carin on tel: 023-626-6260.

A good budget option is **Robertson Backpackers** in Dordrecht Avenue. There are various accommodation options, ranging from a cottage (with its own bathroom, TV and tea/coffee facilities and sleeping 4) to doubles, triples and dorms. There are several communal areas in which to kick back and relax, including the interesting Morrocan Room. Rates for 2, 3 or 4 in the cottage are R280, R320 and R360 respectively; a double room costs R220; triple R270; and a dorm bed costs R80. This is also the home of **Rafting Route 62**, which does Breede River trips. For the nitty gritty, tel: 023-626-1280.

The rural area of **Klaasvoogds West** has a number of good accommodation options. First up, on the right after you've turned off the R60, is the 4-star **Mallowdeen Gardens**, which offers 2 atmospheric African-styled chalets.

Under the thatch you'll find a king-sized bed, fireplace, lounge area, full bathroom, and kitchenette for self-catering. If you prefer B&B, you have a choice of English, Dutch or surprise breakfasts served in the dining room overlooking the pool. Also on offer is a private apartment in converted stables. The solar-heated pool has sunloungers and a thatched gazebo; and there's a large dam nearby with some good birdlife. Ask Wim to point out the resident pair of spotted eagle-owls. Wim and Rita have purposefully kept their establishment small in order to provide personal service. Regrettably, children are not allowed. B&B rates are R385 per person for 1 night, and with good discounts for longer stays. For details, tel: 023-626-5788.

Closer to the Langeberg mountains is the 4-star **Olive Garden Country Lodge** where Ferdinand and Gina have put together a place that has a Zen feel, with a few Buddhas in strategic places, several water features, and plenty of peace and tranquillity. This is the kind of establishment where you book to stay in an environment, rather than just paying for a room. There's lots of emphasis on olives, and some of their trees produce huge quantities. Gina and Ferdinand are certified in olive-oil tasting and their own oil has received a silver medal in the Delicate Oil category. Try their yummy olive jam with rhubarb. Accommodation consists of 2 pool suites, 2 garden suites and 1 family unit. The décor is bohemian afro-chic. They allow all ages if there is a code of conduct and children are properly behaved. Activities include walks through the fynbos up Kranskop for great views, bird watching or just chilling in the hammock. High season B&B rates for suites are R600–R750 per person sharing, and the family unit costs R400 per person sharing B&B. Facilities include a hydrojet Jacuzzi and pool. They offer substantial discounts out of season. Preorder dinner and Ferdinand will serve up a fabulous meal in the attractive dining room. For more information, tel: 023-626-2028 or click on www.olivegarden.co.za.

For those who enjoy self-catering, **Pat Busch Private Nature Reserve**, a little way past Olive Garden, offers fully equipped 1- and 2-bedroom cottages, and a large house, all with indoor fireplaces and outside braai areas. Rates are R175–R300 per person sharing, and activities include game drives, bird watching, fishing and swimming, a 4x4 trail and 2000 hectares of mountain vegetation to explore on foot. For details, tel: 023-626-2033 or visit www.patbusch.co.za.

Just a few kilometres away in Klaasvoogds East lies the **Fraai Uitzicht** wine estate, which has cottages that sleep 4 and suites that sleep 2. The establishment captures the charm of the 1800s and all units have tea/coffee-making facilities, fans/heaters and an honesty bar, while the cottages also have TV. Breakfasts are served in the estate's popular restaurant, as are lunches and suppers. B&B rates for the cottages are R565–R750 per person sharing, and from R480 per person for the suites. To find out more about the Fraai Uitzicht experience, tel: 023-626-6156 or click on www.fraaiuitzicht.com

Eating out in Robertson
Visit Alan and Cynthia at **De Oude Kombuis** coffee shop and restaurant,

The Breede River valley has a reputation of breeding quality racehorses.

alongside Affie Plaas Farmstall, for breakfast, lunch, teas, coffees, cakes, beer and wine 08h00–16h00 Sunday–Friday. Closed Saturdays … but they were talking about opening 7 days a week and might be doing so by the time you read this. Sunday lunch is usually a full house, with favourite dishes like potjiekos and venison pie enticing locals and visitors alike. Alan is also a good source of information on places to stay and things to see and do.

On Robertsons 'strip' in Voortrekker Street, **Café Rosa** is open for breakfasts and lunches, including stuffed croissants, gourmet pizzas, tramezzinis and burgers. They're fully licensed and you can sit inside or out the back. Across the road, **Bourbon Street** is a popular place to chill out around tables inside or on the front deck. There is a large menu, and you can choose fresh Walvis Bay oysters from a glass tank, something from the deli or from a fairly extensive wine selection, or a gourmet burger. Open 11h00–23h00 Monday–Saturday and until 16h00 Sunday. You might think us a bit wacky but, ladies, be sure to check out the loo. It's draped in mosquito net, giving the impression of a … *uhmmm* … throne. If they've taken it down, then complain 'cos it's an absolute winner. On the same side of Voortrekker, but a little further along, is the small **Le Grand Café**, popular for breakfasts and lunches. Open Monday–Saturday.

On the R317, at Bon Courage Wine Estate, **Café Maude Coffee Shop and Restaurant** serves breakfast and lunch. It has a good menu with a range of unusual tramezzinis and huge subs. On cold days, there's a fire in the hearth. We had our meal served in 15 minutes, but, due to the fact that everything is made fresh and the popularity of the place during summer and holiday times, it has been known to take over an hour to get your order. Don't let this put you off, though. Just don't be in a hurry, appoint a driver and sample some of the cellar's excellent wines. Their Prestige Cuveé Chardonnay, depending on year, is fabulous.

For a drink in town try the pub at **De Kaapse Jongens** on the corner of Adderley and Reitz streets. It's popular with the locals and shows sports events on television.

For a fine-dining experience not to be missed, make a beeline for the historic **Fraai Uitzicht** wine estate in Klaasvoogds East. Karl and Sandra are welcoming but casual; they serve great food from a small but distinguished menu and offer a selection of quality wines. Ask them to pair wines with your order, and try their Merlot. There's a fire in the hearth in winter and the front veranda is popular in summer. Regrettably, no children under 12, but those over 12 may dine in the restaurant under very strict adult supervision. Open for lunch and dinner Wednesday–Sunday.

Bon Rouge Bistro on the **Boncap** wine estate is open 10h00–17h00 on weekdays, closed Saturdays, and open until 16h00 on Sundays. A drive out here makes for a great country outing of wholesome food cooked with love and passion by Michelle and her staff. They also produce organic wine, which can be tasted 08h00–17h00 weekdays; and there's a swimming pool and children's

South Africa's national flower, the protea, can be seen among the fynbos of the Winelands region.

sleeping 2–6 people. Michelle, who's also your hostess at the bistro, feels it's more important to keep rates affordable for families than to upgrade facilities regularly, so this is a no-frills stay, but it's comfy and offers a pleasant stay in the country surrounded by vineyards and dams with chirruping frogs. If you don't want to cook, then a 3-course meal from the bistro can be delivered to your unit on a 'heat and eat' option. Self-catering rates are R200–R300 per unit sleeping 2. For more info call 023-626-2073.

The **Amathunzi Nature Reserve** is on the Agterkliphoogte road between Robertson and Villiersdorp, and is run by the very pleasant Martin and Michelle who'll ensure you have everything you need to relax in the stillness and space they offer. Accommodation options include the manor house, which has a big dining room, modern kitchen, TV lounge, huge front stoep with braai, its own swimming pool and pool deck overlooking a dam. It's equipped for self-catering, sleeps 12 and costs R3 000 per night for the house. There's a small self-catering cottage sleeping 2 adults and 2 kids at R200 per person per night, and 5 thatched chalets each sleeping 2, each with its own fireplace and underfloor heating overlooking a dam at the main lodge. The chalets are on a full-board basis with meals served in the reception area and cost from R900 per person, including a game drive. They have mountain bikes for the use of guests. Be sure to ask about winter discounts. For further information, tel: 023-626-1802 or visit the website www.amathunzi.co.za.

play area, all surrounded by vineyards and space. To get here, take the R60 towards Worcester and, after about 25 kilometres turn left at the signboard to Eilandia just after the Rooiberg Winery and then, after another 6 kilometres on this gravel road, Boncap appears on the left.

Near Robertson

Weltevrede Guestfarm on Boncap Wine Estate offers budget accommodation in self-catering cottages or en-suite rooms

Welcome to the Little Karoo 6

The word 'Karoo' is synonymous with semiarid landscapes and vegetation and it is no different here in the Little Karoo. This section of Route 62 (R62) meanders through the region for about 270 kilometres from De Rust in the east to Montagu in the west, and is sometimes referred to as the Mountain Route because the impressive ridges are never out of sight.

On the northern side of Seweweekspoort a gravel road winds along the base of the mountains to the Gamkapoort Dam.

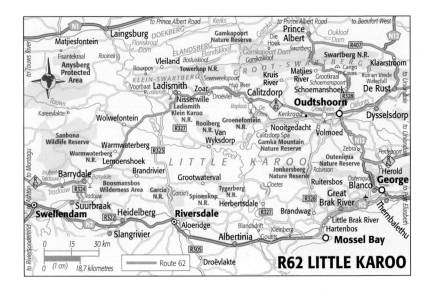

R62 LITTLE KAROO

The reason the Little Karoo is dry is because it lies in the rain shadow between two long ridges of the Cape fold mountains – the Swartberg and Little Swartberg in the north and the Outeniqua and Langeberg in the south. The Swartberg makes up most of the 125 000-hectare Swartberg Nature Reserve, which became South Africa's sixth World Heritage Site in 2004. To traverse these magnificent mountains, you can choose to either go through them – via amazing natural gateways at Meiringspoort and Seweweekspoort – or over them, on scenic passes that include what's considered one of the most spectacular passes in the world, the impressive Swartberg Pass.

Big, bold scenery aside, the Little Karoo also boasts lots of smaller attractions that make it interesting, one of which is its wealth of plant species – the region is part of the Succulent Karoo biome. For those with a penchant for smouldering spearlike flowers, the Little Karoo – best known for its aloes – is the place to be when the *Aloe ferox* lights up the slopes of the Swartberg range during winter. However, for plant lovers, the aloes are not the only reason to visit, as the region also takes a healthy third place in the succulent diversity rankings in South Africa. Many of the succulents are tiny and finding them requires the donning of hiking boots and a sunhat and stepping out into the veld.

> There are two routes from which to choose when travelling between Oudtshoorn and the Langkloof. Either via De Rust and the R341 to Uniondale or via the N12 south of Oudtshoorn, then east along the N9 to Uniondale. The latter is about 10 kilometres shorter, but is busier.

Another safe landing after a morning of hot-air ballooning in Oudtshoorn.

The Little Karoo is delightfully rich in tourist attractions, many of which are centred around the region's biggest town, Oudtshoorn (the Cango Caves attract around 250 000 visitors a year). However, every town along the route has something unique on offer.

As part of the longest wine route in the world, every one of the local towns has either a wine co-operative or wine estates, the vineyards of which each have their own terroir, giving their produce unique bouquets and palates. Running parallel with this viticulture, but not as well known, is the R62 Brandy Route. This should bring a gleam to the eyes of many a South African. Local producers include Mons Ruber near De Rust, Kango Wine Cellar and Grundheim in Oudtshoorn, Boplaas in Calitzdorp, Barrydale Cellar in the town of the same name, and then the big favourite, Klipdrift Distillery, a little beyond the strict confines of Little Karoo in the town of Robertson. Between them they produce some of the finest pot-still brandies in South Africa.

Then there are the people – from east to west we found the Little Karoo to be brimming with salt-of-the-earth folk. The communities here are made up of a parade of characters: yuppies, refined gentlemen and ladies, artists, chefs, skilled craftsmen, winemakers par excellence, cheese-makers extra ordinaire, farmers, retirees, urban refugees and entrepreneurs. Together, these varied individuals bring a twist to what towns have to offer in terms of humour, happenings, facilities, activities, amusement and, of course, great *skinder* (gossip)!

Flowering aloes and cactus pear are seen along the roadsides in much of the Little Karoo.

Route 62:
The Little Karoo

7

As a destination, the Little Karoo is generous in its offerings and, like all good things in life, they should be enjoyed over time. From Barrydale to Vanwyksdorp – and everything in between – this is a region of laid-back generosity and life (and travel) at leisure.

Die Groot Venster (Great Window) is a massive hole eroded through the conglomerate at Red Stone Hills.

BARRYDALE

Barrydale is one of the smaller towns along R62, but what it lacks in size it makes up for in character and feel-good ambience that, rumour has it, has something to do with ley-lines. Apparently, Barrydale is situated at the point at which several of these invisible underground magnetic lines cross and because of this it has a natural air of goodwill. But we were told by one of the locals – a jovial spirit, of course – that as far he was concerned Barrydale was a free-range lunatic asylum. Perhaps he was right, but this is what makes the town's persona so endearing, adding yet another aspect to the Barrydale experience. (The individual who imparted this observation will remain anonymous just in case ley-lines shift and the once laid-back inhabitants try to run him out of town …)

Located, as its name states, in a dale with the Langeberg mountains to the south, the 'Barry' part comes from a well-known trading family of the early 1800s. Like most country towns in South Africa, Barrydale was once inhabited solely by Afrikaans-speaking folk, however, many English-speaking South Africans now reside there, and together the locals provide a good mix of cultures. A lot of what there is in terms of eating and shopping is along R62, which runs through the northern section of the town, but venture into the quieter side streets and you'll find even more. There's also lots to keep you busy in the vicinity, from hot mineral springs, a labyrinth and an internationally renowned rural pub east of town, to wine tasting, a challenging 4x4 trail and quad bike trails to the west.

Out and about in Barrydale

A drive or walk along some of the streets will immediately reveal that Barrydale is a town with a penchant for walls constructed of flat stones, which adds a unique atmosphere to the place. Garden walls aside, there are plenty of shops along R62 in which to whittle away the credit-card limit. These include **Mud Gallery** (selling art and unusual bits and pieces), **Mary's Barn** (selling raffia work from Madagascar and toys cleverly made from recycling cans), and **Desert Fish** (selling crafts, art and alternative décor items – but,

WHY VISIT?

Barrydale is a town of good food, easy conversation, wonderful scenery and fun, relaxing times.

WHAT'S WACKY?

- ◆ The works of art inside the Barrydale Karoo Hotel.
- ◆ Some of the décor creations from Magpie Home Fineware.

WHAT'S WHAT?

The tourism information office is in a small building at No.1 Van Riebeeck Street. To get there, turn into Van Riebeeck Street from R62 opposite the Caltex garage diagonally across from the cellars on the western side of town. The office is on the right. Contact them on tel: 028-572-1572.

as their sign says, definitely not fish and chips).

At the far end of R62 towards Montagu is **Barrydale Cellar**, offering a range of their own wines as well as those produced in the neighbouring town of Ladismith. The cellar (the largest independent producer of pot-still brandy in South Africa) is, however, most famous for its two pot-still brandies – Joseph Barry Pot Still Brandy and Barry & Nephews Muscat Pot Still Brandy. The brandy is twice distilled in traditional copper pots and is a real treat for brandy lovers. But for those not interested in fermented and distilled juices of the grape, there's also the heritage garden to visit.

Venturing off R62 into Van Riebeeck Street, check out **Negosiegat Bric-a-Brac** shop tucked away under a large tree next door to the OK Bazaars. It belongs to Ian and Leonie and is crammed with an unimaginable array of bits and pieces where, if you take the time, you may just find a real gem. Further along and diagonally across from the Barrydale Karoo Hotel, you'll find **Magpie**, where Shane and the other talented young men make wonderful lamp dressings, lamps and other décor items from, wherever possible, recycled goods. This is not a shop as such but rather a studio, so you may want to place your order for a wacky chandelier made from entwined twigs and dressed in fairy lights.

On the farm **The Manger**, situated alongside R62, about 15 kilometres towards Ladismith, lies the labyrinth. It was built in 1998 and is a replica of the 11-circuit labyrinth embedded

Route 62 has a good dollop of humour and a generous helping of wackiness.

in the floor of 12th-century Chartres Cathedral in France. Unlike a maze, which is more for fun, a labyrinth is a meditation tool that offers stable space to quieten and clear the mind, allowing walkers to search for inner peace and harmony. You'll need to make an appointment to walk the labyrinth as it attracts pilgrims from all over. There is no charge for this, but donations are welcomed and go towards upkeep, and helping with the Centre for Rehabilitation of Wildlife. Contact the folk at The Manger on tel: 028-572-1643. At the same location stands the South African **Peace Pagoda**, which was consecrated on 7 December 2000. This 7-metre gold structure, crowned with a spherical crystal and copper umbrella, is a gift that Sayadaw U Thila Wunta, an eminent 90-year-old Burmese monk,

The Blue Cow coffee shop looks across a dam and on to the Langeberg mountains, making it a popular stop for refreshments in Barrydale.

had long wanted to bestow on Africa, thus completing his dream and mission to promote peace and harmony in every continent of the world. Although erected by Burmese monks, the pagoda is interdenominational and represents universal peace and harmony. To visit, make an appointment by calling tel: 028-572-1643.

Overnight in Barrydale

If you're one of those who enjoy something a little out of the ordinary, a touch off the wall, a little eccentric, camp, edgy or risqué, then **The Barrydale Karoo Hotel**, at 30 Van Riebeeck Street, shouldn't be missed. With nude and seminude artworks adorning the walls, it's not for those without a broad outlook and definitely not for kids. Philip Uys is the proprietor and creator and between him, his staff, and a relaxed atmosphere, you're sure to feel at home. The hotel

offers 14 double rooms, some with balconies, and there's a swimming pool in the gardens out back. There's also a ladies' bar for the exclusive use of guests; and the Aloe Bar is where you can enjoy a few beverages with the locals 13h00–20h00 or later if the clientele warrants it. Closed Sunday and Monday. To book, tel: 028-572-1226 or 082-553-1276.

Die Lang Huis is one of the oldest houses in the village and is tastefully furnished with antiques and original artworks. Andrew and Sandra are your hosts and offer 2 rooms in the homestead: The Laird's Chamber with a four-poster bed and the Garden Room with twin beds. Regrettably, no children are allowed, but small friendly dogs are. There's a swimming pool in the garden, a vine-draped pergola to relax under, and in winter enjoy a log fire in the sitting room. They serve amazing breakfasts and Andrew is particularly proud of their selection of porridges, of which the whisky oats is a favourite. (Oh, ask him about Mita the ghost!) B&B rates are R250–R275 per person. Contact Die Lang Huis on tel: 028-572-1954 or www.langhuis.co.za.

If you don't want to venture too far from the action on R62, then **Watercourt Lodge** is well placed for short walks to most restaurants and shops. It has 7 double or twin rooms (2 are disabled-friendly) and a lounge with fireplace overlooking a water courtyard with plunge pool. B&B rates are R275 per person sharing, singles on request. Dinners by prior arrangement. Give Elsa a call on tel: 028-572-1755 or visit www.capestay.co.za/watercourtlodge.

Those preferring to do their own thing need look no further than **Sandy's Place**, a 3-star self-catering establishment, at 52 Van Riebeeck Street, run by Johan and Sterna van Eeden. They offer 1 double, 1 twin, 1 triple, and a family unit, and all are very clean, fully equipped, and have TV (6 channels). Rates are R150–R180 per person. To book tel: 028-572-1415 or visit www.sandysplace.co.za

For a country stay, head to **Lentelus** in the Tradouw Valley, owned and run by the Joubert-Tradauw wine family. They offer 2 units in a double-storey, each consisting of open-plan sitting room/ kitchenette area with tea/coffee facilities (kitted for semi self-catering), an indoor fireplace and a double bedroom en suite. The upstairs unit has a deck and downstairs a patio. Breakfasts are served (weather permitting) in the garden of the farmhouse nearby, and suppers on request. Lunch and wine tasting can be enjoyed at the cellar down the road, where you can also watch farm activities such as cows being milked. Rates are R400–500 per person, children under 10 years R75 and over 10 years R150 if they share a room. For bookings, tel: 028-572-1636 or visit www.lentelus.co.za.

Another country option, this one with a difference, is out at **Warmwaterberg Spa**, where there are hot mineral springs in which to soak and a number of accommodation options, including caravan and campsites. See also page 67.

Eating out in Barrydale

Many of Barrydale's restaurants are located on the 'tourist strip' along R62 and are easy to spot as you drive from one end to the other. **Clarke of the Karoo** is probably the top restaurant when it comes to quality cooking. This isn't just our opinion, but also gets the vote of locals and other visitors too. Mike Clarke has been in the catering business all his life and those who remember Crab's Creek in Knysna, with its delicious pint-of-prawns, will remember Mike. The menu is varied and plenty of blackboards announce a wide range of meals that'll put you in a quandary as to what to choose (they have a budget menu as well). Those who love jams, preserves and unusual ingredients will enjoy browsing the extensive range on offer. The farmstall prides itself on carrying products you won't easily find at other stalls or shops; and they have their own range of quality products too. The place is licensed, with a full bar, and you'll have a choice of different beers from micro-breweries. Open 08h00–16h30.

The **Country Pumpkin** is another favourite on the strip and is open daily 08h00–17h00. There is a varied menu and a deli, which focuses more on snacks (dried fruit and biscuits, for example), but they also sell aloe products.

For fresh-made slow food and relaxed service visit Mike and Beverly at **A Place in Time**. This is where, over mouthfuls of pizza, the locals informed us that there's no dentist, doctor or chemist in town, but if you want beauty treatment there's a choice of places offering hairdos, pedicures and facials. The eatery is a very small establishment, so book in advance if possible, and take your own drinks. On our last visit, it was the only restaurant open on a Sunday evening. The adjoining antique shop stays open until the restaurant closes.

Staying on R62, **Jam Tarts** do pizzas, and the kids will love the Italian ice cream and frozen yoghurts at **Getafix**, which also does excellent value-for-money 'megatoasties' and other takeaways.

Moooving off the R62, try **The Blue Cow**, fondly referred to as Barrydale's 'Waterfront'. Situated on the eastern edge of town at the end of Tennant Street, it is owned by Boetie and Hannette Cooke and looks over a small dam and across pastures to the Langeberg mountains. They serve tea, coffee and cakes, breakfasts and lunches, with the emphasis on slow food, and milkshakes are made with farm-fresh milk. Hannette and a baker in town (who more often than not wins the local baking competition) make the cakes so you're in for a treat. And don't be surprised if Boetie brings his mug of coffee and joins you for a friendly chat.

NEAR BARRYDALE

Along R62 east, there are at least two places that sound more like icons along

With mountains flanking the R62 along its entire length, the Little Karoo has scenery aplenty. Here the Op de Tradouw Pass snakes out of the Tradouw Valley near Barrydale.

the highways of America's Midwest than platteland curiosities. The first is **Ronnie's Sex Shop**, which has become a regional legend of international renown. How did it acquire the name? Well, it all started rather innocently when Ronnie was planning on opening a farmstall called Ronnie's Shop. He'd already painted the name on the outside of the building when, as a joke, his mates added the word *sex* while he was away. He wasn't too pleased but after realising what an attraction that single word was to passing motorists, the pub was born. Ronnie himself, with plaited ponytail, beard and denims, is a larger-than-life character serving drinks from behind the bar, but more often than that he's playing his part in keeping up with the connotation of the name. The pub apparently sees an average of 200 folks a day cross its stoep and is open daily from 08h45 until the last patron leaves. Contrary to what the name implies, the adjoining **Road Kill Café** doesn't serve flattened birds, rabbits and other slow unfortunates scraped off the tarmac, but does offer burgers, sandwiches and various other eats.

Swap the firewater of Ronnie's Sex Shop for the hot waters of the mineral springs at **Warmwaterberg Spa**. About 27 kilometres along R62 towards Ladismith and virtually opposite Ronnie's Sex Shop, turn left at the signboard and a short journey on the gravel road will bring you to the reception of this popular holiday and weekend destination. Here people come to relax and soak in the healing waters of the hot mineral springs. The spa has 2 outdoor pools – one hot

(38–42 °C) and one cold – for the use of all guests. It can get very busy and noisy over school holidays and over long weekends so if your intention is to enjoy peace and quiet, plan carefully. There are a number of accommodation options, including rustic self-catering timber huts and caravan or campsites with electrical points. The most popular options, with their own private baths, are the 2 old bath-houses dating back to 1886. In keeping with the bare necessities of those times, the units have none of the fancier luxuries of modern-day living. There are also 5 units in what was originally the old sanatorium where the Roman baths still operate. These units have their own kitchenettes but the baths are across the passage and the toilets are shared with guests in the other units. The resort has a small kiosk that stocks basic supplies, a liquor store, restaurant and cocktail bar. Rates vary for weekdays, weekends and holidays, but average R300–R420 per person for the bath-houses and sanatorium, R400–R550 per unit for the timber huts (which sleep 6), and R120–R200 for a caravan or campsite (for 4 people). Day visitors are allowed by prior arrangement only. For reservations, tel: 028-572-1609 or visit www.warmwaterbergspa.co.za.

The Tradouw Valley

This 18-kilometre-long valley to the west of Barrydale is fringed to the south by the curves of the Langeberg mountains and to the north by the folded foothills of the Warmwaterberg. The valley is blessed with fertile soils and supports dairy cows on juicy paddocks, as well as fruit orchards, vineyards and lucerne in a patchwork of fields. Irrigation dams filled by mountain streams stand in the shade cast by old oak trees, and rows of beefwoods and poplars shelter the crops from the prevailing winds.

Whatever you do, you can't miss **Joubert-Tradauw Private Wine Cellar** – not only because of the good food and wine (excellent reserve Chardonnay) but because there are regular signs on the R62 for 1.5 kilometres on either side. The boutique cellar offers 4 wines in its range and wine tasting costs just R10 per person, a fee that's deducted from any purchases. They're a very popular venue for a light lunch of Karoo tapas, which often includes something unusual and is enjoyed beneath a vine-covered pergola in summer. The deli sells jams, cheeses, bread and the like.

For 4x4 enthusiasts, Niel Haasbroek of **Klipbok Adventures**, a few kilometres past Joubert-Tradauw towards Montagu, has put together a trail that'll get the adrenaline going. It's a steep, rocky and rough track up the Langeberg mountains requiring good ground clearance and strong nerves. For those who endure, the views of the valley on the way up and south across the Overberg from the top are worth every bump and grind. You can camp at the summit where there's a loo with a view to beat all others. If you don't have a 4x4 but can get a group of 10 together, Niel will take you to the top on a day trip in 'Gogga' the unimog. Rates to ride the trail are R200 per vehicle, to camp R100 per vehicle and a trip in Gogga R200 per head. Call Niel and Manda on tel: 072-297-2088 or 082-339-1089.

> The evergreen klapperbos (*Nymania capensis*) is commonly found throughout the Little Karoo and often mistakenly called Chinese Lantern. This 'lantern' is a papery four-chambered pink 'fruit' containing seeds.

Karoo Saloon is a fairly new roadside pub situated a few kilometres past the Joubert-Tradauw wine farm and deli. You'll most likely be greeted by the proprietor, Willy, who's a lively, friendly character with a soft spot for motorbikes, in particular Harleys, and the biking fraternity. Partnering him in his venture is Titan the Pitbull who, according to Willy, is a legend, and Scrumps, the African Grey. Willy also offers basic camping and accommodation with rates to match, from R50 to R140 per person.

On the Op de Tradouw Pass (about 500 metres past Karoo Saloon in the direction of Montagu) is **Tradouw Quads**. Those who like the wind in their face can hop on a quad bike and experience the scenic beauty of the valley along guided eco-friendly trails. The operation hires out quads to those who don't have their own, and caters for all ages between 2 and 90 (they have helmets to fit all). For information, call Elize Kriel on tel: 082-055-4096.

The Tradouw Pass

South of Barrydale, the R324 traverses the Langeberg mountains via the picturesque Tradouw Pass to the mission town of Suurbraak. The pass was built by master road-builder Thomas Bain between 1869 and 1873, and literally follows the path Khoi maidens took to fetch water from the Buffeljags River long before the first white settlers arrived. The word 'tradouw' comes from the Khoisan description, 'path of the women' (tarras meaning 'women' and daos meaning 'footpath'). The route offers a pleasant drive and there are lookout points where you can stop and enjoy the view.

CALITZDORP

The Port Capital of South Africa. This is the enviable slogan by which Calitzdorp is best known, and a well-deserved one it is to. Although the word 'port' will fall away in the next few years, the sweet liquor will still pour forth from the vineyards here, becoming known as Cape Tawny, Cape Ruby, Cape Vintage and so on. There are several producers

The Calitzdorp Museum nestles under old gum trees in a quiet side street.

in and around the town, from the bigger and better-known Boplaas and De Krans cellars to micro-cellars such as Peter Bayley, Withoek and Axehill. As you imbibe some of these Ports from the smaller producers, take pleasure from the fact that the grapes were probably 'vinified' in the traditional foot-squelching manner. There are also good red and white wines aplenty, but this abundance of juices from the vine is not all the town has to offer. It's a suitable base from which to take exploratory drives along the valleys and winding roads that emanate from the rolling slopes of the Swartberg. If igniting dust trails along gravel roads isn't your idea of a day well spent and you'd rather relax on a front stoep with a beverage, there are enough places to do just that. As you enter town along the R62, Voortrekker Street is where you will find a number of restaurants and shops, mostly in the vicinity of the church.

Out and about in Calitzdorp

A number of cellars in town offer wine and Port, as well as wine tasting. **Boplaas**, **De Krans** and the **Calitzdorp Cellars** are the better-known ones, but try **Withoek** and **Axehill** (the latter by appointment, tel: 044-213-3585) as well. For a pleasant stroll, pick up the *Calitzdorp on Foot* brochure from tourist info and take in some of the historical buildings that make up the older part of town. The museum in Queen Street is worth a look, as is **St Mark's Church** a little further down the road – it's reputedly the second smallest church in the world (tel: 082-952-6765 to have it opened). Appreciators of art need look no further than **Gallery Route 62**, in Queen Street, where Penny Rudder has a good collection of works by local and other artists. At **Posh Junk and Antiques** in Main Street, Lawrence has a good variety of collectibles and some second-hand books to browse through. For something a little different, Dr Noël Jean Creil gives 1-hour organ recitals, which include works of Handel, Bach, Verdi and other masters in the big Dutch Reformed Church 18h00–19h00 Monday–Saturday.

Just past the Calitzdorp Wine Cellar there's a lookout point over the extensive vineyards and fruit orchards cloaking the Gamka River Valley. It's a pretty site at the best of times, but spring and autumn are particularly colourful.

Besides Port, there's one other thing Calitzdorp is known for and that's the healing properties of the mineral baths at **Calitzdorp Spa**, 24 kilometres to the south. Contact the spa on tel: 044-213-3371.

The Little Karoo is an important area when it comes to the diverse succulents for which South Africa is well known. If, like many, you are interested in these fascinating plants that survive so well in harsh conditions, then a walk through the 3-hectare **Hennie Cloete Veldtuin** is well worth it. Call Mike or Judy on tel: 044-213-3181 or 084-657-6648 to make an appointment.

There are a number of scenic drives in the area. If you're not staying at The Retreat at Groenfontein or Red Stone Hills (see 'Overnight in Calitzdorp'), a drive along this loop is well worth it. The **Groenfontein Valley/Kruisrivier Circle** starts at the Groenfontein signboard between the graveyard and big red coffee pot in Calitzdorp's main road. It then follows 50 kilometres of gravel road before joining the R62, about 20 kilometres towards Oudtshoorn. The gravel road winds past the Calitzdorp Dam, widening and narrowing as it swerves around the curves of the foothills. It passes picturesque farms, cottages, and slopes clad in fynbos. In the winter months the spear-like orange flowers of the aloes light up the area.

To the west along the R62 two other drives are recommended if you have time: one to **Matjiesvlei**, the turnoff to which is around 5 kilometres out, and the other through **Seweweekspoort**, about 24 kilometres out, and around to the Gamkapoort Dam (see page 84).

Overnight in Calitzdorp

Anna Sophia's is situated in Voortrekker Street – look out for the metal figures

---

WHY VISIT?
To savour some of the country's finest Port.

WHAT'S WACKY?
The big red *koffie kan* in the main street outside The Red Coffee Pot restaurant.

WHAT'S WHAT?
The tourism office is at the Shell garage on the left as you enter town from the Ladismith side. Tel: 044-213-3776 or visit www.calitzdorp.co.za or www.tourismcalitzdorp.co.za.

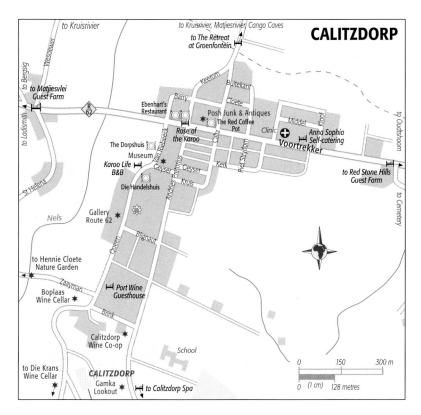

along the roof pitch. There is safe off-street parking accessed from the back, as well as comfortable, fully equipped self-catering units built around a courtyard with a circular firepit/braai as a central feature. Carel and Anita, who own and run the establishment, are both delightful and will be at your beck and call throughout your stay. Ask to try their delicious homemade mustards-with-a-difference, ranging from the mild traditional 'for sissies' to one with chillies 'for consenting adults'. Self-catering rates for units are R150–R165 per person sharing and breakfasts, by prior arrangement, cost R30. Call them on tel: 044-213-3402.

The **Rose of the Karoo** is a long-established landmark in Calitzdorp, and Sandy, your hostess, is somewhat of a living legend in these parts (she appeared on the front cover of the fabulous *Village Life* magazine) and ensures her customers leave with all their expectations fulfilled. Situated across Voortrekker Street from the big church, her establishment is a multi-purpose stopover offering a restaurant, deli, gifts and accommodation. The latter consists of 3 en-suite B&B rooms across the back garden from the restaurant or 2 self-catering units sleeping 5 and 3 in a separate house just up the road. All rooms have tea and coffee facilities, a

THE RED HILLS OF THE LITTLE KAROO

One of the most striking natural features of the area between De Rust and Calitzdorp are the red hills that rise at intervals along the way. These are formed of coarse sediments deposited somewhere between 120 and 250 million years ago. In these sediments are a variety of conglomerates made up of a mass of small rocks embedded in a softer, sandy mixture. The reddish shades are due to the presence of haematite (an oxidised iron mineral) in the soft sandy mass. The hills are most noticeable alongside the R62 near De Rust, on the N12 south of Oudtshoorn, and at Red Stone Hills Guest Farm at Kruisrivier near Calitzdorp.

The red stone formations of the Little Karoo are an unusual geological feature. Some of the best examples are at Red Stone Hills Guest Farm between Oudtshoorn and Calitzdorp.

TV, air conditioning and a fridge. B&B rates are R250–300 per person sharing, while the self-catering units go for R200 per person for the first two nights and R100 per person thereafter. A single costs R250. To book, tel: 044-213-3133 or visit www.roseofthekaroo.co.za.

Away from the main drag in Queen Street try the **Port Wine Guesthouse**, which looks across vineyards from the front stoep. There are 5 double and 5 twin en-suite rooms with coffee/tea facilities and complimentary Port. Facilities include DStv, a pool, fireplaces, air conditioning, a big veranda and a large garden – and it's wheelchair-friendly too. Dinner is, preferably, by prior arrangement and you'll get 3 set courses for R130. The place is fully licensed, and B&B rates are R320–400 per person sharing. For info, tel: 044-213-3131 or visit www.portwine.net.

The **Calitzdorp Spa** has recently had a makeover and offers 3-star campsites and self-catering chalets. Rates for both vary from weekends to mid-week and according to season. Generally, the campsites cost R80–R170 per site a day, with a per-person fee of R13–21. Chalets are around R270–R830 per unit, sleeping 4 or 6. Call them on tel: 044-213-3371 or visit www.calitzdorpspa.co.za.

Near Calitzdorp

Out of town, in the valleys and recesses of the Swartberg mountains not far off the R62, there are a number of places to escape to. For self-catering (or catered), head for the long-established Red Stone Hills, where Petro Potgieter provides 6 cottages, rated 3- to 4-star, scattered among the well-known rock formations from which the establishment takes its name. The units vary from Cape vernacular cottages for 2 people to early Victorian that can sleep 6. All have fireplaces, TV and privacy. Activities include hiking – check out the spectacular Groot Venster (Big Window) carved out of the rock formations nearby – mountain-biking, guided horse trails, great birding, and swimming (at the pool at reception for scorching summer days). Pets are allowed by prior arrangement in certain units. To get there, travel 20 kilometres along the R62 towards Oudtshoorn and take the Kruisrivier turnoff, then from here it's 6.5 kilometres on gravel. From Oudtshoorn, it's 30 kilometres along the R62 to the same Kruisrivier turnoff. Rates are R190–R300 per person bed only. Breakfasts are an optional extra and served in the dining room, while the ingredients for preordered semi-DIY dinners are delivered to your cottage, the table laid and the braai fire lit. Give Petro a call on tel: 044-213-3783 or visit www.redstone.co.za.

Tucked away in the Groenfontein Valley Conservancy **The Retreat at Groenfontein**, owned and run by Grant and Marie Burton, is the perfect place for weary souls to kick back and relax. Choose from rooms in the Victorian farmhouse to modern luxury suites nearby. Stays are on a dinner-bed-and-breakfast (DB&B) basis, with breakfasts on the veranda and dinner around the large communal dining table. Marie is a wizard in the kitchen and caters for vegetarians and guests with special diets (the latter by prior arrangement). They offer good hikes and a cold mountain stream in which to find your own secluded pool for a skinny dip, or there's a swimming pool if you don't want to walk too far. They're also child and pet friendly. To get there from Calitzdorp, turn off in town at the Groenfontein signboard (next to big red coffee pot) onto gravel for 19 kilometres (from Oudtshoorn, after 30 kilometres turn off to Kruisrivier and then 28 kilometres of gravel). DB&B rates are R590–R770 per person sharing October–March, and R350–R530 in winter. For details, call Marie on tel: 044-213-3880 or visit www.groenfontein.com.

On the opposite side of Calitzdorp, try **Matjiesvlei Guest Farm** in the Matjiesvlei Valley, another picturesque off-the-beaten-track valley accessed by only a gravel road. To get there, head towards Ladismith for 5 kilometres and then turn right at the Matjiesvlei sign onto the gravel road and follow the indicators. Here Bennie and Selma have 3 quaint self-catering cottages and grassed campsites – only accessible in a high-ground-clearance vehicle – near the banks of the Gamka River. They also have a 12-kilometre 4x4 Bôjaankop Trail, which traverses the foothills of the Swartberg, crosses the Gamka River and climbs to spectacular views. Accommodation costs R250 for 2 people per house, plus R100 per additional person; camping costs R100 per vehicle; the 4x4 trail costs R150 per vehicle. For more information, tel: 044-213-3756 or 073-174-1028.

Eating out in Calitzdorp

The **Rose of the Karoo** on the main strip has tables inside as well as on the vine-covered patio out back. They serve meals from early until late as well as tea, coffee and cakes. They are licensed, and have a deli stocked with delicious dried fruit and nuts, jams and preserves, pies and bakes. There's also The What Not Shop in which to browse.

Virtually next door is **Ebenharts Restaurant**, which has also been around a good number of years. They're open 07h45–17h00 Monday–Saturday and 09h00–16h00 Sunday for breakfasts and coffees, and do takeaways. Ebenhart himself is South Africa's only pipe-maker and is placed among the top 10 in the world. Some of his hand-crafted pipes are on display.

A little further up the main street is a recent addition: **The Red Coffee Pot**, which is open for breakfast, lunch and supper Tuesday–Sunday. Also new, and located at the kink in Queen Street,

A sign in De Rust reflects the sense of fun here.

is **Die Handelshuis**, a well-renovated and atmospheric establishment – check out the diesel-fired stove. Here Peter and Tracy serve great coffee, cakes and light eats during the day. For those who enjoy a little pampering, Tracy also has a beauty salon on the premises.

Die Dorpshuis, situated just off Route 62 in Van Riebeeck Street opposite the church, is a good place to enjoy a drink on the stoep.

DE RUST

This quaint tree-lined settlement is tucked beneath the southern slopes of the Swartberg mountains at the entrance to Meiringspoort, a famous gateway through the mountains into the Great Karoo. If you're travelling from up north, De Rust lies on the N12 to the Garden Route and the R62 to Cape Town. It's a small attractive village that has many lovely old buildings, some Victorian houses and interesting little shops and galleries hidden in nooks and crannies. If you drive through here during summer, the jacaranda trees that line the N12 will be in full purple bloom.

The town came about when, in the early 1800s, a young man with the surname of Meiring sought and found employment as a foreman on the farm De Rust. The farm flourished under his guidance, and when the owner died, Meiring married his widow. During explorations of the area, he and two friends found a route through the Swartberg mountains, which later became Meiringspoort. The village was established in 1900 on a portion of Meiring's farm. Today, surrounding farms are a mixture of fruit, vegetable seed, grapes, tobacco, dairy, sheep and ostriches, and a few produce excellent dessert wines. The area's exceptional plant life includes the well-known *Pelargonium zonale*, which was first collected in Meiringspoort in 1689 by Hendrik Oldenland, and is said to be the original ancestor of all geraniums found in the world today.

Out and about in De Rust

Meiringspoort is probably De Rust's best-known attraction and, as you wind through its 20-odd kilometres of towering cliffs, you will be awed by its beauty. Contorted rocks lean every which way, patterned by the earth's movement millenniums ago, and somewhere up on the peaks lives the world's most primitive beetle species (*Colophon* species). Make a point of stopping at **Waterfall Drift** picnic site and taking the short stairway to view the waterfall – it's well worth it.

De Rust has had a donkey project on the go for some years now and you can take a donkey cart ride out along a track that passes some farmlands. It's a little bumpy but great fun and you might see onions being planted by colourfully dressed folk all working in neat rows.

The R341 east is flanked by the Kammanassie and Swartberg mountains, and 6 kilometres along here you'll find the turnoff to **Stompdrift Dam**. This is the largest dam in the Little Karoo, and has a 25-kilometre

WHY VISIT?

◆ It's a great base from which to do the Meiringspoort, Prince Albert, Swartberg Pass and Oudtshoorn circular route.
◆ The municipal drinking water comes from a mountain spring and is excellent.

WHAT'S WACKY?

The town and nearby Meiringspoort have inspired great artists, such as Tinus de Jongh, and the composer of 'Die Stem', CJ Langenhoven, is said to have been referring to the poort when he wrote the lines, '… over everlasting mountains, where the echoing crags resound'.

WHAT'S WHAT?

The De Rust Tourism Bureau is on the northern end of the main street as you enter from Meiringspoort. Tel: 044-241-2109, visit www.derust.org.za or www.tourismderust.co.za.

'coastline'. It's a popular venue with anglers and water-sports enthusiasts.

The **Mons Ruber** estate has a wine-tasting facility in a historic double-storey building about 10 kilometres along the N12 towards Oudtshoorn. While you taste, you can explore an exhibition of the 1947 royal visit, and afterwards do the 1.5-hour hiking trail in the famous Red Hills that were formed millions of years ago. The drinking range includes sweet wine, Cabernet, and 'Copper pot-still brandy Witblits'. The latter is a mouthful even before you've tasted it! Of course, the area is known for its excellent Port and dessert wines. The recently upgraded walking trail will take about 3 hours to complete.

At Domein-Doornkraal you'll find sparkling wines, whites, reds and sweet wines. While in the area, explore the pretty loop road that's signposted as Middelplaas, which starts and ends on the N12 on either side of De Rust. It's off here that you'll find the lovely old farmstead and guesthouse called **Die Gat**.

Before you explore the town itself, be sure to get the terrific little *De Rust Historical Hiking Trail* map from the tourist office. It details each building, with a couple of lines of history of each. There's also a list of hikes and walks, detailing the terrain they cover, the distance and contact telephone numbers. While you're wandering around, take note of the exceptional plant life. The diversity in such a small area must be unmatched anywhere. Cycling routes (23–163 kilometres) are similarly detailed on a map and available from tourism, as are 4x4 routes.

On Route 62 you're never far from the mountains. Here De Rust slumbers beneath the curves of the Swartberg range.

The village itself has some quaint shops, such as Village Trading Post, Die Groen Bliktrommel, Mazawattee Antiques, Tolbos Trading Glass Craft, and Schoeman's Gallery.

Horses Helping Humans is a company that offers equine-assisted therapy for individuals and groups. They offer rehabilitation and training of horses, as well as interspecies and inter-life communication workshops. Their 5C Programme uses the 5 Cs of Concentration, Communication, Cooperation, Coordination and Compassion to rehabilitate, heal and grow while working with horses through customised groundwork exercises. For details, tel: 044-241-2225 or 083-592-2867, www.towersigtrust.co.za.

If you'd prefer a people-helping-humans therapy, **The Strawbale House** at No. 2 Le Roux Street is owned by Diana and Pieter, who offer a range of alternative therapies and massages, and have a labyrinth you can walk. They also serve preordered vegetarian, vegan or halaal meals made with organically grown food, and their straw-bale house is filled with natural home-making ideas, including an amazing solar toilet.

Overnight in De Rust

The 4-star **Housemartin Guest Lodge** is a family business whose success is partly due to the professional and friendly people working here. It's owned by Bill and Christina Martin (whose School of Food and Wine in Durban is world renowned) and is run by their bubbly daughter, Candy and her husband Andy. Accommodation is in 12 comfortable en-suite guest rooms, each with its own veranda that leads onto the garden. Roofs are corrugated iron in keeping with the family's Victorian homestead, bathrooms have underfloor heating and linen is percale. Each room is air conditioned and has either a queen or twin beds, and the lodge is wheelchair-friendly. Parking is secure, and there's a secluded pool. It's just a hop and a skip to the communal lounge area, which has a crackling fire in winter, alongside which you'll find The Plough Restaurant (see 'Eating out in De Rust' on page 78). B&B rates are R500–R625. To book, tel: 044-241-2214 or visit www.housemartin.co.za.

For a clean and crisp self-catering option in town, see the guys at The Village Trading Post (see 'Eating out in De Rust' on page 78), but if you prefer a place a little further from town, there's a farm dam and sign (at the town's western entrance) to **Voëlsang**, which offers B&B or a rustic self-catering unit in a quiet garden. Some rooms have separate entrances off a long stoep,

There's nothing like traditional transport to beat the cost of fuel. Take a Donkey *teksie* in De Rust.

while others are in the main house. It's owned by Eunice and Niel Strydom, and B&B rooms cost from R200 per person. For details, tel: 044-241-2270.

About 7 kilometres from town is the historic farmstead **Die Gat**. This is a 4-star guesthouse in the Middelplaas valley that's been in the Schoeman family since the early 1800s. Guest rooms are in outbuildings, such as the one once used as a school and another as a cart-shed, and there's even an ox wagon that's been restored to offer a unique experience. All rooms are air conditioned. Join the owner, Anton, on an open-vehicle drive to explore the farm and braai in the veld. B&B rates are R370–R650 per person, with dinner around R170 per person. To book, tel: 044-241-2406 or visit www.diegat.co.za.

Stompdrift Dam offers camping on grassed sites, some under trees, overlooking the dam. The location is quiet, except in busy holiday times, and rates are R40 per person plus R40–R50 per tent or caravan. They also have rustic reed huts that sleep 2 people for around R300.

Eating out in De Rust

The Plough Restaurant in the main street has been tastefully converted from an old corner shop that still has the corner French doors. Today, the voluminous eatery has deep-red walls offsetting wooden tables and big metal chairs on a screed floor. The manager, Garfield, and his polished staff run a professional establishment that is a great place for breakfast and offers refreshingly different options from the standard bacon-and-eggs fare. Lunch is just as good (the Sunday buffet is so popular that regulars travel for 2-plus hours to get here) and dinner just makes you want to do it all again, starting with breakfast. In summer, dine al fresco on the front veranda and watch the village people. To book, tel: 044-241-2020.

The Village Trading Post is also in the main street and is owned by a couple of city slickers: Niekie is the chef and Soan does front-of-house. It's a restaurant-cum-gift shop that'll tempt you to buy all sorts of goodies for your house and pantry, and the daytime bistro-style eatery is open 08h30–17h00, and Mondays for dinner.

KLAARSTROOM

This Victorian farming village is situated 120 kilometres south of Beaufort West on the N12 just before entering the awesome Meiringspoort, which slices through the Swartberg mountains linking the Great Karoo with the Little Karoo. Villages seldom come smaller than this and its serene atmosphere makes it a great place to unwind. Then, when you've loosened up, there are some super day drives, and neighbouring villages to be explored.

Overnight in Klaarstroom

Klaarstroom Guest House has 5 rooms in a Victorian house and hosts Sharon and Jeremy will fill you in on a number of activities, attractions and day drives in the area. B&B rates are R300 per person sharing and suppers are by prior arrangement and cost R95. To book, tel: 082-488-8370. A little way into Meiringspoort a signboard indicates a gravel road leading to **Wilgemond Guest Farm**, a tranquil protea farm tucked away in the mountains, overlooking vineyards and fynbos-covered slopes. Guillaume and Nelmarie Sweiggers offer accommodation and good wholesome meals in the Cape Dutch-styled farmhouse or a small cottage. The homestead was originally built as a lodge in the 1960s, in anticipation of picking up passing trade on a planned road and tunnel through the Swartberg. The plan was to bypass Meiringspoort because of its susceptibility to flooding. B&B rates in the farmhouse are R300 per person and R300 for 2 in the self-catering cottage. Dinner is by prior arrangement for R150 per person, so call them on tel: 023-541-1756 or 082-471-5351.

> For more information
> on Klaarstroom and what it
> has to offer, visit the website
> www.klaarstroom.co.za.

LADISMITH

The town is named after – and how's this for a mouthful – Juana Maria de los Delores de Leon, for obvious reasons more simply known as Lady Smith because of her marriage to Sir Harry Smith, governor of the Cape at the time. The town's most imposing feature is the towering peaks that form an impressive backdrop to the neat, tree-lined streets and houses built in an interesting mix of architectural styles. The Klein Swartberg, as the range is known, incorporates some of the highest peaks in the Western Cape, with Towerkop (at almost 2 200 metres), being the town's main icon. Ladismith

is well known for its cheese factories and wine cellar, and what better place to enjoy the delicacies of these producers than reclining in a spot with a view of the mountains while watching the sun set across its slopes?

Few towns can boast two large cheese producers and a wine cellar so don't miss the opportunity to settle down with some of the cheese varieties from the Parmalat and Ladismith factories, and spend time pairing them with the local wines. If that's too sedentary, take to the hills along the various mountain trails.

Out and about in Ladismith

If you're just passing through, you may think you're on the main street as you enter and leave on R62. However, the main street and residential area lie towards the mountain and this is where the majority of the shops and small supermarkets are situated. Ladismith is underrated as a destination and a walk along the streets – past bougainvilleas, shady trees, lush gardens and some

Guest farms in the Little Karoo pride themselves on providing meals of both quality and quantity.

lovely houses in many different architectural styles – will quickly put you in touch with the town's rural charm. Among the varied building styles is the town's own vernacular architecture, the 'Ladismith style', a simplified Georgian style. Pick up a leaflet on the architecture, as well as street map, and take yourself on a walking tour.

For those interested in the cheese-making process, the **Ladismith Cheese Factory** can be visited by prior arrangement (tel: 028-551-1613), and the goings-on in the cheese-making room can be viewed through big glass windows while the process is explained to you. The factory does not, however, offer tastings or sell its cheese. The products can be bought at the Route 62 Café at the Total garage in town, next to tourist info. We can recommend the creamy semi-hard Ladismither.

Ladismith Wine Cellar, together with the Barrydale Cellar in the neighbouring town of Barrydale, joined forces in 2005 under the umbrella of Southern Cape Vineyards to actively market each other's products, the towns and the region. It's open 08h00–17h00 Monday–Friday and 09h00–15h00 Saturday for free tasting and sales. The turnoff to the cellars is opposite Keurbosch Farm Stall. If you arrive when they're closed, you can get their wines at the small wine shop alongside the farm stall as well. Brandy lovers can treat themselves to a bottle of Barry & Nephew Muscat Cape pot-still brandy – it's pricey, but in a class of its own. Staying with things delicious, pop into the **Parmalat** shop across from Keurbosch Farm Stall, which sells all their usual products (long-life milk,

yoghurts, cheeses and fruit juices, for example) at bargain prices, so take a cooler box and plan to stop and stock up on your way home.

Where there are mountains there are hiking trails, and here the most popular option is the stiff 12.2-kilometre **Elandsberg Hiking Trail**, climbing 792 metres in altitude. The route takes 5–8 hours and passes the location of Stanley's light at the highest point of the trail. For the not-so-adventurous, the **Towersig** routes start on the edge of town near the hospital and range from 2 to 12 kilometres, taking 1–4 hours. Details from the tourist info office.

WHY VISIT?

To buy cheese.

WHAT'S WACKY?

◆ Stanley's light (make the stiff climb just to see it)
◆ Some of the stuff up for sale at Gert's Junk Stall.

WHAT'S WHAT?

Ladismith's tourist information office is in the old church in South Street near the junction where the R62 does a right angle before continuing through the Little Karoo to the east and west. Speak to Hettie Weymar, and if you have to wait your turn, Kitta Kat, the tourism cat who loves to loll on the large table of pamphlets, will keep you entertained. Tel: 028-551-1378, www.ladismith.org.za or www.tourismladismith.co.za.

If you like browsing through second-hand shops and miscellaneous stores, then Route 62 has a few, like Gert's Junk Stall in Ladismith.

Stanley's light has become something of an icon. It was set up in 1963 by Stanley de Wit, who carried a few bits of equipment, including a bicycle dynamo and headlamp up the mountain, and connected it all together so that the running mountain water would power the light day and night. So why did he go to all this trouble to set up the light? Well, just because he could really. For those who can't face the steep climb to check out the light, the original is on display at the tourism office while new technology now powers the light on the mountain.

If mountaineering is what gets your adrenaline pumping, then Ladismith has at least 6 peaks for you. The most challenging is **Towerkop**, with its 122-metre rock dome tough for even the most experienced enthusiast. If you want to scale the highest in the Western Cape, then the **Seweweekspoort** peak (2 325 metres) is not far away.

Returning to more restful pastimes, spend some time at **Gert's Junk Stall** across from tourist info. The garden will hold a lot of memories for the older generation, and you'd have to be really getting on in years to remember filling the fuel tank using the hand-operated petrol pumps on display. On the enclosed front stoep is a collection of old knick-knacks for sale and old Gert himself is there to assist and inform.

For a short scenic drive, head for the **Hoeko Valley** on the gravel road that curves from the end of North Street. Its claim to fame is that CJ Langenhoven, who wrote 'Die Stem', was born here; the house is now a private museum. In the valley proper, the road is tarred and rejoins R62 12 kilometres east of town. It's a pretty, meandering route, passing little clusters of buildings and palm trees, vineyards and fruit trees, and is particularly picturesque in its spring and autumn colours. To the west of Ladismith lies the **Anysberg Nature Reserve** (see page 20) where you can take 2-day guided horse trails through typical Karoo veld. For further info, tel: 023-551-1922 (the office is manned on a part-time basis, so keep trying).

Overnight in Ladismith

For a country stay with a farm atmosphere head for the 4-star **Ladismith Country House**, about 7 kilometres from town on the Hoeko Valley road or, if approaching from Calitzdorp, take the Hoeko Valley turnoff 12 kilometres before Ladismith – and the establishment is 10 kilometres along, on the left. Your hosts are Isak and Helna, who almost look too young to not only run a comfortable guesthouse, but also produce great food 3 times a day. However, they carry out both these duties with confidence and flair. Accommodation consists of 4 double air-conditioned rooms with mini bars in an old farmhouse, a separate TV lounge, and a dining area on the deep back stoep. The atmosphere is relaxed and down to earth. There's also a self-catering cottage that sleeps 4. B&B rates in the farmhouse are from R500 per person sharing in season, with substantially discounted winter rates on request, and you can enjoy a leisurely 3-course dinner for R120 per person. The self-catering cottage costs R250 per person and breakfasts are R50. For more info, tel: 028-551-1155 or visit www.lcountryhouse.co.za.

In town, visit Carine and her husband Gerrit who own and run the very reasonably priced **Le Roux Self-catering and B&B** at 19 Church Street. They have 8 fully equipped units overlooking a courtyard shaded by old trees, and a small campsite with 6 power points and 3 ablution blocks that can take 4 caravans or tents (more if you're a group and don't mind squeezing in). There's also a pool. The large cooked breakfast, which must be ordered the previous night, costs R40, while the units cost R120 per person sharing (bed only) or R180 single. Campsites cost R90 per caravan and R70 per tent for 1–4 people, tel: 028-551-1439 or 083-306-2494.

Also in town, at 27 Albert Street, is the 4-star **Albert Manor Guest House**, a large Victorian home built in about 1892. It offers 2 en-suite rooms in the main house, while The Coach House is a 2–bedroom cottage set in lovely gardens. There's a lounge with DStv and dinner on request. Rates are R280–R350 per person B&B in the main house, and R310–R370 per person B&B in The Coach House. To book, tel: 028-551-1127.

Ladismith has some pleasant places to eat, ranging from restaurants to tea gardens.

Eating out in Ladismith

A short way out of town on the R62 towards Barrydale, the **Olive Garden** has a motto: 'Eating and drinking well in South Africa is a national pastime, so eat, drink and be merry as we give you a taste of a country that really loves its food and drink with a passion.' A bit like our rugby, I suppose. Traditional fare is recommended: curried offal, *bobotie* (curried mince), oxtail or *bredie* (stew). If you think you've seen clean loos, check these out – to us, it says a lot about the establishment. Meals are served with traditional bread, butter and jam on the side. There's also a pub where you can watch sport on TV or just have a drink, inside or on the stoep.

In town, you have quite a choice of where to eat. **The Flame Tree** is open 09h00–18h00 Monday–Saturday for light meals, such as panninis, cake or breakfast in the lovely front garden of an old house. Don't be in a hurry if you're having anything but tea, coffee or cake, as the emphasis is on slow food and many ingredients are picked fresh from the garden out back when you order. Belinda and Cuen are the owners and, while eavesdropping on some friendly banter between the two and a regular customer, it turns out that when Cuen serves cake the helping is much bigger – it's been known for locals to check who's on duty – as are the breakfasts, which he cooks. The place is also part nursery, part gift shop, selling organic herbs and vegetables, and art supplies. Opposite the Shell garage when you enter from Calitzdorp you'll find Kevin and Barbara at their colourful **Kanna Kombuis**, which is open daily 08h00–20h00. They serve breakfast, lunch, supper and tea, coffee and cakes. The delightful Barbie is very friendly and extremely enthusiastic.

NEAR LADISMITH

Beyond Ladismith, there are three little spots definitely worth a visit: Zoar and Amalienstein, on the road between Ladismith and Calitzdorp, and Seweweekspoort.

Zoar and Amalienstein

These small neighbouring towns, which lie alongside the R62 midway between Ladismith and Calitzdorp, were started as mission stations in the first half of the 19th century. The inhabitants still live a very simple lifestyle, with donkey carts for transport and handmade wire toys for the kids. Check out the impressive Lutheran church in Amalienstein.

Those who enjoy the peaceful spiritual atmosphere of a mission station and would like to stay overnight in Amalienstein contact, **Tant (Aunt) Carolina**, a community-run establishment named after a previously long-standing inhabitant of Amalienstein. It has 3 en-suite double rooms in a house just down the road from the big Lutheran church. Rates are R150 per person sharing, or R500 if you book the entire house. There's also a backpackers' unit at R150 per person, and they do breakfasts and traditional dinners if arranged well in advance. For more info, tel: 028-561-1000. The tearoom/curio shop near the church and guesthouse is also worth a visit but its opening hours are erratic.

Seweweekspoort

For a lovely drive, pack a picnic lunch and head towards Calitzdorp and the take the turnoff to Seweweekspoort, virtually opposite the mission towns of Zoar and Amalienstein. This spectacular gateway through the Swartberg lies below the imposing 2 325-metre Seweweekspoort peak – highest in the Swartberg – and the mountains seem to swallow you as you follow the gravel road into their midst. Steep cliffs of burnt orange, their bases choked with aloes and kiepersol trees, dwarf the narrow gravel road as it meanders through this less-developed version of Meiringspoort. At the other side of the mountains, the road drifts off into the Great Karoo, that vast semiarid plain that covers around one third of South Africa. Before you follow this into the never-never, turn right onto the bumpy track that leads through Bosch Luys Kloof Private Nature Reserve (this new reserve has up-market chalets – for rates tel: 023-581-5046) to Gamkapoort Dam. The scenery along the way is sublime, but the track can be very rough and is not advised in a vehicle without good ground clearance. This whole area is nature reserve so leave your pets at home or you could get into serious trouble. You can also picnic in the *poort* (pass) itself – one spot that's perfect to break out the sandwiches is at the thatched umbrella below the cliffs.

There are several explanations as to where this spectacular poort got its name, one being that brandy smugglers used the route to evade revenue collectors, taking 7 weeks to negotiate the detour in ox-wagons. More likely, it is a corruption of 'Zerwick se poort' after Reverend Zerwick, a founder of the mission at nearby Amalienstein.

OUDTSHOORN

Synonymous with the Cango Caves, ostrich farms and crocodiles, Oudtshoorn has drawn visitors for decades. As early as 1780, when Dutch colonists discovered the caves occupied by southern Africa's earliest people for some 80 000 years, tourists have flocked to the area to sample the exotic. Today, there are so many attractions that you'll need days to discover its delights. Just wander the streets and you'll find roads through tunnels of trees that shade aged buildings, and umbrella-shaded tables scattered around the stoeps of guesthouses and restaurants give it an almost continental feel. Local flavour comes in the form of quaint shops named Boeretroos and Pasella around the corner from which stands a weather-beaten fish-and-chip shop, and around the corner from that is an exquisite old sandstone house.

The surrounding countryside is one of farmers' fields, pretty cottages, ancient stone walls and elaborate ostrich palaces. The smoky aubergine Swartberg mountains north of Oudtshoorn have mysterious depths and serpentine gravel roads leading into the Great Karoo. In winter, flowering aloes enhance the extraordinary beauty here.

Out and about in Oudtshoorn

The *beeeg* deal in Oudtshoorn is the world-famous **Cango Caves**, one of southern Africa's Seven Wonders and an archaeological and historical highlight of

The Queen's Hotel in Oudtshoorn was built in 1880 and is the third oldest hotel in the country.

WHY VISIT?

Numerous activities and attractions, including the annual Klein Karoo Kunstefees, which celebrates local artists and musicians.

WHAT'S WACKY?

♦ Diving with crocodiles.
♦ Checking out the long-legged birds that bat their eyelashes at you.

WHAT'S WHAT?

The tourist office is in the old stone Queen's Hotel building in Baron van Reede Street, right near the imposing CP Nel Museum. Visit the excellent website www.outdshoorn.com or tel: 044-279-2532/3.

the area. You'll find the caves at the end of the R328, about 40 kilometres north of the town. The caverns started forming 20 million years ago with the erosion of 100-million-year-old limestone rock. Today, many have dramatic stalactites and stalagmites. Of the 5.3 kilometres of caves, 1.2 kilometres are open to public and the 60-minute Standard Tour is an easy walk through the first six, largest and most spectacular halls to the African Drum Room. These tours depart every hour on the hour 09h00–16h00, with fees R60 per adult and R30 per child. The Adventure Tour lasts 90 minutes and takes you in deeper but is strictly for lean, fit people who are definitely not claustrophobic (and speleologists, of course!). You'll crawl through narrow passages and drag yourself through Devil's Chimney and The Letterbox. These tours depart every hour on the half-hour 09h30–15h30, and fees are R75 per adult and R50 per child. It's an incredible experience to stand in those vast caverns surrounded by a fantasy of nature's sculpture. There's an interpretive centre, offering a short film, a museum, gift shop, bureau de change, bar and coffee shop, and the photographic Fantasy Theatre, plus a restaurant specialising in ostrich dishes. Wear sensible footwear, and note that the temperature in the caves is a constant 18 °C. Open 364 days a year (closed Christmas Day). For details, tel: 044-272-7410 or visit www. cangocaves.co.za.

En route to the caves, just past Schoemanspoort, turn right off the R328 onto a gravel road that's signposted to **Rus en Vrede Waterfall**. Continuing past this, the road links up with the N12 halfway between De Rust and Oudtshoorn. The waterfall is a short walk through lush forest from the car park, and it's well worth the effort of getting here!

There are several ostrich farms around Oudtshoorn, one of the most popular being **Safari Ostrich Show Farm**, just 6 kilometres south of town along the R328 towards the coast. Ostrich farming started around 1864, and Safari's been going for over 40 years. Stand on an ostrich egg, ride an ostrich (if you weigh less than 75kg) and try their restaurant's divine ostrich-liver pâté and succulent ostrich fillet. Open 07h30–17h00 daily, including public holidays, and a guided tour costs R60 per person. For more info, tel: 044-272-7311/2 or visit www. safariostrich.co.za.

There are those of us who need to try everything once because we're, well,

funny in the head. If you're willing to enter the water with creatures that sport huge gnashers, the **Cango Wildlife Ranch** offers the chance to 'Wet your Pants' and partake in the world's only crocodile cage diving. Sadly, there's no thrashing white water as the beasties gobble up tourists, but being within touching distance of such ancient predatory wildlife as a 4-metre Nile crocodile isn't something you'll experience – and survive – too often (take note how they lick their lips as you step into that cage …). The ranch offers a host of other great attractions, like Jumping Jaws, where crocs get to snatch at keepers holding out food; the Valley of Ancients with its colonial African theme; a reptile encounter; and if you enter the Nyami Nyumi gates, you'll get real close to giant fruit bats in an artificial mangrove forest setting. The limas live on Lima Island, and you

> **TIPS**
> ✦ Try ostrich biltong, dried sausage, and fillet – tis delish. There's a large abattoir shop in the industrial area that's a clinical affair, so don't let the abattoir part put you off. Alternatively, shops in town stock ostrich at higher prices.
> ✦ The Little Karoo's climate has large temperature fluctuations, both diurnal and seasonal, with contrasts of up to 28 °C between day and night not being unusual. So be prepared!
> ✦ There's a taxi service between Oudtshoorn and Cape Town along R62, that is fabulously reasonable at R180 one way. See page 22.

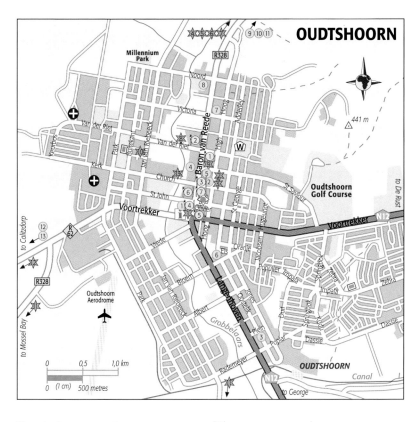

OUDTSHOORN

Places to stay

1. Queen's Hotel
2. 141 High Street B&B
3. Best Little Guest House
4. Yotclub B&B
5. Nostalgie B&B
6. Karoo Soul Travel Lodge
7. Backpacker's Paradise
8. Kleinplaas Caravan Park & Self-catering
9. Buffelsdrift Game Lodge
10. Wilgewandel Holiday Farm B&B / SC
11. Swartberg Country Manor
12. The Retreat at Groenfontein
13. Red Stone Hills

Places to eat

1. Jemina's Restaurant
2. Kalinka's
3. La Dolce Vita

4. The Colony
5. Avocado Pierre
6. Pancake Bazaar
7. Gabby's

Places of interest

☆ CP Nel Museum
☆ Le Roux Town House
☆ Dutch Reformed Church
☆ Cango Caves
☆ Wilgewandel Holiday Farm
☆ Rus en Vrede Waterfall
☆ Cango Wildlife Ranch
☆ Kango Wijnhuis
☆ Art Karoo Gallery
☆ Arbeidsgenot
☆ Safari Ostrich Show Farm
☆ Meerkat Magic
☆ Suspension Bridge

can watch the hippos from a wallow deck that's great for functions. In the cat section, you have a bird's-eye view from a walkway overlooking the enclosures housing big cats, including rare white Bengal tigers. Have a touch experience with hand-raised cheetah and tiger cubs. The wellbeing of the animals is paramount so encounters between the cats and the public take place only with select 'ambassadors' of the species (the policy is never to take animals from the wild). Cost for adults is R85, and R55 per child, but enquire about their annual membership. There's a 'kidzone' with all sorts to keep the little ones entertained

The Cango Wildlife Ranch, on the outskirts of Oudtshoorn, is the place to literally wet your pants getting close to large prehistoric predators.

while you relax at the nearby restaurant, where the menu includes crocodile and ostrich. The ranch is completely wheelchair-friendly, and open 365 days a year. For info, tel: 044-272-5593 or visit www.cango.co.za.

For a truly magical sunrise or sunset, contact Grant McIlrath who started the **Meerkat Magic** experience. This has to be a highlight for any nature-lover. It brings you to within metres of meerkats as they sun themselves at their burrow, and you may even be able to accompany them on their foraging expeditions. Unlike similar experiences, these meerkats are in no way tamed or fed. This is the real thing – they are absolutely wild and in their natural environment. Grant has worked intensively with meerkats for 16 years and his self-taught and entirely ethical habituation techniques allow visitors to get close to these little

beings and witness them going about their daily routine, as if unobserved. He's at pains to explain that although he makes certain noises, and has taught himself to understand their 'language', the meerkats are not interacting with him, but rather, they see him as part of their surrounds, like a rock or tree. Cost is R600 per person, with tours lasting 3–4 hours. This is not an establishment you can pop in to, so phone ahead on tel: 082-413-6895 or 044-272-3077, or visit www.meerkatmagic.com.

Oudtshoorn Ballooning has been sending people into orbit for years now. Okay, so it's not quite orbit, but you lift off just before sunrise and can drift through the air for up to 60 minutes, depending on the weather. Flying at 1 000 feet, the experience offers fantastic views of the mountains and valleys, as well as typical Karoo landscape, when drifting at treetop height. When you land, it's with a gentle plop as the basket touches earth and within minutes you'll have a glass of champagne for the traditional toast to another safe landing. Not a bad start to a perfect day in Oudtshoorn … Flights start anytime from 05h00 in summer, and 07h30 in winter, with the intention of lifting off by sunrise. Launches from Red Stone Hills for 6-plus passengers. Costs R2 100 per person, and discounts for 6-plus bookings. To book, tel: 082-784-8539 or visit www.oudtshoornballooning.co.za.

Artists of Oudtshoorn is a terrific little guide to painting, sculpture and other works of art and is available from the tourist office. It includes an easy-to-follow street map, and details the medium of each artist, plus contact details for those you need an appointment to see, and viewing times for others. There are several galleries in town, but make a point of visiting **Art Karoo** at 107 Baron van Reede Street.

One imposing building you won't miss in Baron van Reede Street is the sandstone **CP Nel Museum**, with its prominent clocktower. It has a long list of great exhibitions, including one on the ostrich, an outstanding collection of porcelain ware, a chemist, general-dealer room, and impressive doll collection. A unique feature of the museum is the reconstructed St John Street Synagogue – the Jewish community, primarily from Lithuania (1881–1890), played a big role in marketing ostrich feathers worldwide. Open 09h00–17h00 Monday–Saturday. **Le Roux Town House** is a fine example of an ostrich palace, and once you have

your ticket from the main museum, you can visit it at 146 High Street Monday–Friday.

If you enjoy wine, the **Kango Wijnhuis** in Van der Riet Street offers tastings and retail sales of an extensive award-winning range of wine, fortified wine, brandy, liqueur and witblits, which can be enjoyed on their stoep in warm weather. In December, they also offer a cheese platter along with your glass of wine; and the garden has plenty of space for the children to let off steam too. Visit the website at www.kangowines.com.

One of the cultural experiences on offer is that of Ma Betty Jantjies, a prominent resident of Bongolethu Township and a Xhosa purist. **Ma Betty's Xhosa Cultural Experience** must be booked in advance, and you'll be treated to an authentic Xhosa meal, prepared in the old tradition, followed by dancing. There is also a *sangoma* (traditional healer) story-telling accompanied by singing. Arrange a visit through the tourism office.

Another cultural stopover is at the **Arbeidsgenot Museum** where the renowned Afrikaans writer, poet, playright and politician CJ Langenhoven was born, lived and died.

Did you know that camels have a fifth foot and can consume up to 100 litres of water at one time? Well, find this out, and more, at **Wilgewandel Holiday Farm**. Situated 2 kilometres before the Cango Caves, the farm offers everything from a restaurant to camel rides, quad buggies, a touch farm, bumper boats, trampolines, a *foefie*-slide and an 18-hole Gwarra-gwarra (like putt-putt) golf course. Relax with a drink on the patio overlooking a dam and mountains while tame peacocks and waterfowl mosey around. It's idyllic for families with small children, and activities are reasonably priced so it won't bankrupt you. Phone ahead to check show times of their award-winning **Pioneer Cultural Experience**, which takes you back to 1823 and includes singing, dancing and eating with the pioneers. The farm is disabled-friendly and offers accommodation. For further information, tel: 044-272-0878, www.wilgewandel.co.za.

Adrenaline junkies who enjoy standing on the edge of a 40-metre cliff while your brain screams survival messages can join Johan Uys of **Swartberg Adventures**. Johan's been exploring the region since he was 'two bricks and a tickey' high and, apart from abseiling, he offers hiking, caving, mountain biking, canyoning and quad biking. Try the 150- to 500-metre cave crawling. Johan has an obsession with safety factors, so you're in safe hands. Call him on tel: 082-926-9389 or visit www.swartbergadventures.co.za.

For outdoor activities with the emphasis on geological, historical and natural treasures, contact Jan Bester of **True South Travel**. On offer here are 4x4 routes, motorcycle tours and hiking trails (tailor-made half- to three-day excursions). Contact Jan on tel: 082-461-8253 or click on www.swartbergexplore.co.za.

Le Petit Karoo Ranch is 12 kilometres north of town on the R328 to the Cango Caves, and offers all levels of horse riding. Rides are available all day, and are on marked trails with a guide. There's

a bistro serving drinks and light meals and, if you have kids, there's a safe games area for them and pony rides on offer. Call Pascal on tel: 044-272-7428.

While in Oudtshoorn, be sure to do the scenic circular route over the **Swartberg Pass**, through Prince Albert and back to Oudtshoorn via Meiringspoort and De Rust. Try to make a day of it, stopping for lunch and taking time to appreciate this spectacular part of our country. The Swartberg Pass is said to rival the most awesome passes in the world, and from the top there's a one-way road into **Gamkaskloof**, commonly known as **Die Hel** (The Hell) – see page 97.

> There are numerous 4x4 routes in the area, depending on how far you want to travel from town. Best is to get a list from the tourist office and make your decision from that.

Another lovely day trip is to Calitzdorp via **Matjiesrivier** and **Kruisrivier**. Take the R328 to the Cango Caves, turn left to Matjiesrivier and follow the base of the mountains. You'll pass the Swartberg Private Wildlife Estate. At the Kruisrivier junction, turn left to **Red Stone Hills**, then backtrack to the junction and continue to or past **The Retreat at Groenfontein** and ultimately to Calitzdorp and R62.

Overnight in Oudtshoorn

The elegant **Queen's Hotel** in Baron van Reede Street is the third-oldest working hotel in the country and was

One of many unforgettable experiences along Route 62 is a few hours spent with a family of wild meerkats near Oudtshoorn.

built in 1880. It is named after the Queen's Medal awarded to its owner in 1886, and today you can still see the original marble flooring, woodwork and other features giving the establishment its historic colonial ambience. The breakfast room opens out onto a pond and courtyard garden, around the corner from which is a secluded swimming pool. Enjoy an aperitif in the luxurious lounge or sip on a Pimm's in the wood-panelled bar before dining in The Colony restaurant. The 40 en-suite rooms are tastefully decorated, with air con, phone and TV. Breakfast is buffet-style and served 07h00–10h00, or you can nip next door to the recently opened **Café Brûlé Coffee Bar and Bakery**. B&B rates per double room are R870 to R1 160, tel: 044-272-2101 or visit www.queenshotel.co.za.

One of the most striking buildings in town is **The Parsonage** at 141 High Street. This double-storey sandstone house, built in 1881 at the time of the ostrich boom, has glorious wooden fretwork detail and a large balcony and veranda. Today, it's a guesthouse run by Gerrit and Ilsa van Schalkwyk, who offer comfy rooms furnished in keeping with the era in which the property was built. In winter, enjoy a log fire in the cosy lounge, and in summer, relax in the stunning rose garden. Gerrit offers a guided tour through the impressive Dutch Reformed church across the road. B&B rates are R280–R330 per person sharing. To book, tel: 044-279-1751 or click on www.oudtshoorn.com.

The Best Little Guest House is 1.7 kilometres from the town centre at 15 Plein Street, which is south of town off Langenhoven Road. There are 8 en-suite air-conditioned rooms, secure undercover parking, a mountain-rock swimming pool, a large deep veranda, DStv lounge, wifi hotspot, fireplace, and outdoor braai area. B&B rates are R270 per person sharing, and R180 for kids 0–12 years. To book, phone Carol or Karl on tel: 044-279-2137 or visit www.oudtshoornaccommodation.co.za.

The 3-star **Yotclub B&B** has different rooms and combinations to suit everyone, from singles to families. This large property leads down to a private 'waterfront' and has uninterrupted mountain views. Enjoy breakfast on the veranda while watching abundant birdlife of 100-plus species recorded. Look out for the large sign next to the Total garage in Baron van Reede Street. B&B rates are from R250 for standard twin, to R450 for the riverside room with king-sized bed. To enquire about family rates, tel: 044-279-2247 or click on www.gardenroute-yotclub.com.

Nostalgie B&B, at 74 Baron van Reede Street, is owned and run by Marietjie Genis, who has 3 en-suite rooms decorated with antiques, lace linen and down duvets in a lovingly restored property that's furnished to create the atmosphere of a bygone time. Visit Marietjie's old-fashioned gift and coffee shop on the same premises for traditional daytime meals and teas. B&B rates are R200–R250 per person

sharing. To book, tel: 044-272-4085 or visit www.oudtshoorn.com.

The 4-star backpackers, **Karoo Soul Travel Lodge**, at 170 Langenhoven Road, has all the usual facilities and adventure activities and is owner-run by Ilze Fisch. Choose from en-suite cottages (with a kitchenette), sleeping 2 for R320 per night; one cottage sleeps 4 and costs R320 for 2, plus R90 per extra person sharing. Double and twin rooms cost R260 for 2 people; triple rooms cost R350 for 3 people; and the 8-bed dormitory costs R90 per person. Do note, however, that these prices are not applicable during the annual KKNK (Klein Karoo Nasionale Kunstefees) festival. Karoo Soul is licensed to serve beer and wine, which you can enjoy at the pool or on the stoep with a fabulous view. Quiet time is from 22h30. This isn't a B&B, but they'll supply breakfast ingredients and you cook your own. For the lowdown, tel: 044-272-0330 or click on www.karoosoul.com.

Backpacker's Paradise, at 148 Baron van Reede Street, is a spacious 4-star backpacker hostel with all the facilities you could want. There's safe parking, DStv, free towel service, tea and coffee, Internet stations, a book-swap library, and a real coffee machine! The bar is situated away from sleeping areas; and you can self-cater or order meals, such as an ostrich fillet braai (R80), or vegetarian. A full, cooked breakfast (R40) includes ostrich egg, and if you're self-catering you get free ostrich egg. Join their company, **Joyrides**, for daily activities that include cycling. Rates are R90 for a dorm room, R290 for an en-suite double, and R250 for a double sharing a bathroom. For

Here's a tip!
Out of season, backpackers are quiet and the ones in Oudtshoorn offer excellent value for money.

Feather palaces stand as testament to the wealth created by the ostrich-feather boom.

details, tel: 044-272-3436 or visit www.backpackersparadise.net.

Kleinplaas, en route to the Cango Caves, offers 50-odd 'modernish' serviced self-catering chalets with a B&B option. Chalets are different sizes: a standard open-plan 4-bed costs R480–R600; 2-bedroom with 6 beds costs R714–R950; and a room with 2 beds (not self-catering) costs R350–R450. Ask about the specials too. The 4-star caravan park has plenty of shady, grassed sites with electricity, modern ablutions and a sparkling swimming pool. There's a central braai area, as well as a laundromat. Camping rates are R140–R190 for 4 people. To book, tel: 044-272-5811 or visit www.kleinplaas.co.za.

Out of town, there are dozens of options. The 4-star **Swartberg Country Manor** lies about 45 kilometres from town at the foot of the Swartberg Pass in Matjiesrivier Valley and is a place to recharge your batteries, whether you prefer to soak up the farm atmosphere or savour sunsets and sunrises overlooking the mountains from the manor's deep veranda. They offer elegant accommodation, great food, and the hosts are delightful. After dinner, join their tour of the skies and take a turn on the telescope. Early morning, before the sun rises, a resident cock starts crowing and the crows start squawking … B&B rates are R570–R620 per person sharing, and dinner costs R150–R180 a head. To book, tel: 044-279-3188 or click on www.swartbergcountrymanor.co.za.

Buffelsdrift Game Lodge is about 7 kilometres from town en route to the Cango Caves, and offers stylishly appointed luxury tents overlooking a huge dam. Tent décor is old colonial and includes a bath with a view over the dam. The main lodge's deck is built over the water and is perfect for spotting any of the 20 game species that come down to drink, including rhino and buffalo. If you're lucky, one of the resident hippos might pop up to say hello or, rather, *harrumpharrumph*. Game-viewing is done from a vehicle or on horseback, but the really special part is the elephant experience where you get to walk with them. Among the 217 recorded bird species are lots of vociferous Egyptian geese. Rates for DB&B, and 2 bush safaris are from around R1 500 per person. For info, tel: 044-272-0106 or visit www.bgamelodge.co.za.

Wilgewandel Holiday Farm has B&B as well as self-catering accommodation in a beautiful old farmhouse that dates back to 1895. It's surrounded by shade trees and lawn, and has a gorgeous view over mountains. The 2 spacious family rooms have 4 single beds each and an en-suite bathroom with shower. The kitchen is shared. Alternatively, there are 2 double rooms, and 1 twin room, both with en-suite showers and kitchenettes. All rooms have tea and coffee, a safe, bar fridge, heater and fan, as well as the use of braai facilities. Rates are R150 per person sharing, breakfast R45, rates for children depends on age. For the lowdown, tel: 044-272-0878 or click on www.wilgewandel.co.za.

> ## Two great farmstays
> between Oudtshoorn and Calitzdorp are **Red Stone Hills** and **The Retreat at Groenfontein**. See page 73.

Eating out in Oudtshoorn

Jemima's Restaurant has been voted one of the country's top restaurants – and rightly so! It's located in an old house in Baron van Reede Street, and tables are set in charmingly decorated rooms, niches and covered verandas leading to the back garden, which supplies all the chef's fresh herbs and many vegetables served. They have some great vegetarian dishes. Although they claim to offer 'plain plaas' fare, this isn't strictly true as many dishes have an extrinsic touch. It's a good idea to book well in advance as this is a very popular eatery-cum-attraction.

Call them on tel: 044-272-0808 or visit www.jemimas.com.

Diagonally opposite is **Kalinka's**, which is open only at night. It's not cheap, but the Russian owner goes out of her way to ensure she has the best quality produce from which to prepare her renowned dishes. Starters include grilled crocodile, Karoo sashimi and smoked croc carpaccio. The ostrich fillet costs R150 and is oven-baked in layers with onion and cheese, or you can have the African Trio of gemsbok, kudu and ostrich ... or the quail breasts.

La Dolce Vita is a favourite with locals and visitors. It's a courtyard restaurant, with a small indoor seating area, and the bright cushions and fun décor touches add to the upbeat atmosphere. The food is a delicious mix of Italian and South African dishes and you can be assured of an enjoyable dining experience, no matter what your age or proclivity. This is also an Internet hotspot. Breakfast is served all day and includes the 'Liver Transplant' – and if you're there for one of their live music events, you may just need a new liver! Portions are generous and this is one eating establishment that's focusing on keeping the locals happy. Open 09h00 until late (kitchen closes at 22h00) Monday–Saturday. For more info, tel: 044-279-3269 or click on www.thesweetlife.co.za.

The Colony restaurant is upstairs in Queen's Hotel next to the CP Nel Museum. It's a stylish place with muted lighting, an extensive wine list that includes reserve wines, and the menu is excellent. There's a good choice for vegetarians – try the roulade of roasted butternut, leeks, spinach and fresh tomato sauce. With your tiny homemade loaf of bread, you get a variety of flavoured butters; salads include roasted beetroot and classic Caesar salad; pasta includes homemade ravioli and cannelloni; and there is Mossel Bay sole, as well as Karoo meat dishes. Open 18h00–22h00. (See also pages 90–91).

Avocado Pierre is owned by Pierre (who also owns Jemima's), and is open from 08h00 until late for all sorts of delicious meals, from breakfast through to cakes, grills, curries, Kassler chops, and more. Sit indoors, or dine al fresco overlooking a small pond and the CP Nel Museum. If you just want a drink, this is a good place too – there's a choice of 11 cocktails, plus a menu of liqueurs, shooters, mixed shooters, ciders and other headache-inducing drinks.

For a reasonably priced breakfast or light daytime eats (the hamburgers are amazing value for money), try the **Pancake Bazaar**, which is in Baron van Reede Street, on the left, about a block up from Queen's Hotel. Opposite, **Gabby's** is a great restaurant to take kids to because there's a play area. It's also a good spot for sports fans to watch main games; if you're a pensioner, head there on a Wednesday; and burger fans can get specials on a Monday. They also do Sunday lunch, have a large, varied menu and have paid attention to their wine list. If the verbose Rindi is on duty, she'll tell you that they even have baby food on the menu! Kids as well as vegetarians are catered for, the homemade chicken pie is huge and good value for money, and they do favourites, such as steak, egg and chips.

The Rus en Vrede waterfall is in a secluded ravine north of Oudtshoorn.

Near Oudtshoorn

Herold is a quiet hamlet in the Outeniqua mountains, and is reached via the N12 south of Oudtshoorn, then east along the N9 towards Uniondale. It's here that you'll find **Over the Mountain Guest Farm**, which offers accommodation as well as a pub and restaurant in renovated buildings that were once the post office, the police station and a 'house of sin' in the early

BIG BIRD

The ostrich (*Struthio camelus*) is the largest of the 8 600-odd bird species in the world, and a flightless one at that, although it can run very fast. It can reach 2.6 metres and a weight of 135 kilograms, and lives on a mostly vegetarian diet of grass, succulents, berries and seeds, with the odd insect to add interest. The large numbers of pebbles they swallow aids their digestion and helps grind hard food. Ostriches are well adapted to living in a dry climate, and are extensively farmed in the Little Karoo. In the 18th century, populations were almost decimated thanks to hunting for feathers – and then we started domesticating them in order to pluck feathers. By the 19th century, numbers had increased due to farming and they're now farmed throughout the world, but particularly in this country, for meat, leather and feathers. The meat is considered extremely healthy due to its very low fat content, while the leather is tanned and used for fashion

One thing you're sure to see lots of in the Little Karoo, and especially around Oudtshoorn, is the world's biggest bird, the ostrich.

items such as handbags and shoes. There are still populations of wild ostriches, the majority of which occur in game reserves. Contrary to popular belief, they do not stick their heads in the sand. Their eggs are so strong that they can take the weight of an average person standing on them without breaking. They mate for life and share the incubation of eggs, which take 35–40 days to hatch, and thereafter the male usually looks after the chicks. He will compete for a flock of 3–5 hens, and in some areas these girls will use a communal nest – a shallow hole in bare ground – holding 14–60 eggs.

20th century. This is an idyllic retreat. Accommodation costs from R300 per person B&B, while self-catering cottages sleeping 4–6 cost R550–R750. Dinner is by arrangement and costs around R100 a head. There are various walking and mountain biking trails, and good bird watching. In season, you can tour the operating hops farm nearby. Call Dave or Gail on tel: 044-888-1700 or 073-170-7120, or click on www.overthemountain.co.za.

Herold is also home to **Herold Wines**, and for wine-tasting call Vivien Harpur on tel: 072-833-8223. The **Outeniqua Power Van** offers trips along old tracks in rail buses from George up the Outeniqua mountains to the top of the historic Montagu Pass, and into Herold. For info, tel: 044-801-8239 or 082-490-5627.

PRINCE ALBERT

Prince Albert is situated on the southern edge of the Great Karoo at the foot of the Swartberg mountains. The quickest way to get here from the R62 is via Oudtshoorn over the Swartberg Pass, but if you're not one for heights and narrow winding roads then take the spectacular Meiringspoort from De Rust to Klaarstroom, then turn onto the R407 and, 55 kilometres later, you'll be soaking up the atmosphere of a bygone era. We first visited Prince Albert some years ago during the Olive Festival, now called the Prince Albert Town and Olive Festival, held towards the end of April each year, and were hooked on the atmosphere of the place. The village came into being in the early 1840s when it was known as Albertsberg, after Queen Victoria's husband. The area saw a gold rush in 1891 and around the same time the price of ostrich feathers peaked and the town experienced a period of prosperity. This affluence can still be seen in the many large Victorian and Cape Dutch homes and buildings that make this town so attractive – our favourite being the Swartberg Hotel. Today the town has a host of activities and attractions to satisfy virtually every preference.

Out and about in Prince Albert

For explorers, the Swartberg Pass over the mountains of the same name is a good starting point. This sinuous road, climbing over the peaks and down into the Little Karoo, is widely regarded as one of the most spectacular mountain roads in the world, rivalled, some say, only by the Darjeeling Pass in Tibet.

A popular day outing is a circular route over the Swartberg Pass to Oudtshoorn, then on to the quaint village of De Rust, through the spectacular Meiringspoort and back. On the way to the top of the Swartberg Pass a road turns off to **Gamkaskloof**, or Die Hel (see page 90), as it's more commonly known. This lost valley, only connected to the outside world in the 1960s, was, for over a century, home to a remote group of people who were described at the time as 'the most isolated community within a community of their own kind in the world'. The valley is now a nature reserve. For walkers, the options around Prince Albert are endless and include the historic walking route (taking in many of the beautiful national monuments – there's a self-guide map available at tourist info) around the town, and those with a penchant for the supernatural can take part in the pre-supper **Ghost Walk** (call Alisa Tudhope on tel: 023-541-1211). The old **Albert Mill** on the edge of town towards the Swartberg Pass was built in 1842 and is nearly fully restored. It's a good place to picnic in the

---

WHY VISIT?

Historic buildings, quiet streets, great accommodation and restaurants, and it's setting at the foot of the Swartberg!

WHAT'S WHAT?

Tourist information is in the main street next to the Fransie Pienaar Museum. Tel: 023-541-1366, www.patourism.co.za.

shade of trees, listening to the gurgle of the water along the canal. When the summer sun gets too hot, use the time to peruse items in the **Fransie Pienaar Museum** in Church Street. One thing this town has, which few others in the region can boast, is a selection of locally grown and produced products for the travelling gastronome. Make time to visit **Gay's Dairy**, to savour and buy award-winning cheeses, **Weltevrede Fig and Fruit Farm**, renowned for their sun-dried Adams figs, oranges and naartjies, and **Swartrivier Olive Farm**. Tours and tastings can be arranged for all.

Overnight in Prince Albert

The town has an abundance of places to stay, from up-market to budget, so you're unlikely to have a sleepless night if you arrive without booking. At the top end is **De Bergkant Lodge** in Church Street, a Cape Dutch gabled house and national monument furnished with antique pieces. There are 8 air-conditioned rooms with en-suite Victorian-style bathrooms, DStv, a swimming pool and a wellness centre offering various treatments. Rates are R800–R1 000 per person B&B, and there is also a self-catering option. For more information, tel: 023-541-1088.

Less expensive and also in Church Street is the 3-star **Swartberg Hotel**, another national monument that is a relic of the Victorian era, with 13 en-suite rooms in the main building and 5 en-suite rondavels in the garden – all with DStv – from R660 per double. To book, tel: 023-541-1332. **Dennehof**, off Christina de Witt Street, has 3 cottages in farm-like settings – either self-catering or B&B costing R325–R375 per person. Call on tel: 023-541-1227. **Karoo Lodge** is in the centre of the

Old architecture and plumbago hedges are a feature of the historic town of Prince Albert.

village, at 66 Church Street, and has 3 en-suite rooms and a 2-bedroom family unit, all with TVs and the usual features. Costs are R285–R385 per person. For info, tel: 023-541-1467.

Budget lodgings come in the form of Tannie Alta and her **Hooggenoeg Holiday Houses**, which are self-contained properties scattered around town from as little as R70 per person (no meals). For details, tel: 023-541-1455. If it's a farmstay you prefer, head 25 kilometres up the Weltevrede Valley to Suzelle Koorts' **Weltevrede** and **De Hoek** farmhouses. Literally translated, Weltevrede means 'well satisfied' and this you will be after a stay in the 19th-century houses surrounded by mountains and orchards. They are self-catering, but meals can be arranged. The costs are R175–R300 per person, so call on tel: 023-541-1715. For lovers of the great outdoors, **Bushman Valley** in the nearby Swartberg Private Nature Reserve has caravan and campsites at R50 per person. To book, tel: 023-541-1322.

Eating out in Prince Albert

During the day, **The Lazy Lizard** at the southern end of Church Street is open 06h00–18h00 for light eats and drinks – and everything is homemade and delicious. They sell curios, and have an Internet café on the mezzanine. **The Bush Pub** does lunches and suppers or just drinks in the atmospheric bar or garden and is open 10h00 until late Tuesday–Saturday, and for lunch until about 16h00 Sunday. **Karoo Kombuis**, in Deurdrift Street, serves traditional Karoo meals, but take your own wine and booking is essential, so call on tel:

023-541-1110. If you can't get enough of the Victorian charm, try the **The Victorian Room** at the Swartberg Hotel for traditional South African fare (it's also fully licensed) or **The Swartberg Arms**, which serves steakhouse fare at wallet-friendly prices.

VANWYKSDORP

This small Little Karoo town involves an excursion away from the R62 but if you are one of those naturally curious explorers then it's worth getting dusty (the town is only accessed via dirt roads). Getting there makes for an interesting circular drive from Ladismith: south on the R62 for 10 kilometres, then left onto the R327, which reaches Vanwyksdorp after 60 kilometres, then take the minor road over the scenic Rooiberg Pass and follow the signs to Calitzdorp, returning to Ladismith via the R62. Vanwyksdorp itself hasn't quite emerged from the dust that settled when inhabitants forsook the countryside for the bright lights of the cities during the latter years of the last century. This, however, is part of the town's charm and the place effuses a rural atmosphere with fruit orchards on

---

WHY VISIT?

Because there are very few such undeveloped spots left to visit …

WHAT'S WHAT?

There's no tourist office in Vanwyksdorp, so contact Calitzdorp Tourism on tel: 044-213-3775, or local estate agent Heidi de Kock on tel: 082-978-4863.

Just about every town has a picturesque church. This one is in the small town of Vanwyksdorp.

the outskirts and large plots complete with grazing cows, sheep and goats slotted among the dwellings.

Out and about in Vanwyksdorp

The Dutch Reformed church, built in 1907, has picturesque grounds with lawns, bougainvillea, hibiscus and lots of roses between which sunbirds flit in the daylight. Look out for the little house overlooking the church and see if you can get a glimpse of the 'Oomie' sitting on his stoep puffing away at his pipe, while his donkey trims his garden. One can't really get more of an idyllic country picture.

Overnight in Vanwyksdorp

There is only one accommodation establishment in town, or rather close to town, and that is **Sonhof Self-catering** owned by Uta Soltau. It's just across the Groot River on the R327 towards Herbertsdale. The house

has 3 bedrooms (1 double, 2 twins), a bathroom and toilet and has the basics for DIY meals, including a braai spot. Rates are R100 per person sharing, with children under 12 years half price. Contact Uta on tel: 072-021-9618.

Eating out in Vanwyksdorp

When we were doing the research for this book there was a local restaurant (open on weekends only), but rumour had it that it was closing and the property was on the market. However, if you feel peckish while idling along the gravel streets, head to **Die Stop Supermarket**. This is one of those funny little-town shops whose dusty shelves carry a surprising variety of stock. There are hot pies for sale, fresh bread, cold drinks and crisps, there's a rudimentary butchery, and a few other things you may want to use to put together an on-the-road meal. Oh, and they even sell Lotto tickets!

Welcome to the Langkloof 8

The Langkloof, meaning 'long ravine', makes up the eastern section of Route 62 and, at around 125 kilometres, it's easy to see how it got its name. For all its length, however, it's hardly more than a few kilometres across, sandwiched between the Outeniqua and Tsitsikamma mountains in the south and the Kouga in the north.

The Langkloof is fondly referred to as the Fruit Route due to extensive orchards of pears, peaches, apricots, plums and, of course, apples.

For many South Africans, the Langkloof came to the fore during the mid-1980s in the form of a novel, *Fiela's Child*, by the late Dalene Matthee. It was set near what is today the small village of Avontuur at the western gateway to the kloof, and the story follows a lost white boy found and raised by a coloured family in the 1800s. The settlement of the Langkloof, however, pre-dates that era by at least another century and a number of the families here today are tenth-generation landowners, some of the longest standing in South Africa.

The kloof has a long history and even today there's a subtle air of mystery surrounding the place, and age-old feuds between families still simmer. Apparently, depending on whom you talk to, there's some dispute as to where the 'true' Langkloof starts and ends. Many of the long-standing *inwoners* (inhabitants) consider it to run

A fruit-packing shed stands alongside a rural road leading into the Tsitsikamma mountains, Langkloof.

only from Avontuur to the bridge on the R62 just south of Joubertina. And if you're on the other side of the bridge, then you're not a 'Kloower'. Taking it further than that, don't think if you move into the area you'll automatically be considered a local. Not even after 20 years. If you're not of the original families, you'll always be an outsider.

That said, the people, whether dyed-in-the-wool or recently settled, have the typically friendly manner of South African country folk and you'll always feel welcome in their territory.

There are only three main towns in the Langkloof. The furthest east is Kareedouw, around which sawmills give an indication of the main industry in the area, with a little sheep and cattle farming undertaken in the foothills. However, as you venture further west, the predominant industry changes to fruit farming, giving rise to the Langkloof's other slogan, The

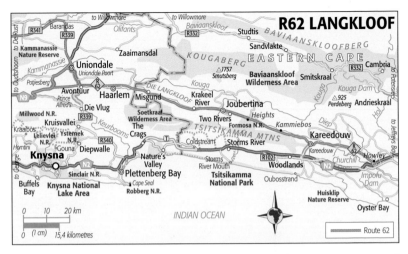

R62 LANGKLOOF

to Willowmore
to Willowmore
Baviaanskloof
Studtis
BAVIAANSKLOOFBERG
Sandvlakte
EASTERN CAPE
Barandas
R341
R339
Olifants
R332
Kammanassie
Nature Reserve
Zaaimansdal
KOUGABERG
△1757
Smutsberg
Baviaanskloof
Wilderness Area
Smitskraal
R332 Cambria
Uniondale
Uniondale Poort
Kammanassie
Kouga
Kouga Dam
△925
Perdeberg Andrieskraal
Potjiesberg
Avontúur
Prince
Alfred's
Haarlem
Misgund
DIE LANGKLOOF
Krakeel
River
Joubertina
Die Vlug
Millwood N.R.
R339
Soetkraal
Wilderness Area
Two Rivers
Heights
Kruisvallei
Keurbooms
The
Crags
TSITSIKAMMA MTNS
Formosa N.R.
Kammiebos
Diep
Kareedouw
Kraaibos
Lelievlei Ysternek
N.R. N.R.
R340
Coldstream
Storms River
Kareedouw
62
Howley
Hornbni
Gouna Diepwalle
Nature's
Valley
Storms
River Mouth
R102
Woodlands
N2
Churchill
Impofu
Dam
Knysna
Sinclair N.R.
Plettenberg Bay
Tsitsikamma
National Park
Oubosstrand
Buffels
Bay
Knysna National
Lake Area
Cape Seal
Robberg N.R.
Huisklip
Nature Reserve
Oyster Bay

0   10   20 km
0   (1 cm)   15,4 kilometres

INDIAN OCEAN

══════ Route 62

Fruit Route. The area's hot summers and frosty winters have made the Langkloof one of South Africa's premier deciduous-fruit regions, which boasts amongst its clients the quality-driven UK supermarket chain of Sainsbury's. This industry is centred around Joubertina and on towards the small farming settlement of Louterwater. Here the main fruits are apples and pears, with peaches, apricots, prunes and youngberries grown on a lesser scale.

At the western extreme of the Langkloof, about 12 kilometres from the junction where the R62 joins the N9, is Uniondale. Because it is situated on the main north–south N9 route, the town is busier than those in the Langkloof itself, and therefore has an extended range of facilities.

A narrow road and stone cottage nestled among the rolling hills of the Langkloof epitomise the rural atmosphere of the broader region.

Route 62: 9
The Langkloof

Much of the natural beauty of the Langkloof region is in the mountains that stretch away from the R62. It's a remarkably untramelled area with a unique and quite spectacular beauty, so it's definitely worth spending a couple of days exploring even the minor gravel roads.

The Langkloof is tinged with a romantic ambience, like here on Bo-Jani Guest Farm, but hasn't yet caught on as a tourist destination.

JOUBERTINA

'Joubertina isn't a destination, but part of the journey.' That is the honest opinion of one of the locals we met when we visited and, yes, he was probably right – you wouldn't want to spend a week in the town, but a few nights getting to know the place won't be time wasted. It's one of those platteland towns where characters make up the fabric of the society, and a chance meeting with one will make for an interesting and unique experience. Their stories will become your stories as you entertain family and friends with them back home. One such individual informed us he had no doubt the town had the 'ugliest' main street in South Africa, and even thought they should market it as a tourist attraction. However, we didn't think it was that bad. Okay, it's not pretty, but we've seen worse. He did have a point about the scrapyard at the far end, though. Rusted skeletons of farm machinery and trucks clutter a large plot, but no matter how persuasive people have been Oom Danie refuses to clean the place up. Town streets aside, Joubertina is set among vast orchards of apples, pears, apricots, peaches and prunes, many of these off the main R62 and up the side kloofs cutting into the Tsitsikamma mountains to the south. Most of what there is to see and do lies in the surrounding mountains.

Out and about in Joubertina

Pick up the *Langkloof Route 62 Tourist Map* from Die Ark and spend half a day on a slow meander on the 'B loop' indicated on the map. It starts near Die Kraaltjie farmstall just west of town and winds its way from hilly heights to valley bottoms, crossing the cool waters of the Kouga and other lesser rivers. You'll pass hidden valleys with cows ambling sedately on green pastures, ponds sporting water lilies reflecting the surrounding scenery, farmsteads and labourers' cottages with their associated menagerie of animals and waving children, perhaps klipspringer and grey rhebok or a baboon on a cement reservoir, and lonely gravestones facing towards the rising sun – all of this embraced by rocky cliffs and distant peaks.

WHY VISIT?

Orchards provide colourful blossoms in spring and juicy fruit in summer.

WHAT'S WACKY?

The quail eggs and meat for sale at Die Kraaltjie farmstall just outside of town.

WHAT'S WHAT?

For clear, concise information, have a chat with Gerrie and Hettie at Die Ark (alongside the R62 at the eastern entrance to the town) or call them on tel: 042-273-1783 or visit www.langklooftourism.co.za.

A market is held on the second Saturday of the month in the parking area at Die Ark, where all sorts of goodies are up for sale.

Breakfasts are served at the farmstall, which also offers light eats. It's open from 07h00 until late afternoon, and sells honey, pickled quails' eggs, and quail and guinea fowl meat fresh from the farm. Activities include hiking, fishing and swimming. Rates are R140–R170 per person self-catering, R100 per campsite plus R10 per person. Breakfast costs R50 and dinner, by prior arrangement, R75 (there's a licensed bar at the farmstall). For further details, tel: 042-273-1313 or 082-498-1045.

Le Bocage Guesthouse, at 20 De Waal Street in town, offers 5 stylish en-suite double/twin rooms in a large house, and all have TV and tea/coffee-making facilities. Breakfasts are served in the dining room. Rates are R250–R300 per person B&B. To book, tel: 042-273-2291 or 082-801-3303.

Eating out in Joubertina

Die Ark is your one-stop info/eat/drink stop alongside the R62 at the eastern entrance to the town. Gerrie and Hettie, who own and run the place, recently moved here from way up north. They're open 07h30–21h00 Monday–Friday, 07h30–14h30 Saturday, and 07h30–15h00 Sunday. The tourist info office takes bookings for accommodation and activities, and the restaurant and takeaways has a good menu, with pizzas as part of their fare. The tramezzinis are massive, so make sure you're really hungry. The restaurant also exhibits artwork for sale, including those of Martin Wessels, a colourful character who lives a hermit's lifestyle at a secret hideaway in the mountains that's known only to a select few. There's a

Surrounded by tall palms, Joubertina's Dutch Reformed church has a unique feel.

Overnight in Joubertina

Die Kraaltjie, on the western edge of town, is more than just a farmstall. Owner Elize van Greunen is your hostess and on duty 24 hours a day – well, it seems that way, anyway … She has 17 self-catering units sleeping a total of 65 as well as 3 farmhouses. There are 10 caravan sites and the establishment caters for conferences and weddings.

bar offering the usual, plus wine tasting and sales from cellars further west on the R62 (Calitzdorp, Kango, Boplaas and Uitvlugt). There is also a theatre underneath – a converted service station – where various singers perform each month. Not bad for a little-out-of-the-way *dorpie*, and like us you'll probably be surprised by the continuous trickle of visitors coming and going, even on a Sunday. For info, tel: 042-273-1783.

Around Joubertina

About 19 kilometres west of Joubertina, on the R62, lies the small settlement of **Louterwater** (meaning 'bubbling water'), and the large number of dams and canals in the area are testament to this abundant effervescent resource.

Oudrif Padstal stands on the left in the shade of a huge tree. It is open 08h00–17h30 Monday–Friday and 08h00–13h30 Saturday, but tel: 042-272-1144 for more information. Here Tannie Marie serves breakfasts and light meals throughout the day and, if you're lucky enough to be there on a Tuesday or Thursday, she serves up plates of wholesome boerekos. Jars of her jams and preserves – made without any preservatives – are for sale, as are crafts made by the local community. This farmstall is associated with **Oudrift Landgoed**, a large fruit-farming concern in the area, and they use the proceeds from the farmstall to fund upliftment projects in the area. In winter there are fires burning in the farmstall's two hearths, which may keep you ensconced in its warmth longer than anticipated. Every second Saturday, Marius and Amanda, the farm's owners and qualified counsellors, mingle with the patrons and freely offer advice to those who seek it. An added bonus to a visit here is the orchards' export-quality fruit, which can be bought by the tray. The best time for soft fruits (apricots and peaches) is November–February, while apples and pears are available year round. You could even take an informative tour of the cooling rooms and pack houses on the premises, and it won't cost you a cent. If you become attached to the place and want to spend a night, then a short distance away, hidden among the orchards with its own hiking trail, is **Oudrift Cottage**, which is available on a self-catering basis and sleeps 4. Rates of R150 per person include a continental breakfast. For details, tel: 083-233-4692.

KAREEDOUW

Depending on the direction in which you are travelling, Kareedouw is either the first or last town on Route 62, lying in the extreme east about 35 kilometres from the N2 highway, which leads to the coastal city of Port Elizabeth. The town is flanked in the south by the peaks of the Tsitsikamma range and to the north by the Suuranys mountains. Around Kareedouw, sawmills give an indication of the main industry of the town with a little sheep and cattle farming undertaken in the surrounding foothills. One important person connected to the town is John Vorster, prime minister of South Africa from 1966 to 1978, who is buried in the cemetery next to the Dutch Reformed church. However, the one thing Kareedouw is most famous for is its *boerewors* (farm sausage) produced by

The Langkloof has some eye-catching places, like this one in Kareedouw.

Kareedouw Slaghuis (butchery), which was established in 1926.

On the eastern edge of the town, and denoted on most maps, lies the small settlement of Assegaaibos, which today consists solely of the **Assegaaibosch Country Lodge**. However, in the days of our forefathers when ox-wagons and horses were the only means of transport, this little place was an important stopover for travellers long before Kareedouw was even thought of. The original hotel was built in 1866, but in 1971 it burned down, sparing just the pub and a stone building that now serves as the chapel. The hotel was rebuilt, however, and although a lot more modern these days, it continues to serve travellers.

Out and about in Kareedouw

The Langkloof Route 62 tourist road map – most establishments will have it – indicates self-drive circular routes, which take you into the depths of

WHY VISIT?

Spend a day or two simply exploring the gravel backroads that loop through the fascinating Suuranys mountains.

WHAT'S WACKY?

◆ Kareedouw *boerewors* surpasses Prime Minister John Vorster's grave as the town's most famous attraction.
◆ The selection of music at Norma Jean's Diner definitely makes it worth a quick stop.

WHAT'S WHAT?

For information, call the Assegaaibosch Country Lodge on tel: 042-288-0700 or visit www.assegaaibosch.co.za.

the Suuranys and Kouga mountains and range from 1.5 to 2.5 hours to complete, although it's worth adding an hour onto that time so you can stop along the way and take in some of the impressive scenery. If you don't want to take your car onto the gravel roads, then Assegaaibosch Country Lodge arranges day excursions.

Stock up your cooler box with a few coils of the town's famous boerewors from Kareedouw Slaghuis. You'd probably expect the butchery to be in the main street, but it's actually located near the sportsfields towards the bottom end of town. A large board in the main street points you in the right direction.

Heading towards Joubertina along the R62, **Herbal Renaissance** stands on the left, about 7 kilometres out. It's open 09h00–17h00 Monday–Saturday, and serves healthy herb-inspired meals and high tea, and also sells gifts.

Kareedouw is only 8 kilometres from the N2 via the R402, and then about 30 kilometres west is Storms River where **Stormsriver Adventures** offers treetop canopy tours and a variety of other adventurous activities.

Overnight in Kareedouw

The surrounds of the 4-star **Assegaaibosch Country Lodge** are a pleasant surprise considering their proximity to a large brick factory. At reception you might get to meet Anton, who owns the lodge and was the inspiration behind its revival, otherwise managers Coenraad and Karin will ensure your stay is a pleasant one. The lodge consists of 13 en-suite rooms with TV and tea/coffee-making facilities, and the majority open onto the expansive swimming pool, which is the central feature of the lodge. At one end is Dezeppi's Pizzeria and on the far side the original pub, which was the

To get to grips with the rolling scenery of the Langkloof, take to the gravel roads in the Suuranys and Kouga mountains.

Attention to detail at Bo-Jani Guest Farm near Kareedouw makes it home away from home.

first establishment in the Eastern Cape to be awarded a liquor licence and still serves up alcoholic beverages. Next door is the new sports bar, where you can watch all the big matches on TV. B&B rates are R425 per person sharing, and R525 per person DB&B. They also cater for conferences and weddings. For information, tel: 042-288-0700.

Bo-Jani is just 24 kilometres west of Kareedouw on the R62: turn right at the signs and follow the gravel road as it winds for 6 kilometres into the Kouga mountains. Thys and Carmen are as down to earth as you can get and want nothing more than for their guests to enjoy their

little piece of paradise. Accommodation is in the old school, which has been renovated and extended into a lovely self-catering cottage sleeping 5, or a fully equipped flat nearer the main house sleeping 6. There are also rustic sites to pitch a tent. Breakfasts and dinners can be preordered – we recommend you experience at least one of each – and are served in the restored stone-and-thatch stables that Thys calls 'Die Plek van die Vleisvreters' (Place of the Meat Eaters) because this is where the indoor braai is situated. Naturally, this is also the place to enjoy a glass of your favourite tipple either outside on the stoep or, when the cold mists settle into the valley, inside in front of the fire. The whole place is warm, cosy, homely and tranquil, with lots of special little touches, and could quite easily become a favourite. There's a real farmyard feeling, with a menagerie of animals, and activities include bird-watching, fishing, horse riding, walks in the fynbos, donkey-cart rides with a picnic basket and, if you can't miss your daily workout, there's a small low-tech gym. Rates are R125–R150 per person sharing, with discounts for children. Dinners must be prearranged and are a steal at R60, which includes a glass of wine, and breakfasts are scrumptious at R35. For details, tel: 042-288-0224 or 082-828-9202.

Eating out in Kareedouw

The Sweaty Dutchman coffee shop and bistro is hard to miss. It's in the main street, with flags flying and an ox-wagon standing outside (open 08h00–17h00 Monday–Friday and 09h00–14h00 Saturday). The title isn't really one that instils confidence in the personal hygiene of the proprietor, especially when they are in the business of preparing food you'll be eating, so it was with some trepidation that we first entered, half expecting to be greeted by a greasy, barrel-chested proprietor with slicked-back hair, a string vest and cigarette loosely clasped in the corner of his mouth. As it turned out, Hans – complete with Dutch accent and bandana tied neatly around his head – was clean-shaven and wearing a spotless apron. Apparently, when he had a coffee-roasting business in Gauteng, he'd arrive home hot and bothered from being in front of the roaster all day and his wife started calling him her sweaty Dutchman. The name stuck. Hans' knowledge of coffee is immediately evident, and he has it roasted to his own specs. Try their Dutch Uitsmijter, a light meal on every menu in Holland. It's perfect sustenance for continued exploring of the area. If the kids need to run their batteries down, there's a neatly trimmed lawn for them to cavort around. For further details, tel: 042-288-0056.

Virtually next door on the main road is **Norma Jean's Diner** run and owned by Tom and Marisa. The restaurant/pub has a distinct music theme throughout, which stems from Tom's fanatical fondness of music – and, with a collection of 800 CDs and 600 LPs, you won't get bored of the background vibes. His signature dishes are the seafood platter, ribs and eisbein, and you won't find French fries here, but rather fresh and chunky potato chips. Portions are generous and offer good value for money. Norma Jean's is open 11h00–midnight Tuesday–Saturday, and 12h00–15h00 Sunday for a buffet lunch. There's a beer garden out back with lots of shade. Call them on tel: 042-288-0664.

Dezeppi's Pizzeria at Assegaaibosch Country Lodge is open Monday, Wednesday and Friday for supper, and Saturday for light lunches. Here, surrounded by murals depicting scenes of rural Italy, Des serves pizzas from a genuine wood-fired clay oven as well as other Italian dishes. **The Copper Pot** is the main restaurant at Assegaaibosch Country Lodge and is open on the nights Dezeppi's isn't. For more info, tel: 042-288-0700.

UNIONDALE

Uniondale is on the N9, a short distance from the small settlement of Avontuur and the Langkloof proper. Locally, the town is probably best known for the occasional sightings of the ghost of a young girl who died in an accident on a lonely stretch of road 20 kilometres from town in 1968. However, this spectral figure is not a tangible tourist attraction and the only time you'll get a glimpse of her is when you least expect it.

The town has lovely guesthouses, some pleasant restaurants, and enough attractions to warrant a few days' stay in a place few think of as a destination.

Out and about in Uniondale

At the **African Aloe** factory, just off Voortrekker Street, health and natural products are manufactured from *Aloe ferox* and *A. arborescens*. They sell these, including health drinks, beauty creams and lotions, from the factory.

Overlooking Uniondale from near the old fort. Beyond lie the Kammanassie mountains.

There's also a restored British fort on a hill (accessed from the road alongside the Dutch Reformed church) at the back of town from where there's a good view. Tucked away behind the showgrounds, the water mill, built in 1854, reputedly has the largest wheel on a mill in South Africa. It houses a restaurant in its historic interior (see 'Eating out in Uniondale').

There's plenty of fascinating San rock art in the area. The best way to view this is on a guided tour at **Mountain Pastures Game Reserve**, where over 500 paintings have been discovered. To book, tel: 044-752-3510.

For a day's outing, take a drive to Knysna or Plettenberg Bay, about 80 kilometres away, via the scenic Prince Alfred Pass, one of Thomas Bain's creations.

Overnight in Uniondale

The 2-star **Townhouse Guesthouse**, next to tourist information in Voortrekker Street, has been offering travellers a place to rest their heads since 1991. The accommodation is made up of 6 en-suite double rooms and a family unit, each with its own entrance, TV and tea/coffee-making facilities. But comfortable beds are not all that's on offer here. There's a swimming pool, braai facilities, lock-up parking, an à la carte restaurant for guests that can seat 24, and a ladies' bar. Your hosts, Dave and Tish, can organise 4x4 trips, hiking trails, game-viewing and trout fishing. B&B rates are R210–R240 per person, but for all the ins and outs, tel: 044-752-1331.

The 3-star **Zeru House**, also in Voortrekker Street, is where Paul and Carol offer B&B or DB&B accommodation in 3 double rooms in the original residence or self-catering in a garden cottage that sleeps 4. There's secure parking, a swimming pool and braai facilities. Rates for the B&B rooms are R250–R280 per person, while the cottage goes for R700 (self-catering, but breakfasts can be ordered for R50 and dinners for R80–R100). For more information, tel: 044-752-1371 or click on www.zeruhouse.co.za.

Another good option in Voortrekker Street is **Uniondale Lodge**, which has 3 en-suite bedrooms, DStv, a guest lounge and a pub. B&B rates are R320–R350 per person. For details, tel: 044-752-1642 or visit www.uniondalelodge.co.za.

Uniondale Caravan Park is alongside African Aloe in Voortrekker Street, not far from the turnoff from the N9 on the Willowmore side of town. It offers level, shady, grassed sites, some of which have electrical points. For the lowdown, tel: 044-752-1266.

A short way out of town, **Mountain Pastures Game Reserve** has 2 accommodation options and a host of activities. At Mountain Pastures itself there are chalets, either double or twin, and one family unit, all with fireplaces and available on a B&B or DB&B basis. Rates are R330–R360 per person. All meals are served in the restaurant; breakfast costs R50, lunch R55 and dinner R70–R100. The self-catering option is located nearby at **San Valley Retreat**, a fully equipped house built in Cape Dutch style, which has 5 en-suite bedrooms. The self-catering unit is booked on an exclusive basis with rates from R600 for 2 people to R2 000 for 10 people (and discounts for stays longer than 1 night and guests can dine at the restaurant). The reserve has about 42 species of game, 130 bird varieties, and a wealth of rock art (over 500 paintings). Activities include quad bike-based activities, game drives, San rock art, fishing, hiking, mountain biking (costs apply). It is also home to many empowerment projects that produce items for sale in the shop. For information, tel: 044-752-3510 or 044-752-3374 or visit www.sanvalley.za.com.

Eating out in Uniondale

If you like historic settings, then they don't come much better than **Die Watermeul Restaurant** situated in the water mill that was built in 1854. To book, tel: 044-752-1079. The **Cracklin Rosy** restaurant and pub – the name could have come straight from one of AC/DC's guitar-screeching hits – is in Voortrekker Street and is open 07h15–18h30 on Monday, Tuesday and Thursday, 07h30 till late on Wednesday, Friday and Saturday, and 08h30–15h00 on Sunday. It offers a formal à la carte restaurant and fast food such as pizzas and hamburgers. If you have time, hostess Susan will relate some amusing stories about the Uniondale ghost – including her personal encounter. For more, tel: 044-752-1152.

The **Uniondale Lodge** serves light lunches and refreshments daily on the stoep or in the lavishly decorated interior, and dinners on Friday and Saturday nights. And by the time you read this, the restaurant at **Zeru Guesthouse** should be open on Sundays for tea/coffee and 'fattening stuff', as Carol puts it, either inside or *al fresco* on the front stoep with views of the Kammanassie mountains.

Welcome to the Overberg 10

The Overberg is a region that's easy on the senses and pleasing to the eye. It's a real tapestry landscape of colours and meandering patterns, both natural and manmade, spilling southwards from the slopes of the Riviersonderend and Langeberg mountains down to the sea.

Windpumps fill up reservoirs to support livestock but the canola and other crops rely solely on rain to come to fruition.

Fishing in paradise? The waters of the Overberg are rich in sea-life and popular with anglers searching for the Big One that doesn't get away.

In summer the farmlands of the Overberg are dominated by shimmering shades of brown, the fields stripped of their winter crops and the bare earth ploughed into meandering combed patterns dotted with tightly compressed wheels of straw awaiting collection. Labourers' cottages hunker down beneath old blue gums and, on a cold day, smoke drifts from their chimneys. Throughout the year the early-morning and late-afternoon sun accentuates the sensual curves of the ridges dressed in fynbos and, when the winter rains return, the undulating and sometimes tiered fields shrug off their brown and slip into the greens of wheat, barley and oats, and the brilliant yellow of the iconic canola. At times, mist glides over the mountains, slipping like a continuous satin throw from origins unseen on the far side, the edges fraying as they dip over the summit and vanishing like a spectre

WHAT'S IN A NAME?

Literally translated, Overberg – derived from the Dutch *over het gebergte* – means 'over the mountains'. But which mountains, was our first question while admiring the many towering ridges to the north and west, with a few strung in between. A visit to the Drostdy Museum in Swellendam informed us. Early European settlers in the Cape Colony, wanting to broaden their horizons, followed an ancient path of the Khoikhoi, the original inhabitants of the area, over what became known as the Hottentots-Holland mountains. Once 'over the mountain', the settlers looked across what is now known as the Elgin Valley, the western extreme of the Overberg region. Today those approaching from Cape Town cross the same mountains via Sir Lowry's Pass, a much quicker journey than in those days of ox-wagons and horses.

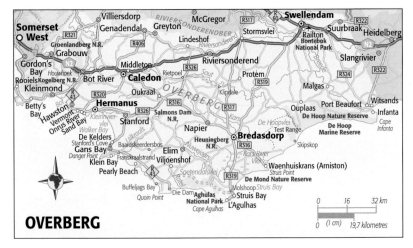

OVERBERG

into thin air in the lower altitudes. On still, sultry mornings, blue cranes float overhead, *craaaaaaking* as they go. A coastline punctuated with long sweeping bays and rocky outcrops fringes the southern boundary of this landscape, and it's here you can spend hours mesmerised by the eternal activity of the sea.

Crammed into this sensual landscape are a host of things to do and see. In

fact, take the alphabet and you can run off attractions starting with any letter – let's say 's': shipwrecks, sailing, shopping, swimming, sunsets, shells, sheep, seafood, sand, southernmost tip, strolling, sleepovers, silence, sea, samba, *ssschardonnay*, swashbucklers … Add to this a scattering of charming inland villages, locally produced beer, cheese and wine, lighthouses, bird watching, wonderful food, and you can start to see why you need plenty of time here.

You won't see the Big 5 here, and you don't need to because the Overberg's coast is bursting with the sea's bounty, including the Big 2 of the oceans: whales and sharks. Get acquainted with this duo at Hermanus and De Kelders, the undisputed world champs of land-based whale-watching (best between July and November), and at Kleinbaai you can cage dive with great white sharks. Another wildlife highlight are the adorable penguins that can be seen from a boardwalk at Stony Point in Betty's Bay.

Nature lovers can spend hours observing African penguins at Stony Point.

The Overberg 11

The Overberg is undoubtedly a fun place to be, whatever your persuasion.
The region's main town, Hermanus, is bursting with life for those who enjoy an
upbeat scene, while quieter souls will find plenty of peaceful corners to which
to escape. Oh, yes, and don't forget the southernmost point on the African
continent, and the true meeting place of the Indian and Atlantic oceans.

The rugged rock outcrops, white sand and clear water of the Overberg coastline.

AGULHAS (L'AGULHAS)

L'Agulhas, or simply Agulhas, is the perfect destination if you're one of those people who like to 'do' the longest-highest-biggest-shortest-lowest-southernmost sort of thing. This is not only the southernmost town on the continent, but also the official tip of Africa, and the place where the Atlantic and Indian oceans meet. Agulhas is more of a settlement of mishmash holiday houses than a town, but there is the odd small café selling basic provisions, as well as some art galleries and restaurants.

Out and about in L'Agulhas

Number one is the **Tip of Africa** where the oceans meet, which is marked by a cairn, but you can't see the meeting point, although many claim to. Some also claim that if you can pee into the water here, you'll have good luck. *Hmmm.* The **Cape Agulhas Lighthouse**, built in Pharos style, has been in operation since 1849, which makes it the country's second-oldest working lighthouse. Today, its lights are 7 500 000 candle power and have a 60-kilometre range, but previously the wicks filled with sheep fat produced a 4 500 candle power light, and in 1905 these were replaced with an oil burner of 470 000 candle power. If you have a head for heights, climb the stairs to the top to get a close-up of the

> Agulhas, like most small towns, is a safe settlement, even for a stroll in relatively isolated areas, but take the usual precautions.

WHY VISIT?
See the most southern point of the African continent where the two oceans meet.

WHAT'S WACKY?
The coastline is dotted with shipwrecks of the poor souls who tried to navigate the notorious Cape of Storms. From the Breede River to Kleinrivier, near Hermanus, there are around 140 wrecks.

WHAT'S WHAT?
Cape Agulhas Tourism is situated at the lighthouse. Open daily 09h00–13h00 and 14h00–17h00. Tel: 028-435-7185, www.tourism-capeagulhas.co.za.

old-fashioned lantern imported from France and installed in 1914. If it's low tide, you may also spot ancient fish traps left by the Khoi people. The resident lighthouse-keeper and staff were withdrawn in December 1968 after the building was declared unsafe due to serious decomposition of the limestone. Later, a restoration programme began. Inside is a museum that's open 09h00–17h00 daily. It offers a graphic account of lighthouse development over the years and has photos of all 56 lighthouses in South Africa, with a map showing where they are.

Agulhas National Park, proclaimed in 1999, is located at the southernmost tip, and was established to conserve the lowland fynbos vegetation types and the all-important wetlands. Although there are currently no roads in the park, the coastal strip is open if you want to walk and explore (it's 72 kilometres long). The park includes important cultural-historical artefacts and national heritage sites, and the Agulhas Plain (the area around the southernmost tip) has a great diversity of indigenous flora and unique vegetation, such as limestone fynbos. The park is of international significance because of its rich plant biodiversity, with species richness equalling that of tropical rainforests. Birdlife here is exceptional and includes a host of migratory and resident water birds. Keep an eye out for the striking orange-breasted sunbirds that frequent the area. The Struisbaai–Elim road goes through the wetlands and birds

The cairn marking the southernmost point on the African continent at Agulhas.

congregate in large flocks here and on the saltpans. Fauna includes porcupines, honeybadgers, spotted otter, tortoises and grysbok. Accommodation is being developed, so call for more information on tel: 028-435-6078 or visit the SANParks website www.sanparks.org.

Coastal Tours offers a fascinating insight into what this area has to offer. It's the only company with a permit to drive on the beach, allowing access to areas otherwise unreachable on a tour. Spend a morning driving through coastal fynbos and taking in incredible coastal scenery. Visit 2 000-year-old stone-age fish traps and middens of the Strandlopers. The tour also passes Lord's House where, in early 1960, British Prime Minister Harold MacMillan apparently wrote his historic Winds of Change speech, signalling the British intention to grant independence to British colonies in Africa. There's also a slim chance of spotting a sea turtle breaststroking its way across the sand. Contact Coastal Tours on tel: 082-774-4448 or 028-435-6903 or click on www. coastaltours.co.za. Birdlife abounds in the area, with large numbers of species, including Caspian terns and African black oystercatchers. The bits of white froth blowing along the beach are likely to be whitefronted plovers that run like the wind. Ask at the tourism office about the best birding spots.

There are three tidal pools for swimming in. In summer, the sea temperature is 20–22 °C, and not much lower in winter.

Spookdraai Hiking Trail is a circular route that takes less than 2 hours. It follows the coastline, and includes a

The Cape Agulhas Lighthouse not only serves to warn ships of the treacherous coastline, but also houses a restaurant and museum.

short walk through town to the top of the mountain, along the ridge, through a deep ravine and back to the start. Get the booklet from the tourist office, which details the 28 points of interest along the way. **Rasperpunt Hiking Trail** is a circular route starting at the wreck of the *Meisho Maru*, meandering through varying landscape, down to the water's edge, up to the ridges and back. It has 34 points of interest detailed in the booklet (also from the tourist office) and takes about 3 hours. While at the tourist office, get directions to the viewpoint overlooking town, the lighthouse and coastline. It's also possible to scuba dive, take a cruise of the bay, horse ride, deep-sea fish and do 4x4 routes in the area. The coast is an angler's paradise and, with the required permits, you may catch cob and galjoen from the rocks, and Cape salmon, yellowtail and red steenbras from a boat.

Overnight in L'Agulhas

The 4-star **Agulhas Country Lodge and Restaurant** is an imposing stone building tucked into the side of the mountain but accessible from the main road and boasts a great ocean view. B&B rates are R595–R895 per person sharing, so call on tel: 028-435-7650 or visit www.agulhascountrylodge. com. The 3-star **Tip of Africa Guest House** is owner-run by Derick and Petro Burger and offers all the comforts you could wish for. It's on the main road and within easy walking distance of the tidal pools. Some rooms have sea views and access to a balcony, and all 7 rooms are en suite. There's a large lounge with DStv, a collection of DVDs and books, and you can help yourself from the fully licensed honesty bar. Parking is secure, and children aged 15-plus are welcome. B&B rates are R350–R550, less 10% in winter. For more information, tel: 028-435-6903, or contact Derick (who also offers tours) on tel: 082-774-4448 or click on www.agulhassouthafrica.co.za.

If you're after something more exclusive, head to **Cornwallis Lodge**. It'll set you back at least a grand per person for B&B, but epitomises understated elegance and luxury. For details, tel: 028-435-6483 or visit www.cornwallis.co.za. **Seashell House**, at 8 Golf Street, offers a private ground-floor self-catering apartment (sleeping 2 people) and a sea view. Situated in an historic gabled home clad in seashells, the unit has outdoor seating, a braai and parking, and is within walking distance of shops and the lighthouse. The owner is an artist and has an innovative home gallery and self-designed labyrinth. Rates depend on the length of your stay, but start at R175 per person sharing. For more info, tel: 028-435-7888 or visit www.seashellhouse.co.za. **South Point** offers units with a private patio and built-in fireplace, plus a laundrette on site, and costs R175–R225 per person sharing. They're 150 metres the sea and 300 metres from the lighthouse. Book on tel: 028-435-7402 or www.south-point.co.za. **Agulhas Heights** has 2-bedroom cottages and claims to be equipped with everything from TV to tot measure. They're situated up on the hill with a 180° sea view. Tel: 028-435-6934. About

5 kilometres from the Tip of Africa and surrounded by the Agulhas National Park, lies **Suiderstrand**, where you'll find the 3-star **Pebble Beach B&B** just steps away from the beach. Rates are from R300 per person. The same proprietors run **Turnstones**, a rustic, thatched fisherman's cottage, perfect for a self-catering holiday away from it all. Enjoy 180° sea views and incredible sunsets right on the seashore. The cottage sleeps 6 and rates start at R550 per night. For details, tel 028-435-7270 or visit www.pebble-beach.co.za. The **Agulhas Municipal Caravan Park** has 76 grassed sites, 40 of which have electricity, and 16 bungalows. Rates range from R90 to R140 for a stand, with a maximum of 6 people. For details, tel: 028-435-6015.

Eating out in L'Agulhas

Zuidste Kaap in the main road is owner-run by Okkie and is very popular with locals and visitors. On offer here are sandwiches, light meals and dinners, with main courses including deboned pork neck and eisbein, which Okkie's German customers reckon he's a master at. The menu includes seafood and local dishes, such as waterblommetjie bredie. Furniture and picture frames are made from okumi logs washed ashore, and there's a large fish tank to add to the atmosphere; and if you just want a drink, there's a pleasant bar at the back of the restaurant. Open daily 10h00–22h00. For the lowdown, tel: 028-435-6034.

The **Lighthouse Restaurant** has a fabulous atmosphere and location, and is the only restaurant based in a lighthouse in South Africa. Although there's no sea view, at night you dine beneath the revolving light of the lighthouse and can watch the beam wash over the houses and hillside every 5 seconds. In fact, this got us thinking that if you lived in the beam of the lighthouse, you wouldn't need an outside light for braaiing and could check your meat every 5 seconds. Dishes include soups, salads, and seafood, steak and chicken. It's a cosy establishment, offering a good night out if you can ignore the noisy staff. Open daily 08h00–22h00, except on Sundays, when they close at 17h00. For details, tel: 028-435-7580 or 083-721-0386. **Agulhas Country Lodge and Restaurant** on main road offers fine dining with uninterrupted sea views, but booking is essential. Lunch is from a small à la carte menu, and dinner is a set menu (usually 4 courses) for R245 a head. Coffee, cigars and cheese are served after dinner in the lounge. For further information, tel: 028-435-7650 or click on www.agulhascountrylodge. com. **Angelo's Trattoria**, also on the main road, serves pizza, pasta and grills. It's very basic and unpretentious and has a kids' menu. Open daily from breakfast to dinner. Call them on tel: 028-435-6417.

ARNISTON

Arniston is a sleepy little village of about 50 permanent residents (or it certainly seems that way) and if you're visiting out of season, you'll experience its tranquillity. Come season, that all changes into frenetic activity. First impressions are of a haven of white buildings and an undeveloped beachfront. Little is known about Arniston prior to the appearance of the first European settlers, except that – as with much of the coastal region – it was inhabited by Khoisan beachcombers known as Strandlopers. Evidence of their existence can be found in the odd shellfish midden and other artefacts occasionally found in the area. There is some confusion regarding its names, which include Waenhuiskrans and Kassiesbaai. Arniston, however, was the geographical name used on early maps of the area (named after a ship that was wrecked here) and is the official (cadastral) name of the village; Waenhuiskrans lies west of Arniston and is translated into 'wagon-house cliff', referring to a nearby limestone cave; and Kassiesbaai, to the east, is the national heritage site where the original fishermen's houses are to be seen.

Out and about in Arniston

The many seaside activities in and around Arniston include angling, swimming, whale-watching (June–

WHY VISIT?
To experience fresh sea air, a pristine coastline and an azure sea.

WHAT'S WACKY?
There are no streetlights, shops, ATM or fuel.

WHAT'S WHAT?
Call the Cape Agulhas Tourism office (see page 120).

The quaint fishing village of Kassiesbaai, with its thatched cottages, is popular with tourists and here Willeen provides refreshments and light meals in her small restaurant.

December), exploring coastal caves, surfing, kite boarding, dune running or just sea-gazing. Although the sea isn't as warm as further east along the coast, it's perfect for snorkelling in clear rock pools and scuba diving among the abundant ocean wrecks.

Spend at least one night so that you can take time to walk around **Kassiesbaai**, the town's national heritage site and one of the last unspoiled fishing villages in the country. Its narrow streets are flanked by white stone cottages, some adorned by fishing paraphernalia, and if you make your way down to the beach, you'll find **Willeen's** wee restaurant and craft shop.

At low tide, explore the massive **Waenhuiskrans Cave**, so named by farmers who said it was large enough to turn an ox-wagon in. It's part of

the picturesque limestone cliffs and you'll need suitable footwear in order to navigate the sharp rocks (you will be getting wet feet!) but it's well worth the effort once you're standing inside, looking out onto the turquoise sea. It's said to be the largest coastal cave in Africa that has no supporting roof pillar.

Arniston fishing boats are called 'chuckies', and a popular pastime is watching them come in and checking the day's catch. It's a chance to absorb the atmosphere of the village's colourful characters and banter.

If you're staying at the Arniston Hotel, you get to use their bicycles for free and it's a great way to totter around the village.

Another way to stretch those limbs is on a 14-kilometre walk (you have to be

At low tide visitors make their way along the rocky coast to Arniston's Waenhuiskrans Cave.

moderately fit) along the beach to **De Mond Nature Reserve** (see page 18), otherwise drive there – just not along the beach! It's a lovely reserve and well worth exploring.

There are plenty of other walks in the area. It is about 3 kilometres west from the hotel to the Beacon at Struis Point; and from the slipway near the hotel it's just 3 kilometres east to the wreck of the *Arniston*, which is covered in sand but occasionally opens up. In 1982, South Africa's first marine archaeology project was to find the wreck of the *Arniston*, and a selection of its bounty – ceramics, metals, coins and jewellery – can be seen today at the Bredasdorp Museum.

Roman Beach, en route to Waenhuiskrans Cave, is the main beach, but there's one in front of the hotel that's popular with the little ones and the elderly.

Etna's Shell Collection is well worth seeing. It's a large private collection on display in her home at 14 Fifth Avenue. She welcomes anyone interested. The collection includes shells from around the world, some of which are extremely rare, and some deadly poisonous. Etna stresses that one should never walk barefoot on the rocks or pick up live shells, and she'll point out those that are as toxic as a puff adder's bite. Phone Etna on tel: 028-445-9657.

Overnight in Arniston

The 4-star **Arniston Spa Hotel** is separated from the sea by a large lawn and road. It has 62 rooms, many sea facing, and the deluxe rooms have private balconies with panoramic ocean views. This is an idyllic place to spend a few days unwinding. If the weather turns blustery, games can be requested from reception; sit and contemplate the awesome power of nature as the waves crash onto the rocks; relax in the hotel lounge with a good book; or head to the in-house Ginko Spa, which offers all sorts of pampering treatments. Each room has a comprehensive summary of information and activities. Large buffet breakfasts are served either on the deck or in a dining room overlooking the sea; and teas, light meals and cakes are offered throughout the day. Rates vary depending on season and time of week and are quoted per 2-person-room from roughly R800 mid-week out of season to R2 100 for a luxury sea-facing room in season. For reservations, tel: 028-445-9000 or visit the website www.arnistonhotel.com. **Arniston-Etnas** is a company offering 46 self-catering houses in the village of

Arniston, and each takes advantage of the unique panoramic views offered. For details, tel: 028-445-9657 or visit www.arniston-etnas.co.za. **Arniston Guest House** at 27 Main Road is a double-storey stone-and-thatch house offering warm hospitality in a homely atmosphere. Ask for the luxury suite, which comes complete with fireplaces in both the bedroom and bathroom. B&B rates are R330–R450. To enquire about prices and winter specials, tel: 028-445-9313 or 082-354-8583 or click on www.arnistonguesthouse. com. **Die Herberg Hotel** outside of town has backpackers' lodgings with double rooms for R120 per person or singles for R150. For info, tel: 028-445-2500 or visit www.dieherberg.co.za. The **Arniston Municipal Caravan Park** has grassed sites separated by hedgerows, and is neat and tidy. In summer it can be packed like the proverbial can of sardines. Sites cost around R130. For details, tel: 028-445-9620.

Eating out in Arniston

Where to drink is the easy part, because as long as you have your own grog, you can enjoy it anywhere overlooking the sea in this part of the world. **Arniston Hotel** has a large à la carte restaurant that's open to the public and a menu that blends traditional South African cuisine with modern innovations from international chefs. The dining area adjoins the bar, which has an aquatic ambience with fish tanks either side and fish beneath the glass bar counter. In winter, a fire in the big hearth adds cosy atmosphere, and in summer you can dine al fresco. Ask about the catch of the day as the chef goes out to meet the chuckies each evening. The hotel has an award-winning wine list.

During the day, you can get soft drinks and light eats from **Willeen's** in Kassiesbaai; or visit the gallery and coffee shop at **Nacht Wacht**, 14 kilometres towards Bredasdorp (see page 131). Rumour has it that **Casa del Sol**, a popular Portuguese restaurant currently based on a farm, will be moving to town.

BETTY'S BAY

The sheer cliffs of the Kogelberg drop steeply to a narrow coastal plain along which Betty's Bay is built between Kleinmond and Pringle Bay. The town stretches about 12 kilometres by road from one side to the other, and the main road is the R44 (approaching from the east you'll pass the Harold Porter National Botanical Garden). Betty's Bay is a quiet seasonal holiday village, ideally suited to those who

WHY VISIT?

To see one of three land-based penguin colonies in the country.

WHAT'S WACKY?

Betty's Bay is full of cute francolin quartets serenading residents.

WHAT'S WHAT?

Contact the Hangklip-Kleinmond Tourism Bureau in Kleinmond, tel: 028-271-5657, www.ecoscape. org.za.

MEET THE PENGUINS

Penguins mate for life, with breeding occurring February–October. Their nests are burrows or small depressions, usually under vegetation or rocks, and their 2 eggs are incubated for about 40 days, with both parents brooding and feeding chicks until they moult their grey fluffy down and can then take to the water. They live 17–23 years, feed on pilchards and anchovies and need about 500 grams of food daily. African Penguins must breathe above water but can dive to a maximum of 130 metres and hold their breath for an average of 45 seconds, and up to 150 seconds. They make a sound like a donkey braying.

---

prefer outdoor living. It has only a handful of shops and one garage, but plenty of great artists.

Out and about in Betty's Bay

Stony Point African penguin colony is the big attraction in Betty's Bay. Until 1982, Africa's only penquin, *Spheniseus demersus*, nested on islands and was inaccessible to bird and nature lovers, until these little waddlers chose to form a colony at Stony Point. The best time to visit is late afternoon when Penny, Guin, and the kids return from their 20-kilometre fishing expedition. The great thing about this colony is that's it's still uncommercialised so you won't find touristy gimmicks for sale. There is, however, a R10 fee to access the boardwalk and, once the ticket office is closed, please be honest and leave your donation in the box. Stony Point is also where you'll see relics of the whaling station and slipway used in the early 1900s to process the southern right whale. The coastline around Betty's Bay is good for swimming, but please stick to obviously safe bathing areas as this coast is notorious for lives claimed by freak waves. To reach the main beach from the R44, turn into Porter Drive (at the BP garage), first left into Anglers, which becomes Access Road, and the parking is at the end of this. Silversands Beach is further towards Hangklip, and its especially important to watch out for those freak waves when fishing from the rocks here. Dawidskraal offers shoreline angling, or you can throw your line in from the harbour wall. Ask the locals how to get to Tom se Klip, also a popular spot, but please get the required permits. You may catch red roman, musselcracker, geelbek, cob, red stumpnose and hottentot. Snorkelling and scuba diving are popular and, according to locals, a lot of the time you can surf here without a wetsuit. If you're an experienced windsurfer, winter is the time for serious winds. Whales can be seen June–November, peaking in September. The southern rights are easily visible from the shoreline when they visit to mate and give birth; and dolphins and seals are also frequent visitors to the area.

Birding is good and, apart from the common seabirds, you will find the

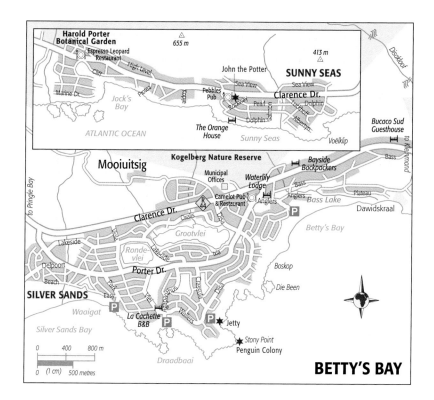

BETTY'S BAY

blue-mantled flycatcher in the Harold Porter National Botanical Garden, which has riverine birds too. Raptors appear in the mountains, often flying high above the valleys and peaks, and the coastal vegetation supports a large variety of other birds as well.

Paddy Starling is arguably one of South Africa's most popular and sought-after water and landscape artists. Self-taught, he started painting in 1970, and his first one-man exhibition sold out on the opening night. The popularity and critical appeal of his art can be measured by the huge demand of his paintings by private collectors, corporate clients and galleries, both locally and internationally; and the success of his

one-man exhibitions, of which he's had more than 30. Paddy's interest in trout and fly-fishing has contributed to his ability to capture water on canvas. He works mainly on commission, so if you are interested, call him on tel: 082-468-4791. **Derric van Rensburg's** works are also very well known, from Overberg

> You can harvest mussels and rock lobster from the shore around Betty's Bay, with required permits obtained from the local post office, but these are seasonal and daily quantities are limited. The authorities are extremely vigilant, so don't risk the hefty fine.

acrylics to wildlife, architectural and figure studies in various media. His studio may be visited by appointment, so call on tel: 083-347-3224. **John the Potter** gallery, on the R44, is open 08h00–17h00 weekdays and 09h00–16h00 on weekends, and sells pottery and artworks.

Set between the mountain and sea on the R44, the 200-hectare **Harold Porter National Botanical Garden** encompasses 10 hectares of cultivated fynbos and 190 hectares of pristine natural fynbos. The main fynbos families (proteas, ericas and restios) are present, along with irises, daisies, orchids and others; and you can see *Disa uniflora* as well as the king protea in their natural habitat. The paths are wheelchair friendly and offer walks through this floral splendour, up Disa Kloof and Leopard's Gorge, revealing its indigenous flowers, fynbos-covered mountain slopes, streams, dark pools and waterfalls. Look out for some of the 88 bird species, including the orange-breasted sunbird and the rare protea canary. There's a restaurant and an indigenous nursery. Open daily 08h00–16h30. For details, tel: 028-272-9311.

The 100 000-hectare **Kogelberg Biosphere Reserve** is a great outdoors venue of mountain landscapes, exceptional fynbos and a pristine coastline – see pages 16–17. For other outdoor activities, contact **Jackazz Eco-Adventures**. It's owner-run by Cuan and Belinda McGeorge, who offer abseiling, black-water tubing, rock-climbing, nature photography, a mountain-top cruise and sand-boarding from a 200-metre dune. Call the McGeorges on tel: 028-272-9080 or click on www.jackazz.co.za.

Overnight in Betty's Bay

The **Buçaco Sud** guesthouse, at 2609 Clarence Drive (the R44 through town), is a Provençal-style house offering wonderful views of both the mountains and the coastline. It has

Stony Point at Betty's Bay is home to the biggest land-based African Penguin colony in South Africa.

lots of atmosphere, colour and original artworks, and some rooms have private decks. B&B rates are R275–R360 per person sharing, and to book tel: 028-272-9750 or visit www.bucacosud.co.za. **Waterlilly Lodge** is a stylish B&B on the corner of Porter and Angler Drive. They have 6 well-appointed en-suite bedrooms, with private lounges, TV and verandas overlooking the sea. Two lounges include books, games and magazines; and one has a fireplace. Owner, Bryan, serves sumptuous breakfasts. B&B rates are from R300. To book, tel: 028-272-9378 or click on www.waterlillylodge.co.za. **La Cachette B&B** has 5 en-suite rooms with balconies and lovely sea views. Rooms have separate entrances and parking in front of each. B&B rates are from R500 per double. For details, tel: 028-272-9117 or visit www.lacachette.co.za.

The Orange House is fully equipped for self-catering, sleeps 6, and has a private path to the coastline. It's surrounded by fynbos and has sea and mountain views. The kitchen leads onto a sheltered sea-facing braai area, and there's an indoor fireplace in the open-plan lounge and dining room. Rates are R500–R800 per night. For info, tel: 028-272-9623 or 083-657-4144. **Woat.co.za Holiday Accommodation** ('Woat' stands for 'Whale Of A Time') offers a range of fully equipped, self-catering villas and cottages by the sea. Call Natalie on tel: 028-272-9892 or visit www.woat.co.za. **Bayside Backpackers** has double rooms for R270 and singles for R90–R120 per person. Call Garth or Lewis on tel: 028-272-9044 or visit www.bettysbaybackpackers.co.za.

Eating out in Betty's Bay

Many locals suggest heading to Pringle Bay for dinner, but it depends on what you're looking for. **Espresso Leopard** on the main road is a licensed coffee shop serving breakfasts and light lunches daily except Mondays, and the food is good. **Camelot** is situated just around the corner from the BP garage off the R44, and has an unmissable kitsch fake-rock façade. You can take the kids there, the food's okay, and it's fine for a drink. If you want to picnic, **De-Nice Deli & Bakery** near the garage is owner-run by Denise Rowan who bakes rolls and breads, has good cuts of meats, preserves, cheeses (including preservative and colourant-free), and pastries including venison pies with all accompaniments. Denise will also take orders, so call her on tel: 028-272-9849. **Pebbles Pub**, although rough around the edges, offers a Sunday roast, but is better known for its pizza, especially the spicy 'Shipwrecked' pizza.

BREDASDORP

En route to Bredasdorp, from whichever direction you're approaching, you're bound to pass sheep silhouetted against the skyline, rustic farm fences and flocks of blue cranes 20 to 40 strong. The black-and-white birds you see will no doubt be sacred ibis, and if they're white with oddly shaped red bills, they'll be spoonbills poking around water lying in the fields. Cows laze and graze, overlooking quaint labourers' cottages flanked by lines of colourful washing, and then you'll reach the economic capital of the Cape Agulhas region, Bredasdorp. It's an unassuming but bustling town with some lovely houses tucked away on side streets, and has all the amenities, including a large Spar supermarket.

Out and about in Bredasdorp

It'll take a while to register that not everyone greeting you is mistaking your car for someone else. This is typical of the Bredasdorpers – they're very friendly and greet everyone, including strangers. Take a drive around to get a feel for the town, and you'll pass interesting little shops, like the Rooi Stoepies Winkel and Oom Loetie se Winkel. The town's best-loved attraction, and one the

locals claim is known everywhere, is the **Shipwreck Museum**, founded in 1975. It houses artefacts and furniture from ships wrecked along the South African coastline; contains showpieces specific to the Overberg; and has the biggest collection of bottles in South Africa. Open 09h00–16h45 Monday–Friday, 11h00–15h45 Saturday–Sunday. For info, tel: 028-424-1240.

Julian's Gallery and Ceramics on the R319 to Swellendam is a landmark. You can't really miss its zany colourful façade, and the warehouse-sized gallery houses fabulous ceramic designs. Owners, Julian and Liz Keyser, have built a highly successful business through sheer hard work and dedication and, due to demand, have recently introduced a matching range of fabric-painted table linen to complement their ceramics. When you've worked up an appetite from all that browsing and shopping, their restaurant menu will impress you too. For further information, tel: 028-425-1201 or click on www.juliankeyserceramics.co.za. The **Kapula Candles** success story started with Ilse Appelgryn making a 'couple of candles' (hence the name) in her kitchen, and has since evolved to an award-winning and dynamic enterprise. They're in the industrial area – turn right just before the silos when heading to Swellendam. The handcrafted candles are colourful and said to spread African warmth to all corners of the globe, with galleries and distributors across the continents. **Intshiba Crafts** is near Kapula and they also do candles, pottery and fabrics. If you're in the market for some goose-down products, **Bel Don**

WHY VISIT?

Stay on a working farm and experience its daily activities.

WHAT'S WACKY?

♦ The unique Shipwreck Museum, which commemorates the hundreds (yes, hundreds) of ships wrecked along the nearby coastline.
♦ A portion of a 170-year-old original wire fence, erected in 1837 to preserve bontebok, can still be seen en route to Arniston.

WHAT'S WHAT?

The Overberg Information office is in the old Victorian building with the attractive garden in Long Street. Open 08h00–17h00 weekdays and 09h00–12h30 Saturday (closed Sundays, but open public holidays). Tel: 028-424-2584, www.tourismcapeagulhas.co.za.

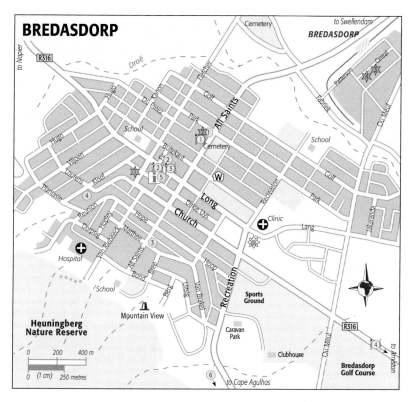

BREDASDORP

Places to stay

1. Julian's B&B
2. Firlane Guesthouse
3. The Coach House B&B
4. De Volkshuijs Self-catering
5. Earl of Clarendon B&B
6. Langrug Lodge en route to Agulhas

Places to eat

1. Julian's Restaurant
2. Bredasdorp Square Restaurant
3. Smaak Restaurant
4. Nacht Wacht Restaurant

Places of interest

- Shipwreck Museum
- Julian's Gallery & Ceramics
- Kapula Candles
- Intshiba Crafts

is also here and sells a range, as well as cotton percale linen. **Bredasdorp Square** (in town, next to the tourism office) focuses on European and French items, and if you need a stylish gift, this is the place to get it. There are several art galleries, and interesting little places to explore, such as **Oom Loetie se Winkel** in Plein Street off the R318. It's a tiny gift shop selling curios, books, art supplies, toys and a lot more, and is open 09h00-17h00 weekdays and Saturday mornings.

The 800-hectare **Heuningberg Nature Reserve** has spectacular views east to Arniston and De Hoop, south to Struisbaai, west along the mountains and north over the town to the Rûens and the Riviersonderend mountains. There's a large variety of erica and protea species in the reserve, and if you visit in April and May, you should see the rare Bredasdorp lily (*Cyrtanthus guthriei*), which is found only on the Heuningberg range. Walking trails are 2–15km in the mountains. Entry is at

Bredasdorp is well known for two craft industries, Kapula Candles, and Julian's Gallery and Ceramics, on sale here in their large showroom.

the top end of Van Riebeeck Street, but pop into the tourism office to check that the gate is being manned. The **Grootberg Hiking Trail** between Bredasdorp and Napier offers hikers the opportunity to see a large variety of fynbos species and birds along a clearly marked route. For information, call Steve Smuts on tel: 028-423-3049 or 076-972-0450. If you're keen to explore the mountains without having to sweat it, **Mountain Fynbos Tractor Rides** are held on a farm between Bredasdorp and Napier. Tours are on Wednesdays and Saturdays at 10h00 and 14h00 and advance bookings are essential. Call Mr Van Zyl on tel: 028-424-2074. Opposite the tourist office in the grand Victorian building is a little centre with art, and a well-stocked second-hand bookshop. Bredasdorp also has the southernmost golf course in Africa. About 4.5km towards Arniston, there's a pull-off and monument alongside the original wire fence erected by Alexander van der Byl in 1837 for the conservation of bontebok.

Overnight in Bredasdorp

One of the top guesthouses is the elegant **Firlane**, which is run by the very cheerful Rosa. Rooms are en suite and have extra-length beds and percale linen, DStv, an honesty bar and coffee trays. There are private balconies for 4 rooms, parking is off-street, and included in the price is use of the new modern gym in the main street. Rates are R300–R750 per person sharing. To book, tel: 028-425-2808. **Julian's B&B** is around the corner from Julian's Gallery and Ceramics and offers a comfy double en-suite room with a small lounge, and breakfast is enjoyed in the restaurant. It's quiet, secure and you're guaranteed total privacy. B&B rates are from R350 per person sharing. Call them on tel: 028-425-1201. **The Coach House B&B** is in a century-old restored thatched cottage with private entrance and off-street parking. It offers space and comfort for up to 5 people and is close to the town centre. Rates are R220–R330 per person sharing. Call

Midge Farquharson, tel: 028-424-2539. **De Volkshuijs** consists of 2 gorgeous little national monuments that are also fully equipped self-catering cottages. One is a double, the other has twin beds. Parking is secure, there's a braai area, and it's within walking distance of town. Rates are R300 for 1 person, R400 for 2, R500 for 3, R550 for 4 people. Contact Elmien Lötter on tel: 082-339-9949. **The Earl of Clarendon** is the upstairs section of the Bredasdorp Square Victorian house and offers accommodation in luxurious upstairs rooms. B&B rates are from R300 per person sharing. For info, tel: 028-425-1420.

Langrug Lodge lies 22 kilometres south of Bredasdorp along the R319 to Agulhas on the banks of **Soetendalsvlei**, one of the largest natural bodies of water in southern Africa. The lodge is surrounded by green fields and, as one soul wrote, is drenched in a gorgeous view of the lake. Built in 1912, it's been tastefully restored in keeping with its history. The ceiling is of rough-hewn beams and reeds, walls are wonky and thick, doorways low, and floors are screed. Furnishings are art deco leather and wood, and the central table and benches in front of the open hearth have seen decades of social occasions and hearty meals shared. The double room is en suite, and a wood-fired donkey boiler supplies hot water. The second room has 2 double bunks and an en-suite bathroom, and the lodge is fully equipped for self-catering. Although there's no electricity, appliances are gas, lamps are paraffin, and there's an endless supply of wood for indoor or outdoor braais. Personal touches, the tranquillity and setting, and the birdlife make this the kind of place you never want to leave.

Rates are R170 per person sharing, with kids under 12 free. Call Jenny Uys on tel: 028-424-1990, cell: 082-493-8872, or e-mail vissersdrift@whalemail.co.za.

Eating out in Bredasdorp

Julian's Restaurant is really quite unexpected, and that's without being rude about Bredasdorp, but if you've never been to the town, its first impression does not lead you to thinking it'll have such an iconic eating establishment. You reach the restaurant by passing through the fabulous gallery, and have a choice of two wings – smoking and non-smoking – overlooking a courtyard through large picture windows. Walls are adorned with original artworks, and in winter there are crackling fires to snuggle around. The contemporary menu makes you wish you were spending a week just so that you can try it all as it offers a range of well-selected dishes with interesting twists. Choose from *smoorsnoek* spring rolls, duck, oriental spicy chicken pasta, vegetable strudel and sweet-potato crisps. Try the popular chicken-liver salad or meltingly tender ostrich fillet, and finish with decadent chocolate pudding. Lunch and dinner menus differ. They also serve luscious cakes during the day, and are open for breakfast, lunch and dinner Monday–Saturday. Liz and Julian are very hands-on, and their loyal kitchen team sends out well-presented dishes. Book in season, by calling tel: 028-425-1201. **Bredasdorp Square** is great for breakfast *al fresco*, and has a large menu. Lunches include everything from soup of the day (including health bread) to catch of the day, cakes, a range of coffees and cocktails (it's fully licensed). Open 07h30–17h00 weekdays and 08h00–14h00 Saturday. **Smaak** is a relatively new restaurant (above the gym) and although already popular, has still to prove its staying power. The menu changes daily and they're open 08h00–17h00 Monday–Saturday and until late Wednesday–Friday (they're not open Saturday nights as this is when they cater for functions). There's another new restaurant at the **Nacht Wacht** farm, about 9 kilometres towards Arniston. The view from the restaurant is through double doors over a field where the odd sheep grazes, and you can dine al fresco. The signature dish is rack of lamb, and the chocolate and cheesecakes are popular. The owner, Melanie Albertyn, is an artist and has a gallery alongside. It's signposted on the R318 and accessed via an avenue of eucalyptus that winds past ancient farm buildings. Open 09h00–17h00 Monday–Saturday (dinner and Sunday lunch on request). For more information, tel: 028-424-1172.

Mac's Sports Bar is a local hangout set a little back off the main street. It has a sign declaring that elbow lifting is a recognised exercise, so no surprise that it's a typical men's bar – rough around the edges and in the middle.

CALEDON

At the risk of being shot by loyal Caledonners, we couldn't find a really good reason to spend much time in Caledon, bar using it as a base to explore the area or a stopover en route to somewhere else. We did our best to get info about the town and activities but the tourist office claimed their members weren't interested in being included in our book. However, during our visit, we did discover that the main street crinkles and snakes past loads of beautiful old houses, some with really gorgeous gardens. From the N2, you will notice the giant silos at the bottom end of town, but several streets have lovely big trees, and if you make a point of driving right to the eastern end of Meul Street you'll surely also find it very appealing.

Out and about in Caledon

If you're exploring the region in spring or summer, you're in for a treat. Green wheat fields roll endlessly over hills and dales, blue cranes do their elegant mating dance, and when the canola is in flower it adds a splash of brilliant yellow to the canvas. Apart from surrounding scenery, Caledon's greatest attraction is 15 kilometres west of it: Dassiesfontein Farmstall. This farmstall is so authentic it even has chickens clucking on the front steps. It's a long, old farm building with rooms leading into others, each revealing farmstall delights. You can find almost anything here, from a good selection of enamelware to old

> ### The Caledon Tourism
> Information office is in Plein Street. Open 09h00–16h00 weekdays. Tel: 028-212-3282, www.tourismcaledon.co.za.

Green and yellow are the official colours of the Overberg in winter.

Dassiesfontein farmstall near Caledon is not just a place for a cuppa or a bite to eat, but a treasure trove for all manner of culinary and household items.

stove parts, cheese, homemade bread, gardening stuff, gifts and décor items. For more information, click on www. dassies.co.za.

Overnight in Caledon

Rouxwil Country House is on a farm 30 kilometres from Caledon just off the R43 towards Villiersdorp. It's owner-run by Thys and O'nel Roux and offers 5 units with lovely landscape views that come complete with grazing zebra, eland and springbok. Each room is individually decorated, and the Happy Room is so bright and colourful it's a perfect pep-up after a long day in the car. Breakfast is included, but dinner is an optional extra starting at R150 per person. B&B rates are from R450 per person. Call on tel: 028-215-8922 or visit www.rouxwil.co.za.

Eating out in Caledon

Your best bet is the **Dassiesfontein** farmstall. Its farm-fresh menu includes divine homemade bread – try the toasted bacon, egg, cheese and tomato breakfast sandwich. They even have such traditional combinations as pork fat and apricot jam open sandwiches, and serve traditional dishes, salads and good *moerkoffie*.

ELIM

Elim is known for its main street, which is lined with old whitewashed and mostly thatched cottages that are as pretty as a picture. Originally a Moravian mission station, the town was founded in 1824, and has the 'oldest working watermill in South Africa' (*er*, except it hasn't worked for some years now …) Its wooden waterwheel, however, remains one of the largest in the country. The road from Bredasdorp to Elim is tarred, but other access roads are not.

Out and about in Elim

Park at one end of the main road, and take your time strolling along it. This is the best way to take in the atmosphere of the village. The old Moravian church is at the top of the street and was completed in 1865, and still houses the oldest working clock in the country (yes, it does …). To the rear of the church is a precinct, much of which is enclosed with a plumbago hedge, and it's here you'll find the watermill built in 1828. During our last visit, the mill was not working as the dam providing the water needed upgrading, but it should be in operation again soon.

The nearby 450-hectare **Geelkop Nature Reserve** is named after the mass of yellow flowering plants, leucadendrons in particular, that cover it in spring. There's a drive offering good views, and you can do a half-day hiking trail.

The area around Elim has several unique wineries, but only some are open to the public. This is the southernmost ward of wine production in the Cape, and aficionados reckon that the climate here allows grapes more time to ripen and develop a balance between acidity and sugar levels, producing particularly good wines. If you're keen on tasting, **Strandveld Wines**, which also produces First Sighting wines, are open 08h00–17h00 weekdays. The signature wine is Sauvignon Blanc and some wines are displayed in the old stable troughs. The garden has an interesting display of 4 distinctly different types of coloured stones from the farm. They also offer 2 self-catering cottages, which sleep 2, for R450. For more information, tel: 028-482-1906 or click on www.strandveld.co.za. **Quoin Rock Winery** is open for tasting and sales by appointment only, so call them on tel: 028-482-1619 or visit www.quoinrock.com – as is **Black Oystercatcher** (contact them on tel: 082-779-5439 or via the website www.blackoystercatcher.co.za). For more about the local wineries, get the Overberg Wine booklet from the tourist information office.

Overnight in Elim

There's accommodation in the church precinct that offers 5 rooms, each sleeping 2. Check it out before booking in. Rates are from R160 per person B&B, and R120 per person for self-catering. For details, tel: 028-482-1806.

Eating out in Elim

The tearoom in the mill behind the church is run by the friendly Jane

African black oystercatchers search for sea snacks along the shoreline.

Speelman and Wilma Gillion. Their hours are 08h00–17h00 weekdays, 09h00–13h00 Saturdays, and on Sundays only by prior arrangement, but out of season hours can be erratic. It's best to phone to ensure they're open if you're planning to have lunch there. They serve bobotie, milk tart, malva pudding and homemade bread. You're welcome to take your own wine for a R10 corkage fee. Call Jane on tel: 073-769-7679 or Wilma on tel: 073-015-2798.

FRANSKRAAL

Just 7 kilometres southeast of Gansbaai, this sizable but quiet seaside village is built along the rocky shoreline, which is open and easily accessible – it doesn't have thick indigenous bush obscuring the view. There are lots of rock pools to explore or from which to simply watch the African black oystercatchers feed. At its eastern edge, Uilenkraalsmond Beach curves past the Uilenkraal River.

Out and about in Franskraal

There's a little maritime museum on the coastal Seaview Drive called the **Strandveld Museum**. It's a private

These old fishing boats are part of the Strandveld Museum in Franskraal.

initiative owned and run by Jan and SD Fourie and is open 10h00–12h00 and 15h00–17h00 or call on tel: 072-235-0694 or 082-255-8509 and they'll open up. You'll most likely find Jan there to show you around and give you a few laughs. Among its interesting exhibits is, allegedly, the most extensive collection of relics from the HMS *Birkenhead*. One fascinating piece is an old double bed with a mattress made from penguin feathers picked up on Dyer Island, giving a new take on grandma's feather bed.

The **Grootmelkhoutbos Trail** is a pleasant 2-kilometre circular walk through a pocket of natural strandveld vegetation containing, among other indigenous species, old milkwood trees. It's particularly pretty in spring when the flowers are in bloom. To get there, take the first road to the right as you enter Franskraal once you've turned off the main R43.

Overnight in Franskraal

Franskraal B&B in Seaview Drive, right on the beachfront, has a number of sea-facing en-suite rooms with tea/coffee-making facilities, a fridge, DStv and spacious bathrooms. It also has a room kitted out for the disabled. B&B rates are from R400 per person sharing and R550 for a single. To book, tel: 028-388-0708 or 082-577-6920.

Campers can head straight to the municipality-run **Uilenkraalsmond Holiday Resort**, which no doubt gets very crowded and noisy during holiday times and over long weekends. It's situated a little further along the R43 towards Pearly Beach at the mouth of the Uilenkraal River. It's great for the kids, with safe swimming in the lagoon, putt-putt, a Supertube, trampoline and, for the adults, a pub with big-screen TV. Caravan/camp sites with electrical connection go for R95–R180, depending on the season. There are also basic 6-bed bungalows from R250–R450. For details, tel: 028-388-0200.

GANSBAAI

The fishing town of Gansbaai has the best of both coastal worlds. Walker Bay lies north of the town, and has a rugged seafront of rock pools and coastal caves, while to the east lies Shark Bay, with its long, white sandy beaches. The name Gansbaai comes from a flock of Egyptian geese that used to hang out at a freshwater fountain that has recently been revamped in the harbour. It's a modern seaside town mixed with old-fashioned *platteland* values and very friendly residents, but its real claim to fame is its reputation for being the Great White Shark Capital of the World. Really, it should be called *Haaibaai* as the waters around Dyer Island teem with hundreds of great white attracted by the rich feeding grounds, thanks to thousands of seals, penguins and other sea life. First impressions of the town are a bustling main street dotted with Norfolk pine trees, a mishmash of old and new shops, smells of the sea and freshly baked bread. You'll get a feel for the place if you look at the vehicles in

WHY VISIT?

◆ To get nose to nose with a great white shark.

◆ Discover what the evocatively named Perlemoen Bay, Shark Alley, and Danger Point are really all about.

WHAT'S WACKY?

Shark Water and shark biltong (the former is mineral water sold locally, the latter not our personal choice of biltong but a good novelty item that is sold by Dyer Island Fisheries).

WHAT'S WHAT?

The very efficient and well-stocked Gansbaai Tourism Bureau is on the eastern end of the main street at the Gateway Centre. Open 08h30–17h30 Monday–Friday, 09h00–16h00 Saturday and 10h00–14h00 Sunday. Tel: 028-384-1439 or visit www.gansbaaiinfo.com or www.danger-point-peninsula.co.za.

the main street, which has everything from cattle trucks and bakkies loaded with sheep and beehives, to shiny four-wheel drives. Thankfully, the town has escaped developers and over-commercialisation so far.

There are several areas that make up greater Gansbaai. When approaching on the R43 from the north, you'll pass the first turnoff to De Kelders, next is the De Kelders/Stanford Bay, then Perlemoen Bay before entering Gansbaai itself. A drive along Cliff Road in De Kelders will give you a very good idea of the size of Walker Bay, and at night you can see the lights of Hermanus twinkling.

Out and about in Gansbaai

Firstly, book a shark-cage diving trip. Even if eyeballing those gnashers up close isn't your thing, you can stay on the boat and still have an amazing experience because viewing from the boat is almost better than from within a secure cage. There are 8 licensed operators, and most trips last several hours, depending on the number of clients on board. Shark cages hold a limited number of people, so the larger the passenger list, the longer the trip. You don't have to be a qualified diver to enter the cage, and will be supplied with all necessary diving gear. Remember to take sun protection and warm clothes, and note that trips are weather-permitting only. Some companies offer free DVDs, and may have a biologist on board to answer questions. Oh, and for those readers who think you can stroke the sharks – *uh uh*! It's strictly a hands-off dive. And just as well, as you're likely to end up without flesh on your bones thanks to their sandpaper skin … or even a little limbless if they're feeling peckish. Lots of famous people have done shark-cage diving, including Brad Pitt, Robbie Williams, Prince Harry, Colin Farrell and the King of Jordan, but alas, they went home some time ago. Two companies well supported by the locals are **Shark Diving Unlimited** and Shark Lady Adventures. The former has been going for years and is a family operation owned by Mike Rutzen, who's one of only a few people who skin dives with the great whites, so you can do a speciality course with him (call Mike on tel: 028-384-2787 or visit www.sharkdivingunlimited.com). **Shark Lady Adventures** takes a maximum of 12 people so you won't wait endlessly for a turn in the cage. Kim Maclean, who holds all the relevant qualifications and is experienced in working with these magnificent predators, leads the company, and can be contacted on tel: 028-312-3287 or via the website www.sharklady.co.za.

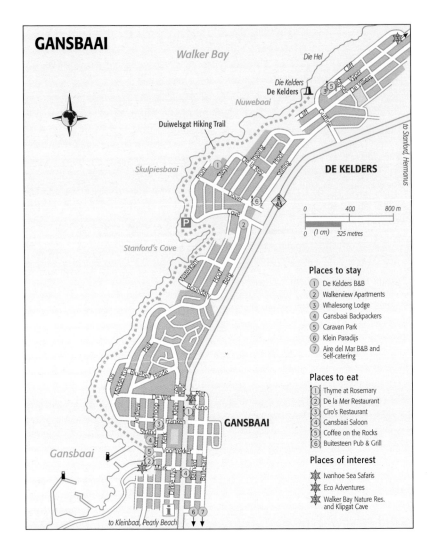

GANSBAAI

Walker Bay

Die Hel

Die Kelders
De Kelders

Nuwebaai

Duiwelsgat Hiking Trail

Skulpiesbaai

DE KELDERS

Stanford's Cove

| 0 | 400 | 800 m |

0 (1 cm) 325 metres

Places to stay
1. De Kelders B&B
2. Walkerview Apartments
3. Whalesong Lodge
4. Gansbaai Backpackers
5. Caravan Park
6. Klein Paradijs
7. Aire del Mar B&B and Self-catering

Places to eat
1. Thyme at Rosemary
2. De la Mer Restaurant
3. Ciro's Restaurant
4. Gansbaai Saloon
5. Coffee on the Rocks
6. Buitesteen Pub & Grill

GANSBAAI

Gansbaai

Places of interest
- Ivanhoe Sea Safaris
- Eco Adventures
- Walker Bay Nature Res. and Klipgat Cave

to Kleinbaai, Pearly Beach

Dyer Island has a huge colony of penguins and about 100 metres away is Geyser Island, home to seals. It's known as Shark Alley, but locals call this gulley 'MacDonalds' because, to the sharks, it's almost like a drive-through takeaway. Whale-watching trips are catered for by several different companies in town, one being **Dyer Island Cruises**, which does a 2.5-hour trip in season (July–December) when you'll get up close to southern right whales. It's a good company to support as they have various community and conservation projects on their books. For more information, call them on tel: 028-384-0406 or visit their website www.whalewatchsouthafrica.com.

Eco Adventures offers kayaking trips that'll get you close to a resident seal colony and, in season, the whales. They also do mountain trips offering spectacular views over the coastline, as well as a tour of **Drup Kelder Caves** (also known as De Kelders), which are known for their crystal water seeping from a freshwater fountain. In fact, these mineral waters have been used for well over 2 centuries for their miraculous cures, and were visited by Lady Ann Barnard, wife of Colonial Secretary Andrew Barnard, in 1798. This is the only known freshwater cave on the African coast. For tours, tel: 028-384-3846/7 or click on www.adventure-centre.co.za for more information.

If you're interested in sealife, you might want to do an abalone tour in the Gansbaai harbour with the **Atlantic Fishing Company**. Tours are Tuesdays and Thursdays and cost R50 per person (as long as there are at least

> **BIRDS OF A FEATHER**
> Here's a question – why are most marine birds black, white and grey? It's said, the white breast camouflages against the shimmering surface from sharks eye-view; the black and grey parts blend with sea and rocks when viewed from above. Isn't nature wonderful … and the *oke* that took the time to work that one out!

4 of you). For details, tel: 028-384-1162. Take a stroll around the harbour while you're there and watch the boats and other fishing activity. On the quayside, fishermen mend their vast nets, and they might even be hauling a trawler onto dry dock. You'll also find the **Gansbaai Marine Factory** here. They produce tins of Lucky Star pilchards – the famous South African brand name.

Shark-cage diving near Gansbaai is a major attraction for visitors to the area, giving them a close-up look at the gnashers of the most feared creature in the sea.

There are numerous other water-related activities, such as deep-sea, rock and beach fishing, kayaking, crayfishing and scuba diving, but as conditions and hotspots vary, it's best to check details with the tourist office, where you'll also get a very detailed map for anglers that covers De Kelders to Pearly Beach. As fishing is the town's main income, you'll find everything you need (including bait, which you can buy from the fish shop in the harbour).

Klipgat Cave is worth a visit, and you'll find it in **Walker Bay Nature Reserve**, which borders the northern end of De Kelders. To get there, drive along De Villiers Street and you'll reach the reserve's CapeNature Gate; pay your R20 per person, and they'll show you where to park and which access path to take down to the cave. It's famous for being home to people of the Middle Stone Age (85 000 to 65 000 years ago) and, more recently, about 2 000 years ago, the Late Stone Age Khoisan lived here. De Kelders also offers fabulous land-based whale-watching from its main road, which runs along the coastline. From this slightly elevated viewpoint, you'll be rewarded in season with sightings of southern right whales that come close to shore.

There are several hiking trails in the area. The **Duiwelsgat Hiking Trail** is about 7 kilometres, with around 3 hours of easy walking. It starts near town at the old harbour and winds north along the coastline past various points of interest, caves and rare coastal limestone fynbos, and finishes at Klipgat Caves. Get the map from the tourism office.

If you're not into swimming in the open sea, there's a tidal pool that's accessible from Kusweg Road. Spend some time exploring the lovely rock pools and beaches in the area. These, with their sea life, birds, beautiful shells and seaweeds, are really rewarding, and of course there are some great beaches nearby. The coastline here is spectacular, but the waters can be treacherous. Be very careful where you swim. Stick to protected coves and bays such as Die Plaat. The closest beach offering safe swimming for families is at Franskraal, about 8 kilometres away, but you can also swim at Stanford's Cove – which is where you'll find the graves of early inhabitants, as well as the fig tree planted here by the first fishermen who lived here.

There is much to discover on drives through the area. About 7 kilometres from Gansbaai, the rocky **Danger Point** peninsula juts 8 kilometres into the sea. To reach the **Danger Point Lighthouse**, take the R43 east out of town and you'll see the road to the right signposted for Kleinbaai. Off the Kleinbaai road, there's a road to the right that leads to the lighthouse, winding just metres from the sea in places. The lighthouse, built in 1895, is open 10h00–15h00 weekdays, and November–April it's open the same hours over weekends. Take a look at the Birkenhead Plaque commemorating one of the most famous shipwrecks in history.

There are various off-road trails in the area, self-drive and guided. **Mount Dyer 4x4 Route** takes about 3 hours and leads you up the mountain, through fynbos. For details, contact Marianne on tel: 028-388-0384. If you're interested in fynbos, make an appointment to visit Mathia Schwegler, who's written a book on the *Medicinal Uses of Fynbos* (see page 152). Mountain bikers might want to try their hand … *er*, legs … at the off-road **Lighthouse-to-Lighthouse Marathon** from Danger Point Lighthouse to Cape Agulhas held in February. The **Strandveld Museum**, in Franskraal, does ghost tours called 'Spookbus Toere'

THE *BIRKENHEAD* TRAGEDY

The reefs and uncharted rocks around the Danger Point peninsula are the reason for it being such a risk to ships coming too close to shore. In January 1852, the HMS *Birkenhead* left Ireland with 479 soldiers, several military and naval officers, over 50 women and children, and a crew of 125 souls. After a couple of days in Simon's Bay, where she took on provisions and fresh water, plus 350 tons of coal, 9 officers' horses and their fodder, she departed on the evening of 25 February. Nobody could have guessed the tragedy that lay ahead. At around 02h00 on 26 February, as she neared Danger Point, she hit an uncharted pinnacle of rock, now known as Birkenhead Rock (visible at low tide a few kilometres off the point), where she broke apart and sank. Of the 638 people aboard, it's reported that about 445 died. The selfless sacrifice of the troops who stood by while the 'women and children first" were put into lifeboats, remains one of the proudest moments in British naval history. Visit the Shipwreck Museum in Bredasdorp, which has artefacts from this wreck.

but these must be booked in advance. You travel to various farms and into the mountains, where you'll hear ghost stories from the legends of the Overberg at each destination, including Napier and Baardskeerdersbos. To book, call SD Fourie on tel: 082-255-8509.

Overnight in Gansbaai
The small and intimate **Whalesong Lodge** stands on the top of the De Kelders cliffs overlooking Walker Bay, and offers excellent land-based whale-watching. It's owner-run by Stanley and Lainey Carpenter and is a professional yet relaxed establishment that has you wishing you'd booked a longer stay. The décor is elegant, its main feature being the awesome view that stretches over the bay. An inviting lounge and dining room leads onto a balcony overlooking the sea, and it's the perfect spot to spend the end of the day, drink in hand, whales in water, and sun sizzling over the skyline. Often, the only sound you'll hear is the waves breaking onto the rocks across the road, and the locals cackling as they cruise the strip in front of the guesthouse (the 'locals' being resident guinea fowl!) The rooms are spacious, each with a small private balcony, and our suite's uninterrupted view through large picture windows allowed us to sit in bed with early-morning coffee, watching slick black bodies turning silver in the sunlight. En-suite bathrooms are under-floor heated and have bath and shower. Breakfast includes homemade croissants, jams and preserves. Rates are R600–R900 per person sharing. For details, tel: 028-384-1865 or visit www.

The lighthouse at Danger Point near Gansbaai.

whalesonglodge.co.za.

Further east, the 4-star **De Kelders B&B** is superbly situated on the seafront and stands surrounded by fynbos, creating a secluded retreat. It also offers excellent land-based whale-watching, and you're bound to see the resident seal colony frolicking beyond the kelp, as well as dassies, mongoose, tortoise, birds and even, on a moonlit night, the occasional porcupine. Owners, Gerhard and Alte Kotze, offer 5 en-suite rooms, 2 of which have terrific sea views. The communal lounge and large wooden deck overlook the bay, and the Kotzes warn that in whale season, breaching and cavorting can interrupt breakfast. B&B rates are R450–R700 per person (children by arrangement). For more information, tel: 028-384-0045 or click on www.dekelders.co.za. **Aire del Mar** is a professionally run establishment in Kleinbaai just a block from the ocean. It offers family units, twins and doubles. Some are luxury B&B rooms, others are 'soft self-catering', and there are also backpacker facilities. Ground-floor units are easily accessible, and have rails for the elderly, and all rooms are spacious. Rates are R250–R370, depending on season and rooms, and breakfast costs an additional R50. Speak to Zelna on tel: 028-384-2848 or visit www.airedelmar. co.za for more information.

If you'd like to self-cater, **Walkerview Apartments** has 3 private units. Although not right on the beach, they do have sea views and cost from R220 per person sharing. Call Leona on tel: 028-384-0430. Alternatively, there are 5 rustic self-catering cottages on the farm **Klein Paradijs**, about 20 kilometres east of Gansbaai (see Pearly Beach on page 190). **Gansbaai Backpackers** is in town, close to all amenities, and it overlooks the harbour and bay. It offers the usual backpacker facilities of dorms, family rooms, en-suite and single rooms, and a communal kitchen. Specials include transfers from Cape Town and a free night in a dorm for those who'd like to dive with the sharks. Rates are from R110 per person for a dorm room and R165 per person for a double en-suite. To book, tel: 028-384-0641 or visit www.gansbaybackpackers. com. There's a caravan park with grassed sites down on the harbour side of town. It doesn't have much shade but some of the sites have views over the harbour and bay. Rates are R90–R110 per site, but call for more information on tel: 028-384-0872.

Eating out in Gansbaai

There are plenty of places to choose from when it comes to eating out, but some are only open during the day, like **Coffee on the Rocks**, which is idyllically located in De Kelders with only a quiet road between you and the sea. They serve breakfast, lunch and excellent cakes (carrot and chocolate are their specialities). All dishes are prepared on a daily basis, and the menu varies but always includes vegetarian fare. Some of their meals are so popular with locals that they'll book portions in advance. Open 10h00–17h00 Wednesday–Sunday or a little later over holidays. For the lowdown, tel: 028-384-2017. **Thyme at Rosemary** is a highlight in Gansbaai, and has a super old-fashioned atmosphere. Yellowed sheet music plasters the walls,

SO WHAT IS FYNBOS?

Fynbos is a part of the Cape Floral Kingdom and it's most commonly found in the winter rainfall region. It's characterised by drought-tolerant plants that grow in poor soil and, as its name suggests, this evergreen shrubland vegetation has fine leaves. Of the incredible 8 000-odd species, the better known are proteas, ericas and restios, but it also has a wealth of bulbous species, several of which are endemic. It has a complex life cycle and, for instance, fire is a necessary part of regeneration. Nearly 400 species of fynbos are very rare, upwards of 200 on the verge of extinction, and nearly 40 of the known species are extinct.

antiques peek out from nooks and crannies, tables are old wood, cutlery is old silver, napkins are embroidered and there are touches of frilliness that's not too excessive. It's owner-run by the somewhat eccentric Rosemary, who – in spite of having had a colourful life that includes being a founder of Biggie Best – looks nothing near the age she claims to be. The back veranda also has tables and the garden brims with healthy-looking veggies and herbs, so if you have a salad, it'll be freshly plucked and organic. The menu is seasonal, with

The harvesting of flowers from the region's fynbos provides income for rural people.

starters being a divine soup in winter and salad in summer. Mains might be traditional oxtail, *skaapkop*, *kerrie afval*, steaks, Karoo lamb chops, line fish, sole, calamari or tiger prawns. The restaurant is in the main street on the right when heading to De Kelders, just before Kino Street. Open daily for lunch and every night except Wednesday and Sunday. Book ahead on tel: 028-384-2076 or 072-884-4936. **The Lighthouse Tavern** is situated south of Gansbaai on the road to Danger Point Lighthouse, and is popular with locals. It's owner-run by a brother-and-sister team, William and Julia, whose eisbein and speciality steaks (with roquefort and escargot, for example) are in high demand. Furnishings are rustic, floors tiled, and there's a large open hearth in the smoking/pub section of the restaurant. The wine list includes local producers, and they also serve cocktails. Starters include perlemoen, while main courses consist of several fish dishes, grills, vegetable pasta and salads, and there's a kiddies' menu too. Open from 08h00 for breakfast, lunch and dinner until late. Residents also frequent **Ciro's Restaurant** in a small stone building at 15 Franken Street en route to the caravan park. Open daily for lunch and dinner from 18h00. Sunday's 3-course lunch is R85 per head, but booking (on tel: 028-384-1106) is essential. **The Great White House** in Kleinbaai has a large restaurant and is a central booking station for shark and whale activities. They're known for their line fish, calamari and grills. Call them on tel: 028-384-3273 or visit www.white-house.co.za.

If you just want a drink, **Ernie's** is en route to the harbour and has a deck overlooking Walker Bay that's ideal for sundowners; and another local hangout is **Buitesteen Pub & Grill** in De Kelders. It's somewhat rough, with the odd redeeming feature, such as perlemoen shells covering the walls and buoys hanging from the ceiling. **Gansbaai Saloon** is a restaurant and pub in the main street that's open 7 days a week for breakfast, lunch and supper.

Whatever you do, don't miss a visit to **Dyer Island Visserye/Fisheries**, a shop in the harbour that does takeaways, and also sells fresh fish. Kingklip, Cape salmon and yellowtail are displayed on crushed ice, and oysters, mussels, prawns, calamari and other ocean delicacies can be selected from various fridges or freezers. Packaging varies from small quantities to bulk, and prices are really reasonable. The takeaway operates 09h00–16h00, and the shop is open 08h00–17h00.

Nearby Gansbaai

Kleinbaai is 6 kilometres south of Gansbaai and from its busy harbour one can see the distant Dyer Island. Years ago, local fishermen in the Dyer Island area told stories of the large sharks in the local waters, which led to the now-famous shark expeditions. Today, shark diving, whale-watching and tours to Dyer and Geyser islands are all launched from Kleinbaai. There's a selection of accommodation here; a tidal pool to the right of the harbour when facing the sea (reach it via Kabeljou Street); and a 9-hole golf course, with plans to expand to 18 holes, that's very popular and even has sea views from some of the holes.

> **For the lowdown on**
> Baardskeerdersbos and what it has to offer, call Helena Swart on tel: 028-381-9206 or 079-528-1919.

About 26 kilometres east of Gansbaai the little village of **Baardskeerdersbos**, more affectionately known among the locals as 'B'bos', is one of those quiet rural places with an air of mystery about them. The name, which literally means 'Beard Shavers' Forest', can be traced back to the mid-1600s and its origin has inspired numerous legends and myths. The most interesting of these is that the name arose because of a fast-running arachnid called a solifugid. These ferocious-looking but non-poisonous creatures (also known as sun spiders or wind scorpions) were thought to pad their nests with beard hair sheared from sleeping men. This is of course entirely untrue. As Brent says, they were 'myth-informed'.

The town has a rural feel and a very small population, but don't think it doesn't have a big following. At their annual church bazaar they are reputed to sell in the region of 1 400 kilograms of boerewors and 2 000 sosaties – not bad for a backwater. Rumour has it that the road from Gansbaai through Baardskeerdersbos to Bredasdorp will be tarred and property prices in B'bos have soared accordingly.

The town and surrounds are popular with artists who let their creativity flow in the tranquillity of the area. To find out more about the **Baardskeerdersbos Art Route** and how to view some of the works of these hidden talents, call Claudette Barnes on tel: 028-381-9636. You can even explore by taking a donkey-cart tour.

About 7 kilometres from Baardskeerdersbos is **Heidehof Fynbos Nature Trails** and here Mathia Schwegler takes visitors on an informative guided walk, explaining the geology and fauna and flora of the region. Her nature trail, which is an easy circular trail of 3–5 hours, is the first in the Western Cape to be accredited with Green Flag status. After the walk, and having worked up a thirst, beer and wine or something a little weaker is enjoyed under the milkwood trees. Mathia also makes creams using oils from certain species of fynbos, which are extremely good for the skin, and has written a book on fynbos. Call her on tel: 028-388-0073 or 082-901-5070.

Visit Barney Otto at the **Strandveld Pub and Grill**, which is open daily from 10h00 and serves lunches. It's housed in the original school, which was built in 1918, and the restaurant tables are a little dwarfed by the size of the hall they're arranged in. There are no frills, but you're guaranteed a genuine *platteland* experience. There's a big-screen TV, a Jetmaster in the bar, and a pool table. Ask Barney to relate the story regarding the money hanging among the bottles behind the bar.

GRABOUW, ELGIN AND BOTRIVER

Grabouw is the commercial centre for what is the largest single export fruit-producing area in southern Africa known as Elgin. Elgin Valley is internationally known as the place in South Africa 'where the apples come from' and it's said to produce over half of the country's export apples. It's an area well liked by nature-lovers but perhaps best known for its annual Elgin Festival, which draws thousands of visitors to displays of flowers, fruit, wines and local products. If you miss the festival, several farmstalls along the N2 sell local produce.

Out and about in the Elgin Valley

Peregrine Farmstall is on the N2 near the junction to Grabouw. It has a fabulous selection of all things 'farmstall-ish', including fresh fruit and veg, homebakes and a selection of wine, and is one of the best-stocked farmstalls in the area. Open daily 08h00–18h00. In the town of Grabouw, you'll find the

---

WHY VISIT?

In spring the fertile valleys of orchards and rambling roses burst into blossom.

WHAT'S WACKY?

It was in this area in 1966, on the farm Applethwaite, that Edmond Lombardi created Appletiser, a pure apple-juice drink that's free of additives and preservatives.

WHAT'S WHAT?

Elgin Valley Tourism has a small office at the Peregrine Farmstall. Open 09h00–17h00 weekdays and 09h00–15h00 weekends. Tel: 021-848-9838 or visit www.elginvalley.co.za.

Elgin Apple Museum, which depicts the history of the fruit industry in the region – but don't expect an up-to-date museum telling you anything about today's apple farming, because it's all about giving you insight to the past. In December holidays it's usually open daily, otherwise arrange with the tourism office to gain access.

Take the Viljoenshoop Road south (just east of Peregrine Farmstall) to **Duncan's Rose Nursery**. Farmers here plant roses along their fences to show the first signs of any of the diseases that might affect their fruit crops, and this road is particularly beautiful in November when the roses are in bloom. Duncan's has a magnificent rose garden comprising hundreds of plants and varieties in glorious shades. Have a chat to one of the rose-growers and if you're a novice you'll pick up invaluable tips. Open 08h00–17h00 Monday–Friday, 08h30–16h00 Saturday, and (August–November) 10h00–16h00 Sunday.

The Houw Hoek Inn next to the N2 has been serving travellers for a very long time.

> Take time to explore back roads in the Elgin Valley. They offer great scenery and views of the majestic mountains.

Off Viljoenshoop Road there's a left turn into Valley Road, which will take you over the mountain to the R44 (Kleinmond Road). It's gravel and not always in good condition but offers some good views.

While in the area, visit **Botriver** to check out the hotel and Shuntin' Shed. There are also a few wine farms here, including Beaumont and Luddite. Take the gravel Goedvertrouw loop north to the edge of the Theewaterskloof Dam, then south again to Grabouw. It's a circular route that winds through stands of trees (including the odd oak) and pretty scenery. Get maps from the tourism office and explore the various mountain passes in the area: Sir Lowry's Pass, Viljoen's Pass and Houwhoek Pass. The area offers several outdoors activities including 4x4, hiking and mountain-biking trails.

Overnight in the Elgin Valley

Mofam River Lodge & Ski School has B&B chalets or you can self-cater. The location is stunning, nestled in a valley on the banks of the Palmiet River – and it's tranquil and ideal for a summer break if you're keen on all sorts of water sports and learning various skiing techniques. Dinner is by prior arrangement, and B&B rates are from R350 per person. For details, tel: 021-846-8345 or visit www.mofam. co.za. **Botrivier Hotel** promises to be something special should their extensive 2008 renovations be completed. For further info, visit www.botrivier.co.za.

Eating out in the Elgin Valley

Pick up something at the **Peregrine Farmstall**, or dine at the **Granny Smith Grill** alongside. Its varied menu runs from breakfasts to sweet treats through light eats to grills and specials. **Orchard Farmstall** also serves meals and is at the western entrance to Grabouw. The **Bear & Barrel** pub is in Grabouw, alongside the Apple Museum and has tables outside in the shade of large trees. If you're spending a few days in the area, pop out to the Elgin/Grabouw Country Club, which has a good view over the Eikenhof Dam and mountains. The Sunday buffet is popular with the locals, and they serve breakfast and lunch.

It's worth driving the 25-odd kilometres to **Botriver** (or Botrivier) for a pizza in the **Shuntin' Shed**, which is a revamped railway shed on the old station. It has great atmosphere and a fab view from the deck. Owners, Russ and Wendy, spent a lot of time authenticating the building as far as possible – the seating, for example, is from ex-railway cars. **Botrivier Hotel** has a restaurant that does 5-course Sunday lunches for around R90, but bookings (on tel: 028-284-9640) are essential.

Near Elgin

Heading east from Elgin, **Paul Cluver Wines** produces great beverages and has a stunning forest amphitheatre that operates in summer. Get the show schedule off their website www.cluver. com. The Houw Hoek Farmstall is a popular stop for a bite, and across the road is the **Houw Hoek Inn**, the oldest (1834) licensed hotel in South Africa. This 3-star establishment, tucked beneath ancient oak trees, has a vast front lawn, squash court, putt-putt, Stage Coach Bar, and serves breakfast, lunch and dinner.

GREYTON

Greyton is not much publicised – and without any valid reason. It's a gorgeous hamlet tucked into the foothills of the Riviersonderend mountains and is particularly resplendent in spring when its numerous rose gardens are in full bloom. While it is generally a tranquil settlement, it can become packed with tourists over weekends and during holidays, but this just adds to the buzz rather than detracting from it. The original village, founded in 1854, is home to an estimated 700-odd very friendly and welcoming permanent residents. There are days when it seems that everyone's on a happy pill, but that comes from having traded their designer city shoes and huge salaries for gumboots and security. It's the kind of place that sings and chirps with summery enthusiasm, and in winter the romantic misty mornings are disturbed only by the tap-tap of a woodpecker. There's a herd of free-roaming horses from Genadendal that wanders the streets; and you can expect to see the odd cow grazing contentedly in the market square.

Out and about in Greyton

The **Saturday Morning Market** offers fresh local produce and has been the place to buy, sell and socialise since the early 1980s. Stock up on organic veg, pies, yoghurt, fresh ice cream, preservative-free cheeses, fresh bread and cakes, and honey. Try the lemon-curd pancakes in winter. Dreamy stuff. The market also sells a range of crafts and other items.

The town's **Rose Festival** is a big event held over the last weekend in October, as close to the 27th of the month as possible. Properties have postage-stamp front gardens, and what's out back isn't visible to those passing by so this is when private gardens are opened to the public. **High Hopes** (see below) is one of the open gardens and has around 1 500 roses.

Spending time in Greyton is about relaxing. Take time to explore the streets, quaint shops and art galleries with evocative names including Inside Story, Scarlett, Blossom, Odz and Mafala. You'll also be tempted into eating out as there's a good choice – then you can work off the calories by taking to the surrounding countryside. There are great hikes, walks and mountain-biking trails. The tourist office has masses of info on these. If you park under the oak trees at the end of Park Street, there's a walk into the mountains where you'll discover lush ponds and fern-filled crevasses. There's also the well-known **Boesmanskloof Trail** that links Greyton to McGregor (see page 38).

Another treat in store is the **High Hopes Healing Energy Centre**, which offers applied kinesiology, massage, reflexology, acupressure, Reiki, attunement, aromatherapy, energy (Chi) massage, and Bach flower consultations.

WHY VISIT?

Greyton is a charming artistic village with lovely old cottages and great restaurants.

WHAT'S WACKY?

The village operates on a 'green belt' concept. Building regulations mean houses are built near the front of their plots, thereby creating large back gardens that form the green belt. This is why the birdlife is fabulous.

WHAT'S WHAT?

Greyton Tourism Bureau is in the main street and is open 09h00–17h00 weekdays and 09h00–14h00 Saturdays. Tel: 028-254-9414/9564, www.greyton.net.

The bed of the Gobos River meanders from the kloofs of the Riviersonderend mountains.

These safe and ancient practices offer ways to heal and rejuvenate. Owner, Angela Craig, also does a 3–4 day Life Renovation Programme, and a Rest/Retreat/Sabbatical Programme. Workshops include healthy meals, yoga sessions and, on the last evening, a concert. There is a twice-weekly half-hour meditation on Mondays and Thursdays at 11h00. For information, tel: 028-254-9898 or visit the High Hopes website on www.highhopes.co.za.

Every Saturday at 08h00 there's a yoga class at **Under the Mountain Yoga Centre** on the corner of Kloof and Park streets. Visitors are welcome but be sure to call Jonathan Blumberg ahead of time on tel: 028-254-9667.

Although having coffee doesn't usually fall under attractions, **The Post House**, in the main street, is an institution. This charming national monument comprises a vibey coffee shop, chocolaterie, restaurant and B&B complete with creaking wooden floors and wonky walls. Better idea, forget the coffee and have their decadent hot chocolate or chocolate milkshake – they're devastating. You can buy hand-crafted Von Geusau chocolates here too.

Wine isn't usually associated with this region but there are 3 wine farms near Greyton: **Andy Mitchell Wines**, **Oewerzicht Cellar** and **Lismore Estate Vineyards**. The latter is Greyton's first wine 'estate' (estate status means growing, making and bottling the wine on said property). Get details on tasting and directions from the tourist office.

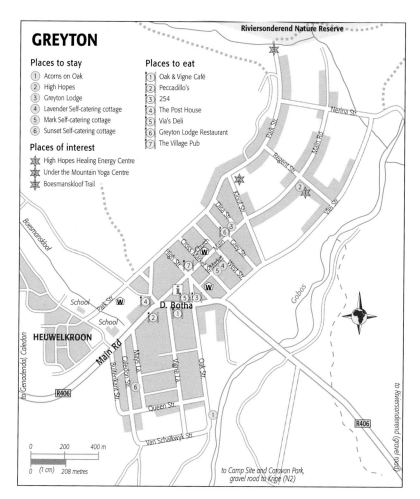

GREYTON

Places to stay
1. Acorns on Oak
2. High Hopes
3. Greyton Lodge
4. Lavender Self-catering cottage
5. Mark Self-catering cottage
6. Sunset Self-catering cottage

Places of interest
- High Hopes Healing Energy Centre
- Under the Mountain Yoga Centre
- Boesmanskloof Trail

Places to eat
1. Oak & Vigne Café
2. Peccadillo's
3. 254
4. The Post House
5. Via's Deli
6. Greyton Lodge Restaurant
7. The Village Pub

Riviersonderend Nature Reserve

Nerina Str.

Park Str.

Main Rd.

Regent Str.

Vlei Str.

Disa Str.

Kloof Str.

Cross Str.

Church Str.

Market Str.

Main

Grey Str.

Oak Str.

West Str.

High Str.

Boesmanskloof

School

Park Str.

School

D. Botha

HEUWELKROON

Main Rd.

Mays La.

Caledon Str.

Butekiam Str.

Vigne La.

Oak Str.

R406

Queen Str.

Van Schalkwyk Str.

Gobos

to Genadendal, Caledon

to Riversonderend (gravel road)

R406

to Camp Site and Caravan Park,
gravel road to Krige (N2)

0   200   400 m

0   (1 cm)   208 metres

Overnight in Greyton

There are just so many fabulous places to stay in and around Greyton – no fewer than 60 establishments and a total of 450 beds, including farmstays. The tourist office has lists, brochures and photos to help you choose, should you arrive without booking, but this isn't advisable over weekends or holidays. If you're after superb personal but non-invasive service and outstanding mountain views as backdrop to a manicured garden, **Acorns on Oak** is a country house offering 5 private luxury units on the edge of town alongside a pretty stream. It's owner-run by Cecil and Mieke, who've travelled extensively and know how to ensure guests are comfortable. Rooms have king-sized beds, the coffee tray comes with an espresso machine, and there's a mini bar and heated towel rails. Cecil and Mieke are award-winning hosts, having beaten 5 000 contenders to earn the

UK's prestigious Inn of the Year Award in 2002. They then bought this property, designed every inch of it, and had the units purpose built, which takes attention to detail to a new level. Guest facilities include a heated 12-metre pool, and thatched braai area overlooking the stream. The garden's water features add an exotic touch and you may need to use the 'stepping stones' to reach your room. Breakfast is enjoyed either on the patio, or in a large dining room with a huge hearth and cosy fire on cooler days, and apart from the standard full-cooked breakfast, you could choose kippers (lusciously plump) with poached eggs, omelettes, Continental, or scrambled egg and smoked salmon. Cutlery is silver and crockery is Wedgwood. Regret no children or pets. B&B rates from R425 per person sharing. For details, tel: 028-254-9567 or visit www.acorns-on-oak.co.za. **High Hopes B&B** offers 5 well-appointed rooms in a gorgeous country garden where exotics live alongside indigenous trees, forming canopies for climbing roses. All rooms sleep 2, and ours had a bay window overlooking the garden. There's something very 'English countryside' about High Hopes, and we could have stayed and stayed, until the owners Sharon and Angela had to prise us from our room. Breakfast is a treat and may start with a fruit kebab, and eggs are free-range from their own chickens. Facilities include a pool and mountain-bike hire; and they hold a music evening every quarter. If you're in the market for a violin, Sharon makes them. B&B rates are from R320 per person for a queen to R475 per person for a king with DStv. Look out for

specials, or call them on tel: 028-254-9898 or click on www.highhopes.co.za.

Greyton Lodge, at 52 Main Street, has 15 en-suite rooms, many opening onto the grounds that are atwitter with birds. Owners, Villi and Boi, have created a homely feel in this historic building. The décor is attractive, walls are adorned with original artworks, and fresh flowers grace all the rooms. The lodge is mostly wheelchair-friendly, and definitely bird-friendly as the feeders and water features in the garden attest. You might be visited by Lucky, the dog, who has a foot fetish, or the pair of resident white ducks. Every Friday afternoon 17h00–19h00 there are live music sessions. Rooms are standard, luxury or suites and B&B rates are R350–R600 per person sharing. Children are welcome on condition that they're well behaved and supervised (children under 12 are charged R150). For details, tel: 028-254-9800 or 028-254-9876 or visit www.greytonlodge.co.za. The self-catering **Lavender Cottage** has an Italian Art deco suite sleeping 2 people. It faces the town square, so on Saturday mornings the market is on your doorstep. Alongside is **Mark Cottage**, also a quaint romantic spot for a couple. Rates are R200–R250 per person sharing. Call Anna Elisabettini on tel: 028-254-9727. **Sunset Self-catering Cottage** in Buitekant Street sleeps 4 and has an interleading bathroom, open-plan lounge and kitchen. The loft sleeps 2 in an open-plan with lounge, kitchen, and separate loo and shower. Rates are R200–R225 per person sharing. To book, tel: 028-254-9895 or click on www.sunsethousegreyton.co.za. There's also a new backpackers, Zebra Moon, in town.

The beautifully situated Acorns on Oak, Greyton's top-of-the-range establishment.

Eating out in Greyton

There's a fine selection of places to eat out in Greyton, and they're all good. In fact, several are great. It's wise to note that as the town continues with its growth spurt, new restaurants open and others close or change hands. Also, many are not licensed, so take your own wine. The best-known eatery is the **Oak & Vigne Café** tucked beneath oak trees in Ds Botha Street. It's owned by foodie, Coenie Visser, who started it about 12 years ago, and comprises a restaurant serving continental and Mediterranean fare, espresso bar, sandwich bar, deli and wine cellar, with an open-air patio courtyard covered in vines. It's a very popular venue, and the in-place to see and be seen by the in-crowd coming into town on weekends. The menu is refreshingly different, from delectable breakfasts (try the kitchen sink pancake) to lunches that include honey-and-sesame coated chicken livers and a divine Delano burger with the thickest patty ever.

The Amangansett Oak is a wholewheat baguette with smoked chicken, crispy bacon, avo, Swiss Emmental and rocket. Beverages include a selection of hot ones including Brazilian hazelnut coffee, and chai tea, and there are also super healthy cold fruit and vegetable juices. The deli also sells home bakes; and adjoining is a good selection of wines. Open daily 08h30–17h30, but times tend to vary according to season, and they trade later in summer. For details, tel: 028-254-9037. **Peccadillo's**, in the main street, is highly recommended by the locals and is a fairly new restaurant owned by the quick-witted Rupert Fage, who does the front of house, and his wife Susan, who's in the kitchen. The décor is simple, and their meals are French style, but the menu is ever-changing. There's a menu for 'Little People', so bring the kids along. Try the warm Roquefort cheesecake with garlic-and-balsamic dressing. Mains may include chicken tikka, pasta or leek-and-marscapone risotto. They're also one of the few places that offer a mixed cheese platter. If you're there for lunch, try their pancake stacks with a delicious choice of fillings. If you're having tagliatelle, it'll be home made, and whenever possible, there's trout on the menu because Rupert and Susan hail from the trout country of Dullstroom. Open 12h00–15h00 Thursday–Monday for lunch, or later in busy times; and from 18h30 until closing for dinner. **254** is another local favourite, and it's definitely best to book here. You'll find it on the corner of Ds Botha and Oak streets in a grand old house owned by Herman and Phillipus. The restaurant flows into different rooms, floors are wooden, and luscious red velvet curtains contrast with snowy tablecloths. They use only the freshest ingredients to produce wholesome dishes with an innovative twist, like deep-fried avo salad and crustless lamb shank pie. Open Wednesday, Friday and Saturday for dinner only. However, it seems that these men are better known for their elaborate Sunday buffet lunches on their farm 18 kilometres from town. If you can get a booking, be warned, this is a slooooow day. If you have a plane to catch at 3 o'clock, you won't make it. Sunday buffet costs R150 per person. The lads do this as a hobby and are much in demand for catering as well, so booking is essential – call them on tel: 028-254-9373.

The Post House, in the main street, is also something of an institution, and serves a divine chocolate brownie. As you sit beneath ancient ceiling beams,

overlooking a wee veranda that runs along two sides of the house, tuck into broccoli-and-blue-cheese soup and chicken crumble with tarragon. Open 09h00–16h30 Monday–Saturday and 09h00–15h00 Sunday, but book in busy times on tel: 028-254-9995. **Greyton Lodge Restaurant**, 46 Main Road, is open to the public for breakfast, lunch and dinner, and teas or light eats in between. In fact, the owners say they're always open, even for a glass of wine, and if you want one, the bar is in the town's original police station. The breakfast and dining rooms overlook the garden. In the evenings, pretty fairy lights illuminate the patio. On Sundays there's a lunch buffet where you can eat as much as you like. Open 7 days a week from 08h00 until late. For more information, tel: 028-254-9800 or 028-254-9876. If you want to meet some of the locals, the well-seasoned **Village Pub**, on the corner of Main

Donkey carts like this one in Greyton are still a traditional mode of transport in the Overberg.

Road and High Street, is open in the evenings from 17h00 until the locals go home, and a little later on weekends, perhaps until 22h00, and closed on Sundays. **Via's** Robert and Via have bought the old Greyt-on-Main, done a great renovation and teamed up with the Naturally Greyton organic shop. Via's deli also serves organic coffee and delectable lunches, including vegetarian meals. The menu changes depending on what's available. On weekends they provide a mezze platter of local meats, cheeses, olives and homemade relishes. To book, tel: 028-254-9190.

Near Greyton

Nearby is Genadendal, established in 1738, which is said to be the oldest mission on the continent. You have to stop in here if you're interested in history or stepping back in time, and be warned that it's one of those places you'll definitely spend longer exploring than you thought. When you turn off onto either leg of the loop road, there is no indication of what lies at their apex – the beautiful old buildings and well-preserved Genadendal Moravian Church Square, with its 20-odd historic buildings dating to the early 1800s. It is regarded as the most authentic church square in the country. The **Genadendal Mission Museum Collection** is housed in 15 exhibition rooms and ranges from household goods to musical instruments, medical equipment and the oldest fire engine and oldest pipe organ in the country. The contents were declared a National Cultural Treasure in 1991, and most of the display has been produced and used at this mission

station. Genadendal was one of the more progressive communities in its time, with members carrying out pioneering work in education, music, printing, vernacular architecture and furniture-making. Today, Dr Balie runs a tight ship with limited resources, managing to put together an impeccably neat and clean museum complex. Open 09h00–13h00 and 14h00–17h00 Monday–Thursday, 09h00–15h30 Friday, and Saturday mornings.

HEMEL-EN-AARDE VALLEY

Tucked between the folds of the Glen Vauloch mountains near Hermanus (see pages 164–177), the valley runs 35 kilometres to Caledon and farmers grow flowers, olives, apples, cherries, pears, berries and grapes for wine. On a clear day, you can see Sandown Bay, Kleinmond and Betty's Bay from the valley. There are 28 wineries, 7 offer tasting and sales, and if you want to lunch here – and you should – be sure to book your table in advance.

The valley has a reputation for award-winning wines, with signature wines being the capricious Pinot Noir, Chardonnay and Sauvignon Blanc. Each winery is a little different from its neighbour. **Newton Johnson** produces wines of the same name, plus the Cape Bay range, and this is where you'll find Heaven, their restaurant. The state-of-the-art cellar is built into the side of the mountain, making this one of the few gravity-fed cellars in the region, and views from their tasting-room windows are spectacular. Open weekdays and Saturday mornings, so check the website www.newtonjohnson.com. **Bouchard**

The Hemel-en-Aarde Valley near Hermanus is a patchwork of orchards and vineyards strung against a backdrop of curvaceous mountain slopes.

Finlayson has a fabulously atmospheric cellar with low light casting shadows on barrels of ageing wine. It's a perfect venue for their classic and operatic concert evenings. Winemaker, Peter Finlayson, was the first to make wine in the valley, and the cellars now produce world-class Pinot Noir. Open Monday–Friday and Saturday mornings. Visit www.bouchardfinlayson.co.za for more information. To reach the restaurant and tasting facility at **La Vierge** you cross a walkway over the wine-making room. There is a deli, a cheese-tasting room, and the 'champagne deck' has a boule court. Open daily, but check the website www.lavierge.co.za. **Sumaridge Wines** has great sea views from the tasting-room balcony. Of the 7 varietals produced exclusively from the farm's own vineyards, they've won awards for their Chardonnay and Pinot Noir. They're open daily, but serve light lunches on bookings only. For details, tel: 028-312-1097 or visit www.sumaridge.co.za.

Eating out in the Hemel-en-Aarde Valley

The heavenly restaurant, called **Heaven**, is in the Newton Johnson wine-tasting barn, and has huge picture windows allowing panoramic views of the valley. They serve breakfast and lunch Tuesday–Sunday, prepared by chefs and owners Bruce Henderson and Yolande Steenkamp. Dishes are contemporary, but be sure to try the peanut chicken salad starter and the Blooming Onion main dish, which is unique – and divine! The menu changes frequently, but the onion is a firm favourite that's always available. The homemade bread is excellent, and if you ask Bruce what's particularly good, he'll twinkle and tell you 'everything's good'. We agree.

Mains cost R60–R120. For reservations, tel: 072-905-3947.

La Vierge winery's restaurant is open daily and serves French country-style meals and breakfast on weekends, and they occasionally have live jazz. The deck is conducive to some very long lunches and too much wine in the sun. Mains cost R60–R120. For details, tel: 028-313-2007.

Moggs Country Cookhouse is not on a wine farm and you won't find anything pretentious here. It lies at the end of a winding gravel road that leads to the converted labourer's cottage in a farmyard setting, tucked into the trees, with lovely valley views. The small menu changes weekly and is seasonal as they grow their own produce as far as possible. Don't miss the homemade ice cream. Open Wednesday–Sunday for lunch, and dinner on Saturdays. Closed in June and July. Mains cost R65–R100. They're not licensed and do not charge a corkage fee. Booking is essential, so call on tel: 028-312-4321.

Near the Hemel-en-Aarde Valley

Sandbaai lies on the coast near the entrance to the Hemel-en-Aarde Valley and is the most recently developed residential area of Greater Hermanus (although many roads are still gravel). Houses are eclectic, but the mix is nicer than many modern-day coastal resorts, and there are a fair number of permanent residents. Sandbaai offers safe swimming in its rock pools and coves at low tide, as well as good snorkelling. A meandering path leads from Sandbaai to Onrus River beach and it takes about half an hour to

> Keep an eye out for baboons along the R43. They tend to dash across the road in front of your car.

walk. It passes secluded coves so it's not advisable to walk here alone, but is fine for groups.

The big attraction of Onrus is the huge caravan park and campsite that runs around the little bay. Camping rates depend on season and site location and run from R75 to R230 for up to 6 people. Nearby is the popular Davies Pool, a natural rock pool ideal for safe swimming, and there's a good beach at Onrus River frequented by surfers and body boarders. (Do note, though, that currents are strong here.) There are several spots to grab a bite to eat in Onrus, including Bella Napoli Pizzeria on Van Blommenstein Road, where you will also find Onrus Gallery. Goddard's Grill is a block up from the caravan park entrance; and there's a pub and restaurant that serves all day breakfast in Molteno Street. Onrus has basic facilities, such as a garage, ATM and a 7-Eleven store.

Vermont is unique in that it has a saltpan that's often full of water birds. Although there's no swimming beach along much of the coast, including Vermont, there is the Jan Rabie Tidal Pool. A 2-hour coastal walk through Vermont Nature Reserve stretches from Brêkvis Bay, with its high dunes and sheltered beach, to Hawston harbour, and takes in the Hoek van die Berg private reserve. There's also a coastal path from Vermont, through Onrus, to Sandbaai.

Hawston's claim to fame is its Blue Flag beach status, but – to be honest – it was not up to scratch the times we visited, and all the locals we spoke to said that it does not maintain the required standards.

Fisherhaven is not a coastal resort, but it borders the Botrivier lagoon and has easy access to this body of water. We couldn't figure out why people have chosen to live and holiday here, but undoubtedly they think it's heaven.

HERMANUS

Harley Street doctors prescribed Hermanus for it's 'Champagne air' as the perfect antidote to the smog of London, but you don't need to come from a polluted city to appreciate this clean environment. Hermanus lies on Walker Bay, which is a marine reserve renowned for the great number of whales that visit July–November. It's the largest town in the region, and a long skinny one at that, stretching approximately 12 kilometres from its eastern to western end. It is built between the steep slopes of the Kleinrivier (or Klein River) mountains and the alternately sandy and rocky coastline. Fernkloof Nature Reserve hugs the town on the northeast side, the Kleinrivier lagoon to the east, and little coastal settlements run along the shore to the west. To the northwest lies the renowned Hemel-en-Aarde Valley.

Hermanus is a relatively large commercial centre, with an estimated total population in the Greater Hermanus area of 70 000. It's an atmospheric town with a good selection of just about everything that makes up a seaside settlement: great restaurants, art galleries, book shops and quaint retail outlets, plus a whole army of accommodation options available to travellers. Add to this a very long list of things to see and do.

The town is trying desperately to hold onto at least some of its past in the form of the remaining historical fishermen's cottages near the old harbour. What

WHY VISIT?

♦ To see whales!
♦ Visit the Hemel-en-Aarde Valley (page 161).

WHAT'S WACKY?

♦ This is the only town in the world that has a whale crier (the most photographed icons in South Africa).
♦ South Africa was the first country outside Europe to win Blue Flag accreditation for some of its beaches – one of which is in Hermanus.
♦ The station is the only one in the world that's never had a train arrive or depart from it.

WHAT'S WHAT?

There's a 4-way stop at Main Road and Lord Roberts Street and if you look to your right (with the sea on your left) you'll see the old station building where the tourism office is situated. Open 08h00–18h00 weekdays, 09h00–17h00 Saturday and 10h00–14h00 Sunday in summer; and 09h00–17h00 Monday–Saturday in winter. Tel: 028-312-2629, www.hermanus.co.za

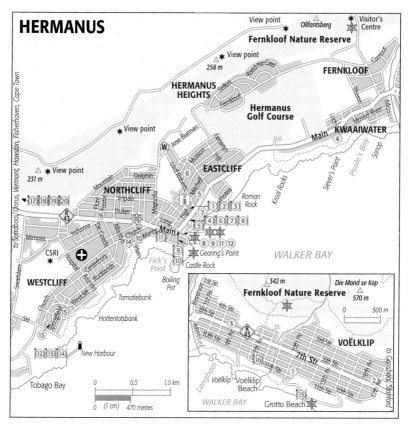

HERMANUS

Places to stay
1. Lavender Manor
2. Breeze Inn
3. Grys Paleis
4. Abalone Guest Lodge
5. Mitchell Street Village
6. The Brown Jug Guest H.
7. Marine Hotel
8. Harbour House
9. Old Harbour Guest H.
10. Pelagus House
11. 45 Marine Drive
12. Hermanus Esplanade
13. Whale Rock Lodge
14. Misty Waves Boutique Hotel
15. Palm Tree Cottage
16. Zoete Inval Backpackers

Places to eat
1. Rossi's
2. Joubert's
3. Cuckoo Tree
4. Meditteria Seafood Rest.
5. Bientang's Cave
6. Cubana Havana Lounge
7. Fusion Cafe
8. Shimmi's Cocktail Bar
9. Fisherman's Cottage Rest.
10. Zebra Coffee Bar
11. Bellini Gallery
12. Quayside Cabin
13. Harbour Rock
14. Gecko Bar
15. Dutchies Beach Rest.
16. Kingfisher Corner Cafe
17. B's Steakhouse
18. Heaven (Hemel-en-Aarde)
19. La Vierge (Hemel-en-Aarde)
20. Moggs Country Cookhouse

Places of interest
- Whale Museum
- De Wet's Huis Photo Mus.
- Old Harbour
- Gearing's Point
- Fernkloof Nature Reserve
- Grotto Beach

used to be the simple homes now house museums, galleries and restaurants. Thankfully, concerned residents have stopped developers destroying these and, although somewhat dwarfed by nearby modern buildings, they still stand.

Roughly speaking, the Greater Hermanus area can be broken down into the suburb of Voëlklip and nearby beaches on the eastern side of town; a little closer to the centre is Eastcliff; then there's the town centre, with its heritage houses; and west of here is the suburb of Westcliff and the new harbour area. Small coastal settlements west of Hermanus are found in the following order: Sandbaai, Onrus and Vermont (the latter two adjoin and it's not clear where one ends and the next starts).

Out and about in Hermanus

It's said that there are something like 300-odd activities and attractions in and around Hermanus, so the best thing to do is visit the tourist office and get brochures and info on those that are of particular interest to you. For many, number one is whale watching. The *Hermanus* info booklet describes favourite whale-watching spots, and gives info about the whale crier. Whale season is roughly June–December, peaking September–October, and you can spot whales from land. If you're on the rocks, you may even get within

Whether it's along the cliff path or in the alleys and side streets, there's lots of strolling to be done in Hermanus.

metres of them. Whale-watching from the air costs around R2 100 for 2–3 people, but it's important to note that prices depend on the cost of aviation fuel. In season, you'll get a refund if you don't have any whale sightings. For details, tel: 028-312-2701 or visit www.africanwings.co.za.

If you're visiting Hermanus out of whale season, there's still a chance you'll see seals and, as you explore the coastline on foot, gulls wheel overhead and plovers scamper along the shoreline. A great way to get the lowdown on whales is to visit the **Whale Museum** just west of the Village Square. It offers fascinating facts and an audio-visual **Whale Show** at 10h00 and 15h00, focusing on the southern right whales that visit the bay. Alongside is **De Wet's Huis Photo Museum**, which has a historical exhibition of the village, giving valuable insight into the early days. The **Village Square** is central to the town and overlooks the sea with only the town's coastal road between it and lawns that lead onto the cliff path. It's a place of trendy shops, good restaurants and a bench for 'tired husbands' and directly in front of the square is an amphitheatre that's handy for tired feet after all that whale-watching. East of the square is the **Whale Fountain**, and there's plenty of parking all around. **Gearing's Point** is a little west of the square on Marine Drive and is just one of the places from which you can spot whales. The 12-kilometre **Cliff Path** offers fabulous sea views and is accessible from several roads and parking areas. It winds through the fynbos along the coastline and, when

Shark Lady Adventures is one of the operators that undertake shark-cage diving near Gansbaai.

you need to rest, there are benches overlooking little coves.

Hermanus has two harbours. Directly in front of the Whale Museum are steps leading to the historic Old Harbour where colourful old fishing skips stand near the doors to the **Old Harbour Museum**, which archives the local whaling history and fishing industry. Today, this natural harbour is used as a focal point for some of the town's festivals and activities, such as Carols by Candlelight and the Easter Passion Play. You can also hire kayaks here and head out to sea. The **New Harbour** is often alive with activity around fishing trawlers and, in summer, the harbour wall looks like a painter's palette of colourful fishermen, all hoping for a bite.

Hermanus also has great beaches and if your hedonistic passions lean towards lying on powdery-white sandy beaches you'll find the best ones east of town in the Voëlklip area. *Please* be aware

that Walker Bay is known for its strong currents and treacherous waters so don't go deep, especially at spring and neap tides. Major beaches have lifeguards at peak times, the most famous being **Grotto Beach**, east of town. Grotto is accessible from the end of 10th Avenue, which heads to the coast off the main road (7th Avenue) through town. Its popularity is in part due to its Blue Flag status. Depending on the season and whether the Kleinrivier lagoon mouth is open or not, this beach can stretch all the way along The Plaat (see Gansbaai on page 142) to De Kelders. At the entrance to Grotto Beach there's a daytime restaurant and behind it a grassed area with braai facilities. The ablutions are usually clean, and you can hire sunloungers and umbrellas. Get there early to nab one of the few parking spaces in deep shade under the milkwood trees. **Voëlklip Beach** is 1 kilometre closer to town and has a grassed slope to sit on, should you not enjoy the sand. This is where the surfers often hang out. Alongside Voëlklip is Kammabaai, which is a favourite with families. West of Kammabaai is the secluded Langbaai, accessed by steps cut into the cliff just off 6th Avenue. From here, the cliffs rise and the path offers lovely views all the way to the new harbour. There are several tidal pools in the area for swimmers; the **Marine**, also known as **Bientang se Baaigat**, is at the foot of steep steps below the Marine Hotel and offers interesting snorkelling; and another is Fick's Pool off Westcliff Road near the Plein Street junction, and although it's a smaller pool, it's more easily accessible and has a sandy bottom so it's great for kids.

Walker Bay offers ideal kayaking and canoeing conditions, as does the Kleinrivier estuary to the east. Whether you hire a boat, or charter a yacht, or join a scuba-diving group, this is prime coastal territory offering numerous water sports. The yacht club is about 12 kilometres east of town on the Kleinrivier lagoon and welcomes day visitors. The best dive sites, or those richest in marine life, are some distance out to sea, and reef depths vary from 9 to 40 metres. Shore entries are possible along the coast, but it's best to get advice, or join a dive group or company on an excursion. There's a good write-up on diving in the *Hermanus* booklet, obtainable from tourism, which describes where to find pinnacles, walls and canyons, and warns about thermoclines, where warm and cold currents collide, resulting in zero visibility.

WATCHING THE WHALES

Whale sightings can be *almost* guaranteed between August and October. The southern rights (so-named because it was considered the 'right' whale to catch for its rich oil and baleen) arrive from their feeding grounds in the Antarctic in June and calve around August–September. The males arrive for mating in October, and the official whale count (done by aerial survey) for Walker Bay (between Hermanus and De Kelders) is around 150 individuals.

Southern rights can weigh as much as 60 tons and have called the southern oceans their home for approximately 60 million years. On average, females produce calves once every 3 years; and the calves feed on around 600 litres of milk daily by sucking, allowing them to grow around 3 centimetres a day. The lifespan of these whales is unknown, but is thought to exceed 50 years. In the 19th and 20th centuries, populations were decimated, but they were the first of the large whales to become a protected species in 1935, and numbers have recovered substantially since. Tourism has played a big part in this revival.

About 1–3% of the whales spotted off the coast of Hermanus are humpbacks, and an orca is seen about once every 10 years. Bryde's whales are rare, but may also be seen.

You'll get good advice from the fishing tackle shops as to where to fish. A brochure of rules and regulations is available from Marine Coastal Management in the New Harbour. Several tourist companies offer guided trips for fly-fishing, lagoon, shore and rock fishing, and deep-sea fishing. Locals say that 30–50 kilometres out to sea one can catch tuna, and closer to shore you may land snoek, dorado and others. In the **Kleinrivier lagoon**, you can catch elf and cob, and it's here you can also fly-fish. The Hemel-en-Aarde valley offers freshwater fly-fishing. While we're talking about catching dinner, in season you can also crayfish but, as with fishing, permits are essential and obtainable from the post office. For info on shark-cage diving, see Gansbaai listing as this is where it happens.

Fernkloof Nature Reserve is north of town in the Kleinrivier mountains. Take the main road east until you reach Fir Avenue just before the circle that leads to the beaches. Turn left into Fir Avenue. It's not well signposted so you're likely to have to double back. The 1800-hectare reserve includes the Cliff Path, fynbos and a small patch of evergreen forest, and it's said that the largest semi-carnivorous plant in the world grows here. Various signs point to the amphitheatre, drinking fountain, aloe garden, fragrance garden and sunbird path. It's known for its 1600+ plant species collected and identified within the reserve, an area of 15 square kilometres, and nowhere else on earth can you see such a variety growing in such close proximity. There's a visitors centre, herbarium, nursery and tarred road all the way to the Botanical Shed, which displays what's flowering each month and is the starting point for the 60-kilometre network of hiking trails. The trails are dog-friendly, although you're less likely to spot any of the wildlife or the 90-odd bird species if you have Fido in tow. Gate hours are 07h00–19h00 in summer, and change with the seasons – www.fernkloof.com. The **Kleinrivier mountains**, which stretch from Hemel-and-Aarde valley to past Stanford, are home to troops of baboons totalling about 150 individuals; and several leopards that've been caught on infra-red camera and are identified by their spoor. It's thought there are 9 leopards in the area. Klipspringers,

---

FESTIVALS & EVENTS

♦ **Hermanus Wine & Food Fair** is held in early August at the Hemel-and-Aarde Village just outside of town. It's voted one of the top 10 Best Wine Shows in SA. It's held at the same time as the Kalfiefees, an Afrikaans cultural event featuring local musicians and live shows: www.kalfiefees-hermanus.co.za.

♦ **Fernkloof Flower Festival** is held a week before the Whale Festival, around mid-September. A colourful showcase of local flora and crafts: www.fernkloof.com.

♦ The famous **Whale Festival** is held the last week in September. It's an arts and enviro experience with around 30 shows, sporting and children's events etc. www.whalefestival.co.za.

grysbok, steenbok, rock hyrax (dassie), all 4 types of mongoose, angulated tortoise, many species of rodents, Cape cobra and puff adders all roam the mountains, as do around 250 bird species. During summer, there are occasionally flamingos and pelicans on the Hermanus lagoon and Vermont saltpan.

The New Harbour stands on a spit of land at the end of Westcliff, and a handful of fishing boats operate from here. Boats may not operate in front of Hermanus as it's a marine reserve, so those leaving the **New Harbour** turn immediately right or travel out of the reserve before turning left. The New Harbour has a few fish plants, and abalone factories. **Abagold** offers tours of their abalone farm on weekdays (excluding public holidays). They have 6 million abalone, which are reared in 24 000 baskets spread out in 1 700 tanks and you'll be taken through the farming process. For tours, contact Marelize on tel: 028-313-0253 or click on www.abagold.com.

One of the best ways to explore Hermanus is to do a tour with **Percy's Tours**. They're a really fun crowd and have a vast knowledge of the area. Their respect for nature and wildlife will enrich your visit, and if you're into wine, wine tours are one of their specialities. The company is owner-run by Percy and Ronel, and comes with all the registrations, accreditations, and bells and whistles to ensure you get the best possible value for money. Tours cost R300–R400 per person for 2–4 hours, and they do day trips and tailor-made itineraries. For details, tel: 072-062-8500 or visit

WHAT'S IT ABOUT ABALONE ...?

Abalone, *Haliotis midae*, is a species endemic to South African waters and occurs between the Eastern and Western Cape. It's found mainly in kelp forests to a depth of 9 metres and, because of this, it's an easy target for divers. Abalone is thought to have aphrodisiac qualities and it's one of three dishes in China that are a measure of respect (shark-fin soup and bird's-nest soup are the other two).

Abalone is sold according to size not age, with small abalone costing around R250 per kilogram, and large dried abalone can fetch R6 000 per kilogram. It's so highly valued that at some farms along the South Cape coast, orders are dispatched under armed escort.

www.percytours.com.

A favourite pastime is horse-riding, and around Hermanus you can do it through the vineyards, fynbos, on farms or along the beach. Several companies offer this activity, so check them out at the tourism office. Other sports facilities, such as hang- and paragliding, and cycling (bikes for hire at **Hermanus Cycles** – tel: 028-313-2052) are well advertised. There's a mountain-bike trail starting at Grotto Beach, but take note that bicycles are not allowed on the cliff path. The **Hermanus Golf Club**, rated one of the best in the country, is in Eastcliff and offers a 27-hole course, and booking is essential (contact them on tel: 028-312-1954 or see the website www.hgc.co.za) and the Arabella golf course is 26 kilometres away on the Botriver lagoon.

There's a craft market in town each Saturday; and numerous galleries, studios, art and craft shops sell locally produced works by painters, sculptors, ceramicists, jewellers, photographers, glass workers, writers and quilters, to name a few media. If you're into holistic activities, there are yoga classes in the area (call Ralph on tel: 028-315-1139 or visit www.yogacoach.co.za), as well as masseuses, reflexologists and practitioners of other alternative therapies (contact Hans on tel: 082-658-6074).

While exploring the town, don't miss **The Wine Village**, about 4 kilometres west at the Hemel-en-Aarde turnoff. Its charming owners, Paul and Cathy du Toit, have created one of the top 10 wine shops in the country, with 1 600-plus varieties from 400-odd estates. Some say this is the largest collection in the country under one roof, and they guarantee door-to-door delivery worldwide. Open 09h00–18h00 weekdays, 09h00–17h00 Saturday and 10h00–15h00 Sunday. For details, tel: 028-316-3988 or visit www.wine-village.co.za. There are also two excellent bookshops in Harbour Road. **The Book Cottage** advertises that it's a village bookshop with a city selection – and it is. **Hemingway's Bookshop** has a wonderful atmosphere, and stocks out-of-print books, Africana and collectibles.

Overnight in Hermanus

The 4-star **Lavender Manor** in 10th Street offers relaxed, up-market hospitality overlooking the sea and is within easy walking distance of Grotto Beach and the cliff path. Rates are seasonal from R500–R1 000 per person sharing and include full breakfast. For details, tel: 028-314-0361 or visit www.lavendermanor.co.za. **Breeze Inn**, at 323 6th Street, is on the very eastern edge of town and offers mid-range-priced rooms from R300. For info, tel: 028-314-0374 or click on www.breeze-inn.co.za. For a self-catering option, it's

MARKETS

◆ Every Saturday 09h00–13h00 at the Hemel-en-Aarde Shopping Village, the Hermanuspietersfontein cellar has a **Food & Wine Market** in their yard. It's a great place to grab a plate and create your own meal, enjoyed with a glass of wine.
◆ Every Saturday 07h30–11h00 in summer and 08h30–12h30 in winter, the **Fernkloof Farmer's Market** is held under the trees at Fernkloof Nature Reserve. It's a mainly organic and home-industry market selling top-quality raw and cooked produce from local cheese and pork pies to cooked dinners. Grab a table under an umbrella and enjoy the marimba band. There's lots to keep the kids happy too. For information, tel: 028-312-2629 or visit www.fernkloof.com.
◆ In addition to the daily stalls in front of the **Whale Museum**, there are additional ones every Saturday 08h30–15h00.

The Whale Fountain honours Hermanus as *the* place to see whales.

A ROOM WITH A VIEW

Be aware that 'sea-facing' properties may be just that – facing the sea, not actually on the seafront, and some don't have sea views. It's said that only a dozen establishments in Hermanus are right on the seafront as such, others have good views, and the variety runs from 5-star to budget. Check out www. hermanusaccommodation.co.za.

hard to beat **Grys Paleis** for quality and price. Owners Heinie and Esther have a large, independent upstairs apartment with a double en suite, and 2 twin rooms that share a bathroom. Rates are R500–R1 000 for the unit, depending on season and the number of guests, and Esther is happy to give good discounts out of season for longer stays. There's also a ground floor B&B double en suite for R560. For more information, contact them on tel: 028-314-1346 or 082-290-5504.

Abalone Guest Lodge is a 4-star lodge on Sievers Point, a prime beachfront position halfway between town and the beaches. It has 8 spacious en-suite rooms that have sea, mountain or garden views. African art and décor create local flavour. B&B rates are R450–R900 per person sharing. To book, tel: 028-312-3744 or visit the website at www.abalonelodge.co.za.

The suburb of Eastcliff is popular as it's the older part of town and has lots of trees. It's said to be safe to walk to town from here, but check with your host first. The 4-star **Mitchell Street Village** is more of a boutique hotel, and offers quiet, luxurious comfort in a welcoming atmosphere. There are 10 elegant suites, each with mini-bar, phone, computer point, TV, safe, robes, slippers and percale linen, as well as a private courtyard or balcony. Facilities include library, 2 swimming pools and manicured gardens. B&B rates are R500–R900 per person sharing. For details, tel: 028-312-4560 or click on www.56.co.za. **The Brown Jug Guest House** has 2 stylish, privately located self-catering units (and 1 B&B) in a tranquil garden with pool. It's 3-star rated, just 3 blocks from the seafront, and within easy walking distance of the village. Self-catering rates are R200–R300 per person sharing. Call them on tel: 028-312-2220.

If you're keen to walk in the footsteps of Brad Pitt and other celebrities, **The Marine Hotel** in the centre of town is the place to go if you can afford the rates, which depend on the type of room. Doubles cost from R2 000–R5 000 in low season to R3 600–R8 000 in high season. **Harbour House** is an up-market establishment comprising a hotel and apartments. The 4-star hotel is on Harbour Road, and gets as close to overlooking the historic Old Harbour as possible, with just the coast road in between, and you can literally whale-watch from your balcony. Décor is modern, rooms have a kitchenette for light catering, there's wifi, and secure off-street parking. Alongside, the **Old Harbour House** guesthouse is a historic building with 5 luxurious en-suite rooms overlooking the sea. B&B rates are from R1 295 per double room per night, including breakfast, or R1 095 excluding breakfast. Self-catering apartments cost R2 500

per night. For more info, tel: 028-312-1799 or click on www.harbourhouse-hermanus.co.za. **Pelagus House**, at 31 Marine Drive, is another up-market establishment within walking distance of the centre, or stroll across the road to watch the whales. They offer various rooms as well as a 2-room penthouse. Rates in low season are R450–R600, and in high season R550–R1 000. To book, tel: 028-312-4955 or visit www.pelagus.co.za. **45 Marine Drive**, and the affiliated **Hermanus Esplanade** in the same road, offer 2–3-star seafront self-catering apartments for 2–6 people from R300 for 2 in a non-sea-facing to R1 400 for a 3-bedroom in peak season. For details, tel: 028-312-3610.

The suburb of Westcliff is west of the centre of town and comes with an abundance of places to stay and francolins that cruise the area. Marine Drive, the main drag along the coastline through town, becomes Westcliff Road, and 2 kilometres from here you'll reach the entrance to the New Harbour. Turn right here into Stil Street and 100 metres further you'll see 2 large palm trees and electronic gates, which is the entrance to our favourite B&B, the 4-star **Whale Rock Lodge**. It's a large corner property with rolling lawns, a manicured garden, and a thatched main house that's flanked by various suites that all open onto the garden. Owner, Shelagh Milton, and her staff will warmly welcome you, and whichever of the 11 en-suite rooms you book into you can be assured of privacy and space. Rates are R450–R700 per person sharing. For more information, tel: 028-313-0014/5 or visit the website at www.whalerock.co.za.

The 5-star **Misty Waves Boutique Hotel** on Marine Drive has sea views and opulent décor, and is just a short walk from the sea and cliff path. There are 25 rooms, and suites come with various features such as sea views, spa bath and private verandas. Rates are R1 200–R3 000 per room, and there's a roof-top restaurant that's open 19h00–22h00 every night. For details, tel: 028-313-8460 or click on www. hermanusmistybeach.co.za.

The quaint **Palm Tree Cottage** at 94 Westcliff Road is owner-run by Helen Tait, who started it in 1990 when she realised there was virtually no really reasonably priced self-catering in town. Today her prices are still very affordable at R150–R200 per person sharing 1 of 2 rooms in the house. They're not en suite but each has its own bathroom. The twin is the better option as it's more spacious. There's also a cottage that sleeps 3 and it's fully equipped for self-catering, with rates from R260 for 2 and R300 for 3. Book well in advance as Helen has a lot of repeat business. Call her on tel: 028-312-3563.

Zoete Inval Backpackers, at 23 Main Road, is 1 of 3 backpackers in town. With a 4-star grading, it's a little more up-market and one of the quieter backpackers. It's been going 15 years and is 1 of the 2 original backpackers in the Western Cape, so owners Jan and Marilyn really know their stuff. A variety of rooms cater to most needs, from dorms to private en-suite to a

A visit to the barrel cellar of Bouchard Finlayson is a real treat.

family flat. Rates are seasonal, but average R75–R100 for a dorm bed to R350–R425 for an en-suite double. To book, tel: 028-312-1242 or click on www.zoeteinval.co.za.

Eating out in Hermanus

In many restaurants you'll be paying for the location, which is reflected in the prices on the menu. We did an exercise of noting line fish prices, which varied from R45 to R115, and the more expensive restaurants don't necessarily come out tops in terms of taste, quality or portion size. A lot of what happens in terms of food and beverage activity occurs along the seafront near the Old Harbour from where you can watch the sea and its creatures at play.

With around 70 restaurants in town, we tried our best but could unfortunately not eat at all of them so we spoke to dozens of locals and guesthouse owners during our numerous visits, and the favoured restaurants in town are Rossi's, Meditteria, Joubert's and B's Steakhouse at the turnoff to R320. Favourites in the Hemel-en-Aarde Valley are Heaven, La Vierge and Moggs. Be sure to book at these restaurants. There are the usual chain restaurants where you know what you'll get for your rand. Look out for specials out of holiday seasons.

Rossi's is an Italian restaurant in High Street that has an extensive pizza menu, but also a reputation for serving consistently good pasta, steak and seafood – all in a lively environment that's overlooked by some quizzy fish in a tank. Pizzas come with side dishes of garlic, chilli and Parmesan, and cost

Hermanus offers the best land-based viewing of whales anywhere in the world.

R55–R90. They are open for lunch and dinner daily. To book, tel: 028-312-2848. A little further up the road from Rossi's is **Joubert's,** owner-run by a husband-and-wife team, who have a small but fabulously prepared menu that's more international than local and includes great flavour and ingredient combinations. Open daily for dinner in season. Closed Sunday–Monday in low season. For details, tel: 028-312-4983.

Meditteria Seafood Restaurant is above the golf shop in Marine Drive near the Village Square. It's a mellow place of neutral tones, candlelight, a great view and understated service. Dishes are mainly seafood, but there are good meat dishes and the chef's always inventive. Mains cost R70–R150. Open from 18h00 daily. No children under 12. For more information, tel: 028-313-1655.

Bientang's Cave Restaurant is one of our favourites and scores top points for its location in a cave below the town centre's cliffs. There are 4 levels

The Cliff Path along the Hermanus coastline is a great place for lengthy strolls and an occasional cooling dip at some of the beaches along the way.

of tables, including 2 on the rocks, and this must be the best whale-watching restaurant in the world, where whales come within metres of diners. The à la carte menu of mainly seafood includes their famous bouillabaisse and flame-grilled line fish. Open daily 11h30–16h00, year round and subject to the weather, and 19h00–21h30 in season (at night over weekends in low season). It's advisable to book, so call them on tel: 028-312-3454.

Cubaña Havana Lounge & Latino Caffé is South Africa's only authentic franchised Latino Social Caffé and eatery that combines a cocktail bar, cigar lounge and themed cuisine. If you like something a little different and a little spicy, with an ambience to match, you'll like Cubaña. Breakfast includes vegetarian and spicy dishes served until 14h00; and the rest of

the vast menu runs from tostados (open toasted samis) to *hamburguesas* and *baskettas*. They also have an extensive cocktail menu set up by 'professional mixologists'. I have visions of Tom Cruise flexing his pecs and flicking bottles into the air à la the movie *Cocktail*. They have a rule of no under-23s.

If you feel like Sex on the Beach, **Fusion Café**, under Cubaña, has great cocktail specials during Happy Hour, and a stunning view of the bay. Although every second restaurant specialises in 'fusion' food, this one has some refreshingly interesting dishes. Open 07h00–17h00 Sunday–Monday and 07h00–21h00 Tuesday–Saturday. To book, tel: 028-312-4277.

The **Fisherman's Cottage Restaurant** is a genuine old fisherman's cottage and one of the town's historic buildings, behind the Whale Museum. It's a bit pricey but the historic atmosphere is great. The bar opens at 16h00 and must be one of the smallest public bars in the country at about 2 metres by 4 metres. Open for dinner from 18h00 Monday–Saturday, and for lunch on Saturday. For details, tel: 028-312-3642.

If you're just after a quick bite or take away, try **Hermanus Fish Shoppe** in the Gateway Centre (near the main entrance to Pick n Pay). They also sell fresh oysters.

For breakfast or coffee head to **Bellini Gallery & Cappuccino Bar** on the corner of Marine Drive and Park Lane. The modern **Shimmi's** cocktail bar is above Cubaña and has an awesome view of the sea and Old Harbour. It's perfect for sipping a cocktail while whale-watching, and has a small dance floor that's packed most weekend nights. **Zebra** is another popular nightspot. It's on the main road where the traffic

lights dogleg with Harbour Road.

There are two places to eat at the **New Harbour**, and both have fabulous views and atmospheric locations. Harbour Rock does grills, seafood and sushi, and overlooks the harbour through picture windows. Open for breakfast, lunch and dinner daily. The adjoining **Gecko Bar** serves pizza and is a popular weekend hangout when it has live music. **Quayside Cabin** is on the lower slipway in a quaint building that's half container, half wood and decking, but don't let this put you off. It's ideal for long, lazy lunches of wine and seafood, and the menu includes abalone casserole with lime, dill and fresh cream. Yummy!

In Voëlklip, **Dutchies Beach Restaurant** is at Grotto Beach and is a fully licensed spot offering lunches, snacks, breakfasts, teas and sundowners. Open 08h00–20h00 in summer and 09h00–17h00 in winter. The Kingfisher corner café and takeaways on 7th Avenue is just 2 blocks from the beach.

Hemel-en-Aarde Village, at the junction of the R43 (4 kilometres west of Hermanus) and the R320 into the Hemel-en-Aarde Valley, is where you'll find **B's Steakhouse**, which comes highly recommended by every soul we asked in the area. These people know their meat, and if you want a perfectly grilled, meltingly tender steak, don't even *think* about going anywhere but to B's. B stands for Bruce, who's the daytime chef at the Heaven restaurant in the valley. They're fully licensed and have an award-winning wine list. For further information call them on tel: 023-316-3625.

HERMANUS FACT FILE

◆ Walker Bay is a marine reserve – there are certain rules and regulations that go with this, so become informed.
◆ Hermanus Public Protection (HPP) officers patrol the cliff path and town, but follow basic safety precautions and don't walk alone in isolated areas.
◆ Various parts of the cliff path are wheelchair friendly.
◆ Water is scarce, especially in summer when there's a large influx of visitors. Please limit your water usage.

INFANTA

The small holiday resort and fishing hamlet of Infanta is situated on the western side of the Breede River mouth, opposite Witsand. It's reached by following a somewhat undulating gravel road for about 40 kilometres from the Malgas junction near the Breede River Trading Post, and has fortunately been saved from development so far. It's a scattering of 70-odd mostly holiday houses near St Sebastian Point, which stands surrounded by fynbos-cloaked hills. There are no facilities here, although we heard about a tiny shop that operates on an erratic schedule, but we couldn't find it. There's a wee shop 2 kilometres before you reach Infanta called Grasrug Winkel (aka Ellas Mall). It sells the basics, some DIY stuff, books, shoes, clothing, fishing tackle, fresh meat and ice cream, but it doesn't stock much fresh fruit and veg (although it does store boats and repairs punctures …).

WHY VISIT?

This is the ideal getaway (out of holiday season) from which to enjoy the coastline and pristine surroundings.

WHAT'S WACKY?

The fish eagles breeding on the Breede River.

WHAT'S WHAT?

There's no tourist office but Tim and Hilary at the Mudlark (see pages 179–180) are an excellent source of info on the area.

Out and about in Infanta

Like Witsand (see page 216), Infanta has the advantage of not only being on St Sebastian Bay, but also at the mouth of the Breede River, which makes it ideal for all kinds of water sports – just be sure you know where the conservancy starts and ends, or you'll be fined! The Breede River is recognised as the best fishing estuary in South Africa, but please note that the lower reaches are a conservancy (see Witsand). Swimming, surfing, windsurfing, fishing (deep-sea, river, rock, boat and fly-fishing), river cruises, canoeing and sailing – you can do it all from here. There's a boat-launching facility, but you can also fish the rocky shoreline. Tidal action reaches 60 kilometres upstream where cob, spotted grunter and garrick are caught. The lower reaches of the river are a cob fisherman's paradise, and it's not unusual for specimens weighing 50 kilograms to be caught. The nearest post offices for angling licences are at Witsand and a postal agency is rumoured to be opening at the Trading Post at Malgas in 2009. Boat licences can be obtained from Grasrug Winkel near the Mudlark. If you follow the road into Infanta to where it ends in a small parking area, there's a path along the coastline and up onto the cliffs from where you have a grandstand view of the whales in season. It's generally accepted that the greatest whale nursery runs from Witsand, past Infanta and west to De Hoop Nature Reserve. As early as the first week in June you might spot whales. Following the coastline around to the river mouth, you can see the remains of a ship, the *SS Kadie*

steamer that was wrecked in 1865. Alternatively, when leaving Infanta, a road that's not signposted (opposite the road is a sign: Kabeljoubank) runs diagonally to the right and ends in a small parking area from where it's easy to access the sandbank. At low tide, an extensive rock bank is exposed, offering some good rock-pool exploring, and although there's not much left of the *Kadie*, it's amazing that the salt water hasn't eroded the chunks of metal away completely. Bird watching along the Breede River is spectacular. For birding details, see the listing under Mudlark that follow.

Overnight in Infanta

Our favourite place is the **Mudlark River Front Lodge** on the banks of the Breede River, about 2 kilometres before you reach Infanta. This 22-hectare retreat is owner-run by Tim and Hilary Arnott and comprises wooden cabins in a thickly planted indigenous garden that slopes gently down to the river. It's one of those places that immediately

Up the lazy Breede River for a day's fishing near Infanta.

speaks to your soul. Views over and up the river are uninterrupted, the setting is tranquil, and the garden alive with birds. Your hosts will organise river cruises and horse-riding trails through the conservancy, and tell you about walks along the riverbank and through surrounding fynbos, but allow yourself time to relax as well. If you're keen on fishing and birding, you'll be in paradise. The Mudlark offers trips in small boats for around R120 an hour. You get your own gillie, who'll show you the best fishing spots; and if you want to deep-sea fish, Tim's an old sea dog and will take you out for the day at a cost of around R2 000 for up to 4 people. For those of you who think women can't fish, Hilary's story will make you weep. She's won several fishing awards and still holds the record for the largest swordfish ever caught by a South African woman – a 138-kilogram broadbill swordfish. Check out the awesome photo in their boathouse. Hilary also earned a reputation for being a local fundi at catching spotted grunter. Fishing season is traditionally from October to Easter.

The last bird count was 206 recorded species, and Hilary's garden resonates with the chatter of birds flitting between the flowering aloes and large milkwood trees. There are pairs of resident francolins, 3 sunbird species, southern boubou, tchagara, cardinal and Knysna woodpeckers, to name a few. From the little deck off our room we saw a fairy flycatcher and spotted prinia. Estuary birds include terns, sandpipers, turnstones, sanderlings, kingfishers, Cape shovellers and fish eagles. You may also spot a striped mouse sunning itself, a mongoose peering curiously from behind a tree, or a duiker tripping down the driveway.

Accommodation is on a dinner, bed and breakfast basis. Hilary specialises in country cuisine and meals are served at a communal dining table overlooking the river or *al fresco* on the deck. The **Mudlark** is somewhat of an institution in these parts and has lots of repeat business, so it's best to book well in advance. Rates include a full English breakfast and a 3-course dinner, and are R450–R520. To book, tel: 028-542-1161 or visit www.mudlark.co.za.

> By the way, 'Mudlark' is not a bird. There are various definitions in the dictionary, the gist of which is a 'beach bum' who made a living from picking up bits and pieces mainly on tidal rivers in England.

KLEINMOND

Kleinmond lies at the foot of the Palmietberg between the mouth of the Palmiet River and the Botrivier Vlei. Approaching on the R44 from Hermanus in the east, you'll pass the Kleinmond lagoon estuary on your left, where the famous wild horses live. The R44 runs through town and forms Kleinmond's main street, which is lined with modern buildings, businesses, banks and about a thousand estate agents. Follow this road west, and you'll reach the junction, indicated by a large signboard, to Harbour Road where it's all happening. This is where you'll find the tourist office, restaurants, coffee shops and curio shops. It's a trendy spot compared to the main street and has enticingly named retail outlets, such as Rainspider, Sunshine Trading and The Fishing Cat.

Out and about in Kleinmond

The town is surrounded by the **Kleinmond Coastal and Mountain Reserve**, which is crisscrossed with trails and easy walking paths, the most popular being the coastal path. Details of these can be found in the book *Where to Walk* in Kleinmond from the tourism office. Kleinmond is well known for its wild horses, which live in the Rooisand Reserve wetland east of town. It's an area that stretches about 6 kilometres to the river mouth at Kleinmond, and the feral horses roam freely, using this as their grazing grounds. Various romantic tales account for their existence and they can even be spotted in the far distance from the R44. They're of significant historical importance and, according to

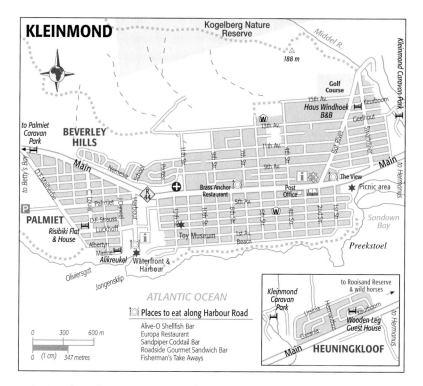

KLEINMOND

Kogelberg Nature Reserve

Middel R.

188 m

Kleinmond Caravan Park

Golf Course

15th Av.
Haus Windhoek B&B
Keurboom

Geelhout

13th Av.

to Palmiet Caravan Park

BEVERLEY HILLS

11th Av.

Main

Nemesia

9th Av.

to Hermanus

to Betty's Bay

D.F. Malherbe

Main

Porter

i

The View

Picnic area

Brass Anchor Restaurant

Post Office

R 44

Palmiet

5th Av.

Sandown Bay

PALMIET

D.F. Strauss

Luckhoff

Toy Museum

Risibiki Flat & House

1st Av.

Beach

Preekstoel

Albertyn

Marine

i

Alikreukel

Waterfront & Harbour

Oliviersgat

Jongensklip

ATLANTIC OCEAN

Kleinmond Caravan Park

to Rooisand Reserve & wild horses

Ursina

Hermanus

Keurboom

Wooden Leg Guest House

to Hermanus

Gazania

Main

HEUNINGKLOOF

Places to eat along Harbour Road

0   300   600 m

0 (1 cm) 347 metres

Alive-O Shellfish Bar
Europa Restaurant
Sandpiper Cocktail Bar
Roadside Gourmet Sandwich Bar
Fisherman's Take Aways

ecologists they play an important role in the wetland ecology. The easiest way to find them is to join a horse trail; alternatively, walk along Kleinmond's main beach towards Fisherhaven and the wetlands. Please note that, although they appear tame, they are wild animals and should be treated with caution. The stallions, especially the youngsters, may be aggressive. The **Equestrian Centre Arabella** offers guided whale-watching, fynbos trails, beach rides as well as viewing of the wild horses. Transfers to and from stables on request, so call them on tel: 082-463-8285 or 083-362-1046. Kleinmond's main beach is Blue Flag rated; however, its lagoon on the eastern side of town is – according to the warning signs in

2008 – too polluted to swim in. On the western side, the **Palmiet Lagoon** is great for swimming, canoeing and boardsailing and has a beach ideal for games and sunbathing. The whole area has good fishing spots and you are most likely to catch steenbras, cob and galjoen. Please get required permits for angling and for collecting bait. There are coastal walks, and a long list of various inland hikes, but it's best to get up-to-date info from the tourism office, and for obvious safety reasons don't walk alone. There's good land-based whale-watching from Kleinmond June–November, and if you spend enough time at the sea you're also likely to spot dolphins and seals. The **Kogelberg Biosphere Reserve** (see page 16) lies only 8 kilometres southeast of here. Along the road to Kogelberg you'll find **Gravity Adventures**, which offers white-water rafting and tubing trips on the Palmiet River during the high-water winter months when the river's classed Grade 3+, and more relaxed float trips in the summer months. All boating and safety equipment is provided with fully qualified and experienced guides. For details, tel: 021-683-3698 or visit www. gravity.co.za.

Golfers have the 9-hole **Kleinmond Golf Course** at the foot of the Three Sisters, and just 5 kilometres away is the world-renowned 18-hole **Arabella Country Estate**, rated one of the top in the country, near the junction of the R43 and R44. The latter runs along the Botrivier lagoon. Near the top of Harbour Road, check out the **Bee & Kie** honey factory, which sells various flavours of honey, mementos and honey-related gifts. There's a window one can look through into their factory to watch the honey processing. Open 09h00–17h00 Monday–Friday, 09h00–16h00 Saturday and 10h00–15h00 Sunday and public holidays. At the bottom of Harbour Road, turn left and visit Ann and Danie Fourie's **Road Side Studio**, which has a great selection of arts, crafts and interesting bits.

Overnight in Kleinmond

There are dozens of B&Bs and self-catering options. The modern **Wooden Leg Guest House** at 2 Keurboom Street in the suburb of Heuningkloof has 5 rooms, 2 with separate entrances, 2 are self-catering, and all are well equipped. Breakfast is served at a communal table, and dinner must be pre-ordered. No children or pets allowed, but you can use the pool, jacuzzi, sauna, TV lounge, DVDs and bar. There's secure off-street parking, and they also offer boat trips. B&B doubles cost from R800 or R700 for a twin. To book, call Jeanette Lategan on tel:082-579-3735 or visit www. woodenleg.co.za. **Alikreukel**, at 4 Marine Avenue, has two self-catering units a stone's throw from the sea. One unit has a kitchenette and braai, twin beds, a double sleeper couch, shared en-suite bathroom, TV and outside braai. The other is a spacious en-suite double with TV, tea/coffee facilities and bar fridge. It's a 15-minute walk to the secluded beach at the Palmiet lagoon mouth, and

---

WHY VISIT?

◆ See the wild horses that have lived here for over half a century.
◆ Dine *al fresco* on fresh seafood while overlooking the sea.

WHAT'S WACKY?

The private Toy Museum has an amazing collection of old toys (but be sure to make an appointment on tel: 028-271-3798 or 082-774-3899).

WHAT'S WHAT?

Hangklip-Kleinmond Tourism Bureau is on the left as you drive down Harbour Road. Tel 028-271-5657. It has a very comprehensive website that includes sections on events, nature, fauna and a bird list – click on www.ecoscape.org.za.

Canoes for hire line the grass verge of the Kleinmond Lagoon.

3 minutes to the restaurants and shops of Harbour Road. Rates are R300 per unit (R260 for the second night), and the establishment is run by the very pleasant Corinne. For info, call her on tel: 082-928-1193 or after hours on 028-271-3917.

The 3-star **Risibiki** consists of a flat and a house (both self-catering) at 25 CR Louw Street. The flat sleeps 6 in 2 spacious rooms, and is wheelchair friendly, whereas the house sleeps 8 in 3 rooms. Both have lounge-cum-dining rooms with M-Net, safe parking, balcony decks with sea views, and braai facilities. Call Isabel du Plessis on tel: 028-271-3414 or 072-677-8832 or click on www.kleinmond.com. For something a little more up-market, **Haus Windhoek B&B** is 4-star graded, and is situated next to the Kleinmond Golf Course at 35 Swartrivierweg on the east of town (up the hill a little). It's been operating for 25-plus years and offers 6 well-decorated en-suite rooms in a stylish establishment. Five rooms have a private patio or balcony, and all have a bar fridge, safe and DStv. Rates are from R450 per person B&B. Call them on tel: 028-271-3554 or visit www.hauswindhoek.co.za. The municipal **Kleinmond Caravan Park** is on the mountain side of the national road on the eastern side of town and has 112 caravan and 12 tent sites, all with electricity. It's an open park with a few trees and has a subway to the beach. Contact them on tel: 028-271-8158. The municipal Palmiet Caravan Park is clearly signposted west of town and lies on the mouth of the Palmiet River. Here the 84 caravan and 20 tent sites are electrified, plus there are 34 tent sites without electricity. All sites are grassed and separated by thick bush, some overlooking the sea, and there's a kiosk. There are swings on the edge of the lagoon mouth, beach access is easy, and boats can be launched nearby.

Ablution blocks are disabled friendly, and there are even disposable septic tanks for motor homes. Rates depend on where a site is located and the time of year, and range from R70 out of season to R220 in high season. For details, tel: 028-271-8158.

Eating out in Kleinmond

Locals recommend **The Brass Anchor** for a really good meal, and you'll find it at 68 Main Road. Down in the Harbour Road area there are several restaurants to choose from, some overlooking the sea. The **Alive Alive O Shellfish Bar** operates from a blue container but has tables spread out on a bed of mussel shells, some under awnings. It's also the only place to get sushi in town, so prices are a little high but the location is great. We didn't get to try any of their food the day we were there because they were so busy, they neglected to serve us. The **Fisherman's Take Aways** is popular with locals; and around the corner from Europa is the **Road Side Gourmet Sandwich Bar**, which is open on weekends and holidays. Try their bacon, Camembert and fig combo. The **Europa** restaurant and coffee bar is reasonably priced, and serves breakfasts, light meals, lunch and dinner from a full à la carte menu. Tables are inside or on the stoep, and they're licensed. Closed Sunday–Tuesday evenings. They can be contacted on tel: 028-271-5107 or visit www.europarestaurant.co.za.

The **View Restaurant** is a large orange building, known locally as the Pumpkin Palace, and if it hasn't been repainted, you'll easily spot it on the main road as you enter town from the east. The restaurant is upstairs and has good views across Sandown Bay. The menu is contemporary (a separate one for children), and there's also a licensed bar, smoking area, fireplace, and terrace. For details, tel: 028-271-4937. For drinks, drive down to the bottom of Harbour Road, turn left, and you'll see a large veranda that's shared by a couple of places – it's a good spot for sundowners. The **Sandpiper Restaurant and Cocktail Bar** has a kids' playground.

MALGAS

Hardly a hiccup on the map, Malgas is a settlement of 2 gravel roads scattered along which are a few houses, a 150-year-old church, hotel and a very old general dealer, but the place is best known for its pont river-crossing. It's a great place to relax in warmer weather, if you enjoy spending time on the water, but take note that the Breede River is tidal and therefore has currents. It's a very deep and dark body of water so please ensure everyone on your boat is wearing a life jacket – and be sensible when swimming.

Out and about in Malgas

The most important reason to visit Malgas is to cross the Breede River on the last hand-pulled pont in the country. It runs daily from, theoretically, dawn until dusk, and it's a good idea not to be in a hurry when using it. If the pont is on the opposite side of the river, it takes the guys a while to pull it back to your side, before repeating the task to pull you across the river. What's more, in busier times, there can be quite a queue as the pont can only accommodate 3 cars at a time. Oom Nicolaas, who owns the old general dealer up the hill, says there are days when, from his shop door, he can see the back of the queue.

The upper reaches of the Breede River are renowned for bass fishing. Tidal action reaches 60 kilometres upstream, supporting a rich diversity of fish and birdlife. Various water sports, such as water-skiing, wakeboarding and tubing, can be done if you have your own boat. The area is also excellent for bird watching. Make a point of popping into the old shop, **Malagas Algemene Handelaar**, owned and run by Oom Nicolaas and Tannie Hendrika. It's been in the Van As family for 100 years, and still has that lovely old general-dealer feel to it, with ancient wooden shelves that display a range of dusty goods, both new and old, and an antique Coca-Cola bottle opener. Check out the amazing yellowwood ceiling and counter. Its operating hours can be erratic out of season, but it's usually open on Fridays and Saturdays.

Up the road at the Malgas junction, as its locally known, where the road forks east to Infanta and west to Bredasdorp, is the **Breede River Trading Post**. It's a new establishment owner-run by Tony and Veronica McPherson, who're bringing various services to the community. They sell basic groceries, meat (including excellent sirloins, say the locals), good homemade bread and bottled water. Take your own water bottles and fill up. This is also where you'll find diesel (petrol's available at the Malgas Hotel). Open daily 08h00–17h30.

Overnight in Malgas

At the junction where the Breede River Trading Post is situated, take the road to Infanta and, after a short distance, turn left again to **Lemoentuin**, which is a dead-end leading to various properties along the river. Where the road takes a sharp right, there are signboards to **Whispering Waters**, also referenced as 'Plot 241', a well-equipped self-catering house that's highly recommended by AA and is owner-run by Petra Brits and Celia Roux who've been there 8 years. You get the whole house, whether you're 2 or 9 people. The 4 rooms are en suite, there's a large open-plan lounge/dining room/kitchen (the latter includes a large fridge and a freezer for all those fish you're going to catch). The deep front stoep and braai area overlooks the river, and when it's sunny, you need just walk to the end of the lawn to dangle those toes in the water or launch your boat. Do note, however, that children are not allowed near, or on, the water without life jackets.

If you're after peace and quiet, don't book over peak holidays. Rates are R245–R300 per person for self-catering (dinner and breakfast on request). For more information, tel: 028-542-1787 or click on www.whisperingwaters.co.za.

Potteberg Guest Farm is 9 kilometres from Malgas at the foot of the Potberg mountain on the boundary of De Hoop reserve and it's owner-run by Niel and Saartjie Neethling. It's an ideal base from which to explore the Potberg, and offers easy access to hiking trails and whale-watching off De Hoop. The private flat has a stoep, small living room with open-plan kitchen, and double en-suite bedroom with brass bed. It's equipped for self-catering or you can pre-order dinner and breakfast. Activities include farm experiences and an excellent chance of seeing the Cape griffon vultures that feed on the farm. The Neethlings also have a bird hide

overlooking the Potberg. Rates are R360–R400 for the flat (meals extra). For details, tel: 028-542-1876 or 082-096-6631 or visit www.sleeping-out.co.za (see also Mudlark River Front Lodge on page 179 and Waterkloof Guest House on page 219).

Eating out in Malgas

If you just want a drink, the **Malgas Hotel** is fine, and has a lovely river view. The **Breede River Trading Post** does takeaways and light eats, and if you book well in advance you can join them on the *kuierstoep* of the store for Sunday lunch, which varies from a traditional roast to a 'bottomless' hamburger. Along the road to Infanta you'll find **The Boathouse** pub and pizzeria renowned for its pizzas. Open daily in season, otherwise 16h00–23h00 Wednesday, 11h00–23h00 Friday–Saturday, 11h00–17h00 Sunday. Further towards Infanta

There's only one way to cross the Breede River at Malgas and that is on the last hand-operated pont in South Africa.

there's a sign and a farm road on the left that winds through fynbos down to the river, where you'll find **The Bush Pub**. It's owner-run by Peter and his wife Pietie and has been going for about 10 years. If you have a boat on the river, their jetty can moor 10 boats comfortably. The pub consists of tables under shelters tucked into the riverine bush around the main bar area. In season they serve meals but out of season they sell cook-it-yourself braai packs and, occasionally, hamburgers. One of the big attractions, which has become somewhat of an institution, is trying to hit a target on the opposite side of the river using a golf club and ball. There's a play area for kids, a 9-hole 21-par bush putt-putt course through the veld, a boule court, and a TV for important sporting events. Open 11h00–19h00 Friday–Sunday.

NAPIER

The little village of Napier sits at the foot of the Soetmuisberg in the heart of the Overberg. Rolling wheat and barley fields surround it, and it's a place that speaks of laid-back country town bliss that creeps into your soul. There's a good feel to Napier, which has lots of newcomers bringing great ideas and renewing the energy of the town, and you'll meet an interesting mix of people that are hip, modern, young, old, arty and just plain chilled. The main street is called Sarel Cilliers Street, and is also the R316 where most things happen (a tour of the residential streets will reveal large town plots where cows, sheep, horses, donkeys, chickens and ducks are also resident).

Out and about in Napier

A visit to Napier is all about relaxing and breathing that crisp country air deep into your lungs while sitting at one of the main-street eateries and watching the locals do their thing. Sarel Cilliers Street has a few interesting shops, so take your time to explore. Pop into **The Gallery**, owned by Janet Hall and Helen Vale Xenos. It offers a variety of works on several subjects and you may well be tempted to spend your life's savings here. Across the road is a stained-glass shop worth browsing through, and further east is **Art & Toy World**, owned by Alan and Rose Raubenheimer. Alan makes unique handcrafted tin-plate steamboats that are candle-fired, and the toy museum has an excellent display of old and rare toys. Alan's also an artist, and you can view his impressionist watercolours too. Open 10h00–16h00 most days including Sundays and public holidays, but they are usually closed Tuesday–Wednesday. One of the most recent and exciting additions to town is the **Napier Brewery**. Phone ahead to arrange a visit but don't expect a glossy tour – this is still a small company – but they'll offer you a taste of their excellent ale and lager or you can buy it from a local pub. Call Mark on tel: 083-703-8004 or clock on www.napierbrewery.co.za. Napier also now has its own winery thanks to Jean Daneel. Although it's not open to the public, you can buy his wine at the great wine shop next to Napier farmstall called **Vindigo's**. If you're in the market for garden wares and plants, **Groei** is just east of town alongside a gorgeous old house and Gert can advise you on gardening;

The area around Napier is fast becoming known for some good wines and they're all on sale at Vindigo on the outskirts of town.

WHY VISIT?

♦ Absorb the tranquil village atmosphere of Napier.
♦ Sample the local Napier lager and ale.

WHAT'S WACKY?

The candle-fired steamboats and other nostalgic toys at Art & Toy World.

WHAT'S WHAT?

The tourist office is at the garage at the northwestern end of Sarel Cilliers Street. Open 08h30–17h00 weekdays and 09h00–13h00 Saturday (closed on Sundays, but open public holidays if they don't fall on a Sunday). Tel: 028-423-3325, www.tourismcapeagulhas.co.za.

or head to the town's original herb garden by taking the road between the farmstall and the ox-wagon monument, turn left into Wouter Street and you'll find **Foyle's Herbs & Plants**. On the opposite side of town is the **Moerse Farm Stall** where you will meet the *moerse* friendly owner, who'll sell you *moerse* bottles of earthworm wee, which promise *moerse* growth for your plants. The farmstall sells home bakes, light meals and much more.

To stretch your legs, do the 8-kilometre **Grootberg Hiking Trail** that starts at the FM tower southeast of town. It's a chance to see birds, enjoy the fynbos and take in fabulous views across the Agulhas Plain to the south, and the rolling hills of the Ruggens to the north. To book, call Stephen

Smuts on tel: 028-423-3325. There are also horse trails that range from 1 hour to overnight – to book, tel: 082-817-0263. If you really want to relax, join a group for a **Wellness Weekend** at **Peace Valley** (see the website www.peacevalleyguesthouse.co.za).

Overnight in Napier

The 4-star **Peace Valley Guest House** is, as the name states, in a peaceful valley on the edge of town. Accommodation is self-catering in a large unit that's completely separate from the main house where the charming owner, Lorna Young, lives. It consists of 1 double en suite with its own balcony overlooking the dams and garden; a twin with separate bathroom; and beds in the loft. The property has a river and 2 dams to keep web-footed family members happy. Bed-and-health-breakfast rates are R350–R400 per person sharing. To book, tel: 028-423-3372 or visit www.peacevalleyguesthouse.co.za. **Suntouched Inn Travellers Lodge** in the main street, has backpacker accommodation in a garden cottage for R100 per person (bed only) or R130 (including breakfast). It also has 4 double rooms above the restaurant, each with its own theme inspired by the owner's travels. Rates are R250 per person sharing B&B. If you're a group, ask Angela to organise the self-catering house, which costs R750 and sleeps 7. For more info, tel: 028-423-3131 or visit www.suntouchedinn.co.za. **Sunbird Lodge**, on the road to Grootberg Hiking Trail, is also self-catering and has marvellous fynbos views, walks and great birding. For details, tel: 028-423-

3049 or click on www.overberginfo.com/sunbird. **Horseshoe Cove Cottage**, on a large plot in West Street, is a spacious self-catering cottage that sleeps 4–5 people and has a cot. Rates are from R200 per person sharing. Call Sue on tel: 028-423-3509. Although backpackers can camp at Suntouched Inn, the nearest proper campsite is in Bredasdorp. **Oom Attie's Ossewa Camp & Agricultural Museum** offers overnight accommodation in ox-wagons on his farm, and you can view a variety of old implements. He doesn't use a cell, so best time to phone him is in the evening, on tel: 023-423-3630.

Eating out in Napier

All Napier's restaurants are in the main street. Our favourite place to eat and drink is **The Fox** at the northern end of Sarel Cilliers Street. It's as close to a real English pub as you can get in South Africa, and Mike and Louise Williams

Napier Farm Stall is known far and wide for its delicious meals and freshly baked goodies.

were so keen to open a genuine English pub here that they went and lived in the UK for several years to earn their licences as 'publicans'. Louise runs the bar and is justifiably proud of the fact that she is the only publican in the entire region to have Guinness on tap; and Mike does all the cooking. The food is fabulous and they go to a lot of trouble to source high-quality ingredients. Everything is homemade and very fresh. Mike's menu is seasonal, and in winter you can pre-order his excellent steak-and-Guinness pie (it has to marinate). On Sundays they do a full roast that includes beef, one other meat, and Yorkshire pudding. Closed Tuesdays. To book, tel: 028-423-3293. **Napier Farm Stall & Restaurant** has been a popular stopover for years and they still make great home bakes and comfort food. According to locals, their cakes are excellent. They also serve farm-style breakfasts all day, and are open daily 08h00–17h00. **Suntouched Inn** has an upbeat restaurant and pub owner-run by Craigan and Angela Millar. They're renowned for their pizza, which comes in wonderful combinations. Open most evenings and all day Saturday–Sunday. **Gunner's Mess** markets itself as a coffee shop, diner and pub. Open 09h00–21h00 Tuesday–Saturday and 08h30–15h00 Sunday. The **Good FoodCafé and Deli** is a large white double-storey building with blue woodwork that you can't miss. It opened in December 2007 and had earned a good name within a year. Try the blackforest ham and Gruyère ciabatta. They're open from 09h00 until lunchtime in winter, but closed on

Tuesdays and Wednesdays; and 08h00–17h00 in summer, and were talking about opening in the evenings too. **Pascal's Bistro** serves a combination of French country and local cuisine and occasionally has live entertainers; and the newly opened **Renéessance**, next to the Napier Farm Stall, is already popular with the locals for it's upmarket décor and Mediterranean fare.

PEARLY BEACH

The name of this small seaside village is indicative of the colour of the sand on the beaches here. It's a rather narrow village fronted by a rocky shore, on either side of which are long uninterrupted stretches of sand. To the northwest the beach stretches to Uilenkraalsmond, about 16 kilometres away, which is great for extended strolls. It's a sleepy little place that gets busy over the summer school holidays in December/January.

Overnight in Pearly Beach

Klein Paradijs, owner-run by Susanne and Michael Fuchs, offers the best of both worlds from a 5-star fully catered country guesthouse to quaint self-

WHY VISIT?
To take *looong* walks on the beach.

WHAT'S WHAT?
There's no tourist office as such but Fine & Country Estates, at the first intersection after you've turned into town off the R43, is happy to be of assistance to all visitors. Tel: 028-381-9033.

catering cottages. They're situated on a 140-hectare fynbos farm on the opposite side of the R43 to Pearly Beach (instead of turning right into town when approaching from Gansbaai, turn left and follow the signs for a few hundred metres to their front door). They offer 5 en-suite rooms in the thatched house, and meals are prepared by Michael, who is a Swiss-trained chef. A 4-course dinner costs R250 a head, and they have an extensive wine list. B&B rates are seasonal, R550–R950 per person sharing. For those who enjoy doing their own thing, there are 5 fully equipped farm cottages. The 3 flat-roofed units sleep 6 in 3 bedrooms, and 2 thatched units sleep 2 and 6. The latter have walled gardens and are ideal for travelling pets, which are welcome. There's a dam where you can fish or paddle among the water lilies in the rowing boat or canoe, and walks through the fynbos offer good birdlife and views. Self-catering rates are also seasonal, R135–R225 per person sharing, depending on cottage type and number of people. For details, tel: 028-381-9760.

If you prefer to stay near the beach, try **The Ark**, which has 3 stars and is one block away from the lapping waves. It's well signposted as you enter town and you can watch whales from the deck. B&B rates are R260 per person sharing and R300 a single (discounts for stays of more than 1 night). For more information, tel: 028-381-9180.

Eating out in Pearly Beach

There's not much choice in Pearly Beach when it comes to dining out, but the food and hospitality at **The RooiBier** restaurant, which doesn't look like much from the outside, are good and honest and you're sure to meet a few locals here. They're at the Pearly Village Centre at the junction of Main Road and Newey Street as you enter the village. In the same centre is **Cuppa's**, which serves hot and cold drinks, light lunches and takeaways.

Near Pearly Beach

Die Dam is a coastal spot 20 kilometres southeast of Pearly Beach at the end of the R43. The origin of its name seems to be a bit of a mystery as there isn't a dam in sight, although on a calm day the waters of the bay may give the impression of one. There's nothing here except for **Die Dam Holiday Resort**,

A stairway leads to yet another perfect white sandy beach, this time at Pearly Beach.

which is just metres from the beach. It's municipal-run so the facilities are dated and basic, but because it's fairly popular it's well maintained. Of all the chalets, most are privately owned but there are 2 for hire at R250–R360 per night (take your own bedding). Camp and caravan sites cost R115–R165 per night for up to 8 people and 2 vehicles. For details, tel: 028-482-1710. It's most popular with rock and surf fishermen who spend their days on the rock outcrop in front of the resort or along the white beach on either side. It's a good spot to hook kabeljou, musselcracker and geelbek. If you're not a fisherman, the stunning beaches are great for strolls, and on a warm, still day they have a distinct tropical paradise feel.

PRINGLE BAY

Pringle Bay lies within the Kogelberg Biosphere Reserve about 90 kilometres from Cape Town on the scenic Clarence Drive that runs to and from Gordon's Bay. It's a relatively undeveloped settlement of mostly holiday houses comprising a mishmash of architectural styles, all overlooked by the mountains. There's no fuel in Pringle Bay, but there are good restaurants serving breakfast, lunch and dinner, as well as a mini-supermarket that's also a postal agency, and a country shop that sells basic supplies, fresh produce, frozen meat, wood and various bakes – and is also the satellite tourism office. This is the perfect place to watch the sunset. In the evenings, you can almost hear the sun sizzling over the horizon beyond False Bay as you take in a view encompassing the whole Cape Peninsula from Cape Point to Table Mountain. Nearby you'll find

the promontory called Cape Hangklip, and the peak called Hangklip – and the view north from the point at Pringle Bay shows Rooiels with its nearby Klein Hangklip.

WHY VISIT?
For the seaside idyll and a slice of unspoiled nature.

WHAT'S WACKY?
Pringle Bay only obtained electrical power in 1992.

WHAT'S WHAT?
Speak to Mr or Mrs Pink at Pringle Bay Country Shop, which is a satellite tourism office (tel: 028-273-8068) or contact the Hangklip-Kleinmond Tourism Bureau in Kleinmond (tel: 028-271-5657, www.ecoscape.org.za).

Out and about in Pringle Bay

Pringle Bay is a river and beach environment that'll have nature-lovers in raptures. The fine-white-sand beaches are perfect for walking along, or just catching some rays. It's a place to swim – but be aware that the sea can be treacherous so get local advice before going in too deep – surf or kayak, fish (directly from the rocks along the shoreline), dive for crayfish in season (with required permit), and from May to December you can even spot whales from the shoreline. There are hikes and quiet roads to cycle or run along if you need to stretch your limbs. The Buffels River and its estuary at the northern

end of Pringle Bay beach provide a haven for shy otters, and birders can spot both fynbos and estuarine species.

A rocky stretch of coastline and hanging cliffs at Pringle Bay.

Overnight in Pringle Bay

There are plenty of accommodation options, including the 3-star **Barnacle B&B**, which offers 2 units furnished in Cape Country style. Each has a kitchenette and DStv. The Cottage has a separate entrance, an antique brass double bed and an alcove with twin three-quarter beds. The Sunshine Suite sleeps 3 and faces the river and rugged mountains. They're connected to the beach by pathways over the dunes or through the reeds to the lagoon. Prices start at R330 per person sharing, and include an English breakfast served on the deck (in summer) of the main house overlooking the beach and ocean. To book, tel: 028-273-8343 or visit www.barnacle.co.za. **Road Side** self-catering accommodation at 272 Hangklip Road is within walking distance of the beach. It's fully equipped and sleeps 5 in 3

BABOONS AT THE BAY

Local baboon populations also consider Pringle Bay a haven, and are a major problem here. We heard stories that they've even learned how to remove glass sliding doors in order to enter houses for the sake of pillaging. Take the signs, 'Feeding of baboons prohibited' seriously – baboons can be extremely dangerous, so give them a wide berth.

bedrooms. The lounge has an indoor braai, as does the patio, which also has a sea view. Parking is undercover, and guests have use of a boule court. Rates are R200 per person per night, and substantially less for those staying more than 5 nights. Call Ann on tel: 082-873-6931 or Danie on tel: 082-770-0015.

Eating out in Pringle Bay

@365 Restaurant and Pub is owner-run by Sammy, the very charming maître'd, and Morné, cook extraordinaire, and comes highly recommended by residents of Betty's Bay and Rooiels. They serve breakfast, lunch and supper Friday–Sunday, but are closed Mondays and open evenings only on other days. Their ever-changing blackboard menu offers all sorts from poached kippers to seafood curry, excellent steaks, venison and good old home cooking. They're full most nights, even out of season, so be sure to book a table in advance on tel: 028-273-8931 or 082-894-3019. **Gators** is around the corner and serves wood-fired pizza, has a fully licensed bar and does takeaways – contact them on tel: 082-457-9403. Although we couldn't get to eat or drink there, we were told that **Miems** has a pub upstairs and meals are priced a little more reasonably than elsewhere. Then there's **Hook, Line & Sinker** and **The Anchor Restaurant**, where it's best to reserve your table for Sunday lunch.

RIVIERSONDEREND

Riviersonderend is a small farming village on the N2 between the Garden Route and Cape Town. It has stunning mountain scenery, some hectically bright houses, a good wine shop called The Wine Rack, and an even better pie shop.

Out and about in Riviersonderend

The big attraction is exploring the mountains on foot, which will allow you to see the beautiful wildflowers and fynbos and suck fresh air deep into your

Riviersonderend stands dwarfed by the rolling landscape and a big sky.

lungs – and then the scenery will suck that air right out and leave you breathless. The **Kleinbergie Hiking Trail** takes you past signal canons that were part of the former Overberg Signal Canon system when they were used to call residents who served in the military if there were indications of war in the Cape. That was some time ago, in 1795 and 1806 actually,

WHY VISIT?
The wine and the pies …

WHAT'S WACKY?
In 1923, when the first plots were auctioned, the new owners were allowed to keep one cow for milk, and two oxen. Only butchers were allowed to keep sheep.

WHAT'S WHAT?
The best place to get info on the area is to contact Valerie Loveall of Loveall's Guest House (see page 195).

during the first and second occupation of the Cape. If you're heading from here down the R317 to Bredasdorp, keep a sharp eye out for wildlife. You might see a steenbok in a sheep paddock, blue cranes, jackal buzzards, the ubiquitous Egyptian geese, and there's a section of game fencing behind which eland live.

Overnight in Riviersonderend

Loveall's Guest House is a no-frills, spotlessly clean and quiet establishment owned by Val, who's a real tonic. She's full of enthusiasm about her town, and when she's not raving about the area she's pursuing her other passion, painting. Rooms overlook a rustic garden; breakfast is light, and is included in the rates of R260–R300 per person sharing. Call Val on tel: 028-261-1048 or 072-216-5073.

Eating out in Riviersonderend

If you enjoy homemade pies, you'll find excellent ones behind the unassuming façade of **Homemade Pies** at the **Ou Meul Bakkery** in the main street.

There's a pizza takeaway that closes around 17h00; a restaurant and takeaway at the Caltex garage on the eastern side of town that advertises it's open 24 hours; and a Steers diner at the Shell garage. And that's pretty much it …

ROOIELS

The village of Rooiels lies on the slopes of Klein Hangklip at the western gateway to the Overberg. The R44 enters the Kogelberg Biosphere Reserve just beyond Gordon's Bay, and after another 20 picturesque kilometres, you'll be in Rooiels, which is a scattering of houses that hardly makes a blip on the radar. But this is its appeal. You get to explore the shoreline and, depending on which month you visit, may even have it to yourself. On windy days, even the sea doesn't lose its deep turquoise as it swells and dips bejewelled with sparkling white horses and rainbow spray.

Out and about in Rooiels

The locals say the best months to visit Rooiels are from late March through winter, and the best beach is at the mouth of the Rooiels River – unless the southeaster is blowing, which can be daily in summer. In that case, head to the boat slipway area. Fishing (from the rocks) can also be good. Drive through the village to the last road, turn right down to the beach, or catch directly from the slipway. There's a cave in the Rooiels River Valley that is thought to have seen

THE CRANES OF THE OVERBERG

The blue crane (*Anthropoides paradiseus*) is South Africa's national bird and a common sight in open farmlands of the Overberg region, where breeding pairs are easily spotted in spring to summer. They roost on the ground, perform display dances in groups or pairs, and can be heard calling from great heights when soaring above the fields. Although these elegant birds often occur in large flocks, specifically in winter, according to IUCN criteria, their status is vulnerable.

Waves curl into the bay at Rooiels, the most westerly town in the Overberg region.

An ideal and quiet base from which to explore the western parts of the Overberg.

WHAT'S WACKY?

◆ When the baboons come on a raiding trip to town, a red flag is flown at the Country Village Shop in the centre of town.
◆ The cross near Rooiels is in memory of Dr Marais, Rector of the Stellenbosch Gymnasium (later Stellenbosch University), who was swept off the rocks here in 1901.

WHAT'S WHAT?

The Rooiels Village Shop stocks all the basics and is owned by Margaret Hensen, who also runs a satellite tourism office here. Contact Margaret on tel: 028-273-8383. Alternatively, contact Hangklip-Kleinmond Tourism Bureau in Kleinmond on tel: 028-271-5657 or visit www.ecoscape.org.za.

continuous human occupation for thousands of years, as indicated by extensive sea-shell middens. During the early period of Dutch colonisation, the cave was home to parties of *drosters* (absconders), as was the case with the caves at Kogelbaai, on Klein Hangklip, on Hangklip et al.

Overnight in Rooiels

The 4-star **Wonderlings B&B** is up on the mountain overlooking Rooiels and False Bay. It's ideal for a weekend and offers pampered comfort in 2 large, modern suites. The views from every window are spectacular and you can spend hours just gazing at the ever-changing play of light on the ocean. It's owner-run by Jenny Stark and Koos Smit. Koos does 'catch-and-cook-your-own-crayfish' canoeing trips April–December. Rates are from R240 self-catering to R400 B&B in season. To enquire, tel: 028-273-8961 or click on www.wonderlingsbandb.com.

Eating out in Rooiels

The **Drummond Arms Pub & Restaurant** is situated at the central 'hub' of the village where you'll also find a little shop open daily 08h30–17h30. Next door is the **Something Else Restaurant and Art Gallery**.

STANFORD

Known as the 'alternative to Prozac', Stanford is licensed to chill. First impressions are of an old English village surrounded by green fields that turn canola yellow in spring. Tractors pattern the lands, leaving symmetric lines, and in contrast the sometimes verdant, sometimes dry lands are overlooked by a sky that always seems to have the odd tuft of white cloud in it.

Stanford's history dates back to 1729, when a farmer from Caledon spotted land in the area and was awarded a grazing permit by the government. Over time, the permit changed hands, a farmhouse was built and in 1838 Robert Stanford, who'd retired from the British Army on half pay, bought the property. He used the land to supply the Cape with fresh produce, then in 1849 he became embroiled in anti-convict protests against the British government's decision to settle prisoners in the Cape. Although in agreement with the protest, Stanford was still in the employ of the British Army and was forced to provide the convict ship, army and government with supplies. This enraged the masses, who then ostracised him to the point where he lost everything. His labourers were chased off the farm, his family pelted in the streets, his children expelled from school, and his dying child refused medical help. The farm was sold on auction, and in 1857 the new owner subdivided the property into erven for a town. Today, however, it's all peace and serenity. It's one of the best-preserved villages in the Cape and claims its market square, dating to 1785, is the only undeveloped one in the country.

Out and about in Stanford

The streets are quiet and full of interesting architecture, some of which is 300 years old. Get info on the self-guided walking tours from the tourist office. Do a cruise down the Kleinrivier (or Klein River, as it is equally commonly known) with **Platanna River Cruises** (contact Janice Gilman on tel: 084-583-5389), covering 8 kilometres of river, then marsh, and 8 kilometres of lagoon. If you're on your own water vessel, make your way quietly down the river and there's a

---

WHY VISIT?

For that Prozac effect, and to buy some fabulous cheese and beer.

WHAT'S WACKY?

◆ The only traffic light is on the veranda of Hennie's Pub & Grill!
◆ Stanford is home to *Village Life* magazine.

WHAT'S WHAT?

The very helpful Stanford tourist office in the main street is open all day Monday–Saturday, and until 13h00 Sunday. Tel: 028-341-0340, www.stanfordinfo.co.za.

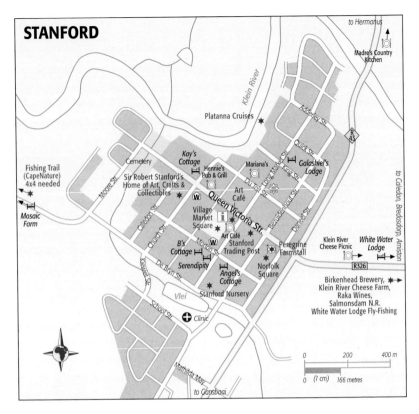

STANFORD

to Hermanus

Madre's Country Kitchen

Klein River

Platanna Cruises

Adderley Str.

Quick Str.

R43

Kay's Cottage

Fishing Trail (CapeNature) 4x4 needed

Cemetery

Hennie's Pub & Grill

Mariana's

Galashiel's Lodge

Sir Robert Stanford's Home of Art, Crafts & Collectibles

Art Café

Moore Str.

Du Toit Str.

Long Market Str.

King Str.

Queen Victoria Str.

Bezuidenhout Str.

Caledon Str.

Church Str.

Village Market Square

Art Café

B's Cottage

Stanford Trading Post

Peregrine Farmstall

Daneel Str.

Klein River Cheese Picnic

White Water Lodge

Mosaic Farm

Morton Str.

De Bruyn Str.

Serendipity

Norfolk Square

R326

Angel's Cottage

Kleiner Str.

Stanford Nursery

Birkenhead Brewery,
Klein River Cheese Farm,
Raka Wines,
Salmonsdam N.R.
White Water Lodge Fly-Fishing

Vlei

School Str.

Clinic

Mathilda May

to Gansbaai

to Caledon, Bredasdorp, Arniston

0   200   400 m

0   (1 cm)   166 metres

good chance of spotting some of the 120 bird species and perhaps even an otter. Look out for the heronry, where dozens of herons roost in a mass of orange bills and slinky grey feathers. If you're a birder, visit October–November when hundreds of flamingos feed at the Kleinrivier lagoon. The **Stanford Walking Trail** meanders along the river and also offers sightings; and in late September and early October, the **Stanford Glendower Bird Fair** has bird-related stands and events, entertainment and stalls. While strolling around town, pop into **Sir Robert Stanford's Home of Art, Crafts and Collectibles**, which is situated in the original farmhouse that was owned by old Robbie himself. **Stanford Trading Post & New Junk Shop** sells local art and high class junk. Then, if you're foot-weary, stop at **Art Café** (open Tuesday–Sunday) for refreshments and a view of the passing traffic on the main road. The artworks adorn the walls, and on display in a glass cabinet are the equally artistic cakes that are served with coffee. **Peregrine Farmstall** sells gifts and meals, and behind it is **Norfolk Square** offering a range of shops (but note that it's closed Tuesdays).

Just a hop (s'cuse the pun) and skip along the R326 you'll find the **Birkenhead Micro-brewery**, which

also produces wine and bottled water, and is the only company doing all 3 in the country. It's best to phone ahead to book a tour or check if the pub is open. Tours are usually at 11h00 and 15h00 and include tasting, and you can buy directly from them to stock up for the rest of your holiday. Their beers are mostly German style, plus one English bitter. Contact the brewery on tel: 028-341-0183 or visit www.birkenhead.co.za. Further along the R326 is **Klein River Dairy**, which has won numerous awards for their cheese, of which the most famous is their Gruyère and Leiden. What's more, this is virtually the only place in South Africa where these 2 varieties are made. Their raclette is just as good and, thankfully, they produce about 10 tons of cheese per month so you can taste and buy to your heart's content. The cheese-making process can be viewed through large picture windows, as can the maturing room. For details, tel: 028-341-0693 or www.

Leisurely breakfasts in soothing settings, like here at Galashiels Lodge in Stanford, are part of the Overberg experience.

> Many businesses in
> Stanford operate on erratic hours
> during the off-season winter months.

kleinriviercheese.co.za. Further north along the R326 is **Raka Wines**, where you can taste and buy wine (tel: 028-341-0676). To reach **Salmonsdam Nature Reserve** (a fynbos reserve, rather than a wildlife one), travel 5 kilometres along the R326 from Stanford, turn right onto the gravel Papiesvlei road and follow the signs for 14 kilometres. Next door is the Grade-3 **Shannonea 4x4 Trail**, which offers good scenery over 40 kilometres. Vehicles climb 900 metres above sea level and it takes 3–6 hours. Costs are R160 per vehicle, so call Christiaan Swart on tel: 082-324-1133. About 14 kilometres west of Stanford there's a fishing trail that gives anglers with 4x4s easy access to popular sites. There's a CapeNature brochure available from the tourism office, and the gatehouse to the trail is open 07h00–10h00. Fees must be paid, and driving on the beach is strictly prohibited. **Platbos**, Africa's southernmost forest, is also in this area. It's a 30-hectare privately owned indigenous woodland with specimens up to 1000 years old. Pre-booking is essential, so call on tel: 082-411-0448. Fly-fishing is possible on the other side of town at White Water Lodge for R250 per day.

Overnight in Stanford

There's accommodation to suit every budget, from luxurious full board to self-catering. Our favourite guesthouse is **Galashiels Lodge**, which stands

The sandwich board says it all, but the fun in Stanford is not limited to the trendy Art Café.

tucked beneath a canopy of trees. It's a restored Victorian guesthouse that comes complete with a Scottish owner, Brian, his lovely wife, Jill, and a Scottish terrier. Jill is a wealth of information on the town and runs their stylish guesthouse with flair. It's clear that her previous career was as an interior decorator, and the garden is full of nooks and crannies to rest your tired body and soul. B&B rates are from R450 per person sharing. For details, tel: 028-341-0181 or visit www.guesthouse-southafrica.com. **Mosaic Farm**, on the Hermanus lagoon, is a sanctuary for flora, fauna (with up to 247 bird species) and people. Accommodation is in luxury stone, thatch and canvas chalets at **Lagoon Lodge**, where wooden walkways link the units to the main lodge. The camp stands beneath huge milkwoods, one of which is estimated at 2000 years old. It's a great base from which to kayak, explore the dunes, and see the hundreds of flamingos. B&B rates are R760–R800 per person sharing in low season, and R990–R1150 in high season, with children at half price, and dinner additional. There are also 2 cottages on another part of the farm: 1 sleeps 9, the other 2 adults and 2 children, and rates depend on the number of guests. For info, tel: 028-313-2814 or click on www.mosaicfarm.net. **White Water Lodge** is not only great for trout and bass fly-fishing, but also offers elegant accommodation in 5 chalets, 1 self-catering cottage and a honeymoon suite. Rooms are spacious, air conditioned, and have a fireplace plus other luxuries. The main lodge has a bar and a large pool, and there are

On a sunny day, head to Klein River Dairy and enjoy a picnic by the river.

also quad-bike eco-trails, walks and a boule court. B&B rates are from R500 per person sharing; the honeymoon suite costs R2 000, and self-catering is R900 for a cottage sleeping a young family. To book, tel: 028-341-0762 or visit www.whitewaterlodge.co.za.

UNDER MILKWOODS

The white milkwood, *Sideroxylon inerme*, is an often-knobbly evergreen shrub that, under optimum conditions, can grow into a large umbrella-shaped tree. Its name comes from the milky latex in its fruit and bark, the fruit being particularly sought-after by baboons and birds. These trees are adapted to withstand harsh coastal winds, and their white flowers have a characteristic smell. Milkwoods are a protected indigenous species and may not even be pruned without the relevant permits.

The tourist office has a long list of self-catering and budget accommodation, but one that caught our eye is the historic **Angel Cottage**. Built around 1910, it's named after the 'angel evening' held the first weekend of December when hundreds of angels are on display, much to the delight of the local children. It sleeps a couple and 1 child, and offers total privacy. Rates are R300 per double (R50 per additional person). Call on tel: 028-341-0083. **B's Cottage** is a quaint self-catering thatched cottage, in a picturesque garden with views of the village market square and the Kleinrivier mountains. It also sleeps a couple and 1 child (pets are allowed by prior arrangement, and weekend visits must be a 2-night minimum). Rates for the cottage are R400 per night. **Serendipity** sleeps 6 at R500 for 2, plus R100 per extra person. For info on B's Cottage and Serendipity, call Bea Whittaker on tel: 028-341-0430. **Kay's Cottage** is a 'granny flat' self-catering cottage with a double room just 2 minutes' walk from the river. Rates are R250 per night (minimum 2-night stay). To book, tel: 028-341-0709. Campers have only 1 option: **Salmonsdam Nature Reserve** (see page 16). There's a large grassed site, and rather tatty ablutions. Rates are R25 per person entrance, plus R100 per campsite. For details, tel: 028-341-0018 or 082-429-4775.

Eating out in Stanford

There's a good choice of eateries, one of which is 2 kilometres from town on the Robert Stanford Estate. **Madré's Country Kitchen** is owner-run by

Madré, who serves really good country food that depends on what the farm is currently producing. Ingredients might include asparagus and artichokes straight from the garden, and everything zings with homemade appeal. Tables overlook a large pond, young vineyards and the mountains. Usually open Friday–Monday and most days over Easter and December holidays from 08h00–16h00, but it's best to book on tel: 028-341-0647. The other highlight is a **Klein River Cheese Picnic**. Pre-order a picnic basket, buy a bottle of wine from their shop, and head down to the grassed banks of the Kleinrivier where tables nestle beneath trees or you can spread a blanket on the lawn. Quantities aren't huge, but the food is rich and includes paté, cheese, cold meat, fresh bread and salads. It's idyllic and romantic, and you should do this at least once. The picnics are only available September–April, but call on tel: 028-341-0693 for more information. The award-winning **Mariana's** has been around for years. The décor here is simple and the menu changes regularly, offering unpretentious dishes and delectable desserts. To book, tel: 028-341-0272. **Hennie's Pub & Grill** indicates whether it's open or closed with the use of a genuine traffic light. It's where many locals drink and watch rugby, and is open from 16h00 until late. **Peregrine Farmstall**, at the entrance to Stanford, serves light eats and has a good selection of preserves.

STRUISBAAI

As you enter Struisbaai from the east, you'll pass historic lime-washed fishermen's cottages called the **Hotagterklip Cottages**. They're national monuments that feature prominently in many paintings of the town, but the rest of the buildings are mostly modern. Struisbaai is a holiday town that thrums in summer, and goes into a sleepy lull out of season. Its main street is lined with estate agents and the odd commercial outlet, and is the through-road to Agulhas.

WHY VISIT?
Enjoy the southern hemisphere's longest white-sand beach.

WHAT'S WACKY?
The giant stingrays in the harbour at Struisbaai.

WHAT'S WHAT?
Contact Cape Agulhas Tourism in Agulhas. Tel: 028-424-2584, www.tourismcapeagulhas.co.za.

Out and about in Struisbaai

Struisbaai is known for its long 14-kilometre beach that runs all the way to De Mond Nature Reserve at low tide. It also has the longest boardwalk in the southern hemisphere, starting at the main beach and meandering to the harbour. There's nothing quite like an 'endless' white beach to soothe the soul and conjure up romantic ideas of other 'endless' things, like summers, G&Ts and bank accounts. You can swim off the beach, but be aware of tides and currents. Struisbaai is also said to be a kite boarding and windsurfing hotspot. If you'd like to

A thatched fisherman's cottage at Hotagterklip near Struisbaai typifies the simplicity of the Overberg region.

enjoy the beach on horseback, **Morning Glory Stables** are owned and run by the Johnsons, who are renowned for their compassionate horse care, and if it happens to be full moon and low tide when you're there, it's a memorable ride. For info, tel: 082-853-6732. **Struisbaai Harbour** is small and quaint and has colourful fishing boats bobbing within its seawalls. There's always some activity to be seen here, even if it is just the coming and going of seagulls, and it's a good place to absorb the beauty of nature manifesting in the turquoise

swells, frothy waves and tingling ocean smells. At low tide you can see the white sandy bottom and if you take time to meditate on a clear, still day, you might be privileged to see the big stingrays gliding past or even an otter or seal. If you want a sea cruise, contact Piet-Steyn Marais (tel: 079-354-3080), who runs a boat called *Ipitombi*. **Awesome Charters** offers deep-sea fishing and pleasure trips (you may even spot whales if you do a boat trip from May to December). They supply bait and equipment, and you keep your own catch. Contact Anna on tel: 082-870-2783 or visit the website www.awesomecharters.co.za. De Mond Nature Reserve is about 30 kilometres from Struisbaai (see page 18).

When in Struisbaai, hire a bike and cycle to the tip at Agulhas. It's a lovely 6-kilometre ride on a calm day. Ask about bike rentals at Cape Agulhas Tourism (see page 120).

Overnight in Struisbaai

There are lots of accommodation establishments in town, but the Agulhas tourist office has photos and brochures to help you choose. The 3-star **Cape Agulhas Backpackers** is on the right at the first stop in Struisbaai, and offers a variety of accommodation options, from an 8-bed dormitory costing R80 per person per day to R175 per person for a self-catering unit with its own entrance. Double rooms cost R220 and come with down duvets, while a double en suite is R280. This is a vibey, colourful place just 400 metres from the beach and a 10-minute walk to the nearest shop. There's a TV lounge, licensed bar (not open to the public), and the communal kitchen stocks everything from spices to loo paper. Order the meal of the day for R50. Camping costs R50 per person. Pick-up and drop-off in Swellendam by arrangement for around R500 both ways. They offer bicycles and kayak hire, and do harbour trips. For more information, call Stefné on tel: 082-372-3354 or click on www.capeagulhasbackpackers.com. **Harbour Lights** is a 3-star guesthouse with 4 en-suite rooms and a self-catering unit. Rooms have TV, heated towel rails, electric blankets, ceiling fans and hairdryers. The breakfast room and balcony have panoramic sea views, dinner is served every evening, and they're fully licensed. Rates are R150–R230 (bed only) or R170–R450 B&B. For details, call Lydia Brown on tel: 028-435-6053. **Struisbaai Caravan Park** has 248 grassed sites with electricity but there is no shade and hardly a tree in sight. Although totally exposed, some sites are right on the beachfront and there are access gates to the beach for all residents. Rates range from R90 to R140 for a stand of maximum 6 people. To book, tel: 028-435-6820.

Eating out in Struisbaai

On a windless day, treat yourself to fish and chips and a bottle of wine at one of the outdoor tables at **Pelican's Harbour Café**. It's not cheap at around R50 for fish and chips, but the view is as great as the ambience. Also popular are the seafood pan of prawns, hake, calamari, mussels, rice and chips (a mini costs R90 and large R180) and the 12-mussel pot (at R40). The place claims to be licensed to sell abalone. A whole one costs R130 and is served in a creamy sauce with rice, while minced abalone costs R50. Open 10h30–20h00 weekdays and 10h00–22h00 weekends. Call them on tel: 072-742-5824. Alongside is a fresh fish shop if you prefer to cook your own, but the hours depend on how well the fish are biting. **The Bistro on Main** is at number 66 and is open 7 days a week, with an à la carte or a set menu on Sundays. Pop in for a light meal or speciality coffee and confectionary during the day, or join them for a dinner. Open 08h00–22h00 Monday–Saturday and 08h00–17h00 Sunday – tel: 028-435-6651 to book. The only place to eat right 'on' the beach is at **Nostra Pub & Grill** and, because of its location, it tends to get really busy, but is an ideal place for sundowners. They serve pizza, pasta, steak and seafood, and also do takeaways. There's also a pizza takeaway at the back of the 'Struisbaai Mall', and around the corner is **Michael Collins** Irish-themed pub. It's bright red, so you can't really miss it, and if you drink too much, there are doctors' rooms right across the road.

SUURBRAAK

This small village nestles at the base of the Langeberg mountains, 10 kilometres from the N2, between Swellendam and the scenic Tradouw Pass. The London Missionary Society established the place as a mission station in 1812 and it retains an air of peace and wellbeing to this day – so much so that a number of city folk have settled in the community and on smallholdings along the banks of the Buffeljags River. The main road is lined with little traditional cottages and shaded by old oak trees.

Pop into **Paradise Organic**, a restaurant in the main road serving breakfasts and light meals 09h00–16h00 Tuesday–Sunday. Greg and Louis grow the organic produce and every meal is prepared fresh. In summer they also sell organic vegetables and fruit.

SWELLENDAM

Situated at the foot of the majestic Langeberg, Swellendam is the country's third-oldest magisterial district – after Cape Town and Stellenbosch. It was established in about 1746, and today it's one of the best-preserved towns with regards to architecture and history. There are a couple of entrances to the town off the N2, and Voortrek Street (the main street) is several kilometres long and strewn with accommodation and a few restaurants. The eastern entrance takes you down the hill past the Drostdy Museum, over a wee bridge, around the corner past the amazing church, and into the main hubbub of the main street where you'll find retail outlets. However, there are fabulous restaurants and guesthouses off the main street, so make sure you explore the town thoroughly in order not to miss these. Many of the streets are lined with ancient oak trees.

Out and about in Swellendam

The best way to appreciate the history and architecture of the town is to get information on the historical walk from the tourist office. Its details include what's considered one of the finest structures in the district, Auld House, and dozens of others. The most imposing is undoubtedly the **Moederkerk** (Mother Church) in the main street. This is no ordinary church, but an amazing mixture of Gothic, Renaissance, Baroque

WHY VISIT?
- Explore beautifully preserved historical buildings.
- Visit the Bontebok National Park.

WHAT'S WACKY?
- The fairy sanctuary.
- The mountain peaks behind Swellendam are numbered (as in Eenuurkop and Twaalfuurkop) and the locals reckon they can tell the time by looking at the mountains.

WHAT'S WHAT?

The large tourist office is in the main street, opposite the Spar, and has a good range of mostly dusty brochures. Open 09h00–17h00 weekdays and 09h00–13h00 weekends. Tel: 028-514-2770.

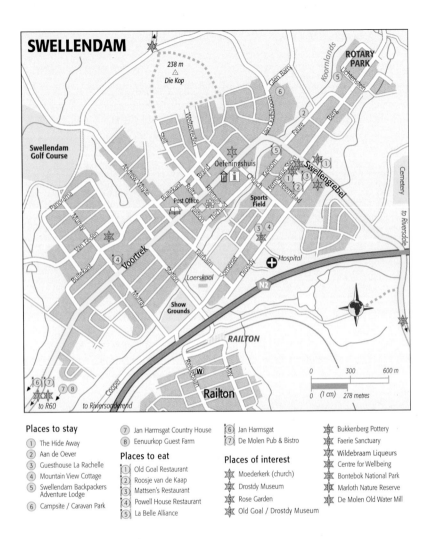

SWELLENDAM

238 m
△
Die Kop

ROTARY PARK

Swellendam Golf Course

Oefeningshuis

Post Office

Sports Field

Swellengrebel

Hospital

N2

Voortrek

Laerskool

Show Grounds

RAILTON

Railton

0   300   600 m

0   (1 cm)   278 metres

to Riversdale

to R60   to Riversonderend

Places to stay

1. The Hide Away
2. Aan de Oever
3. Guesthouse La Rachelle
4. Mountain View Cottage
5. Swellendam Backpackers Adventure Lodge
6. Campsite / Caravan Park
7. Jan Harmsgat Country House
8. Eenuurkop Guest Farm

Places to eat

1. Old Goal Restaurant
2. Roosje van de Kaap
3. Mattsen's Restaurant
4. Powell House Restaurant
5. La Belle Alliance

6. Jan Harmsgat
7. De Molen Pub & Bistro

Places of interest

Moederkerk (church)
Drostdy Museum
Rose Garden
Old Goal / Drostdy Museum

Bukkenberg Pottery
Faerie Sanctuary
Wildebraam Liqueurs
Centre for Wellbeing
Bontebok National Park
Marloth Nature Reserve
De Molen Old Water Mill

and Cape architecture. It was built in 1911 and includes Baroque gables, Gothic windows, an Eastern-styled cupola, and the steeple is a replica of a famous Belgian steeple. Visiting hours are 08h00–13h00 and 14h00–16h00 (Monday, Wednesday and Friday) and 08h00–13h00 (Thursday). Just up the road, off Van Oudtshoorn Street, is a magnificent Victorian house, now

called Schoone Oordt Country House, with incredible cast-iron filigree detail. You can easily spend a couple of days viewing Swellendam's old buildings.

Drostdy Museum in Swellengrebel Street was once home to the original magistrate in 1747 and is dominated by beautiful yellowwood fittings and displays of antique furniture. It's part of the greater museum complex that

Swellendam is famed for its fine accommodation in tranquil settings, like here at The Hideaway B&B.

includes an **Ambagswerf** (tradesmen's yard), rose garden and the **Old Gaol Restaurant**. The mill in the Ambagswerf is still in operation and you can watch wheat being ground between 2 flat stones turned by the waterwheel. On Fridays, the museum bakes 20 loaves of bread in a wood-fired oven, and visitors are welcome to watch the process, from start to sealing the chimney vent with mud, and finally removing the perfect loaves. The Old Gaol Restaurant will also be making *roosterbrood* nearby (see page 211).

When you tire of old buildings, hit some of the galleries and craft shops. Swellendam has attracted creative souls for years, and some have studios that can be visited. **Bukkenberg Pottery**, in Hermanus Steyn Street, is set in a lovely garden that may be explored, but the highlight is their pottery, which includes pots large enough to fit a 6-foot genie

in. For really wacky and wonderful ceramics, make an appointment to visit **Jan du Toit**. He's a renowned potter and painter who's at pains to point out that he has a working studio, not a gallery. Jan's head-and-shoulders vases are famous, and each is a masterpiece. Jan loves people visiting, but you need to phone ahead on tel: 028-514-2955.

Another innovative Swellendam company is **Rain**. You'll find one of the shops at 274 Voortrek Street. Rain produces handmade body and bath commodities and is the brainchild of Bev Missing, who came up with the concept 10 years ago. Today she employs 65 people and has shops all over the country. Her ranges bring the aroma of Africa into your home and include Kalahari Melon, Mongongo Nut and Mafura Butter. If you appreciate the environment and ethical business practices, you'll love this shop. Open

08h00–17h00 weekdays, 09h00–16h00 Saturday, and 11h00–15h00 Sunday and public holidays. Visit the website www.rainafrica.com.

Swellendam is also famous for its fairy sanctuary, the **Continent of Sulina**, much-loved by children and adults alike. It's been going for 18 years and the owners, Ian and Minky Sulina, who call themselves the 'faerie-nuf folk', have created a magical world of wishing wells and winding pathways, hidden creatures and mushroom rings. Mysterious corners lure and entice you into being 5 years old again, and if you have kids you'll score top points for bringing them to this fantasy land. Sulina's has an extraordinary selection of fairy, goblin, elf-like gifts including dragons, mobiles and books. Open 09h00–16h30 Wednesday–Sunday and

Against a backdrop of the Langeberg mountains the mother church in Swellendam peeps above the trees that line the town's streets.

on public holidays (except Christmas Day and New Year) and every day in school holidays, but closed for the month of June. You'll find them in Buitenkant Street, which runs parallel with, and north of, the main road. Call the sanctuary on tel: 028-514-1786.

Wildebraam Liqueurs is on a youngberry farm in the Hermitage Valley, east of town (turn right off the R60 to Ashton). Tasting is a relaxed affair, starting with their range of Marguerite preserves, then come the liqueurs over crushed ice, and finally the credit card comes out so that you can leave with your choice of edibles and drinkables. Their liqueur range includes youngberry, honey, hazelnut and rooibos. You can also visit to pick your own berries for R10 a kilogram from mid-November to mid-December. For details, tel: 028-514-3132 or visit www.wildebraam.co.za.

If you want a relaxing experience, head to **The Centre for Wellbeing** and have one of Jeanette Visser's soothing foot and back massages. She offers a range of therapies, including reflexology, which helps clear the body of any blockages, and aromatherapy. For an appointment, call Jeanette on tel: 028-514-3799 or 083-703-7986 or click on www.mountainviewcottage.co.za.

If the outdoors is your thing then Swellendam's a good base for river-rafting on the Breede River and doing horse or other trails through the forest and fynbos. There are several operators, so ask your host to recommend one, or pick up brochures from the tourist office.

Bordered by the Breede River, the **Bontebok National Park** is no more than 5 kilometres south of Swellendam see pages 14–15; and **Marloth Nature Reserve** is north in the foothills of the mountain (see page 18).

Overnight in Swellendam

A huge selection of overnight stopovers awaits visitors to Swellendam. One establishment even has a rate per pet! The **Hideaway B&B** in Hermanus Steyn Street is 5-star rated, and owner-run by Mark Stevens and Diana Tye. Mark is related to Adin and Sharon Greaves, the previous owners who spent 20 years in the hospitality industry and had perfected the art of hosting to a very high standard – not an easy act to follow, but Mark and Diana run a flawless show and do so effortlessly. The main house is Victorian, and behind it are 5 garden rooms, with separate entrances. Each is equipped with every conceivable facility you might wish for, and some you'd never have thought of. The mini-bar is complimentary, there's homemade shortbread, and emphasis is on service and guest satisfaction. The garden overflows with roses and dahlias in summer and we guarantee that, once ensconced, you will not want to leave. Breakfast is sumptuous to say the least. Rates are R400–R650. For details, tel: 028-514-3316 or visit www.hideawaybb.co.za.

The 4-star **Aan de Oever**, in leafy Faure Street, offers 4 garden and 3 standard rooms with private entrances and en-suite bathrooms. All are stylish, and our spacious loft room came with free-standing bath, double basins, shower, air con, comfy chairs, full DStv and wireless connection. The large

Melktert is still made over hot coals and served at The Old Gaol Restaurant.

grounds offer several places in which to wind down. Lawns are manicured, there's a pool, and the garden runs down to the Koornlands River. There's an abundance of birdlife, and awesome mountain views. Breakfast is a cold buffet and then hot to order. B&B rates are R350–R650 per person. For more info, tel: 028-514-1066 or see the website at www.aandeoever.com.

Guesthouse La Rachelle, at 8 Somerset Street, is a restored Cape vernacular home dating to about 1910. It also has 4 stars and the en-suite units each have a separate entrance off a central courtyard and pool area. It's compact, cosy and within easy walking distance of restaurants and places of interest, to which owners Marius and Rachelle Potgieter will direct you. B&B

rates are seasonal from R300–R450 per person. To book, tel: 028-514-2383 or click on www.larachelle.co.za.

Mountain View Cottage is a cute timber-and-thatch place in Drostdy Street with a fantastic view across the town to the slopes of the Langeberg. It's spotless and comfortable, with 1 double room, a loft with 2 single beds reached by a stepladder, a fully equipped kitchen, and small lounge with fireplace and TV. Self-catering rates are from R170 per person, with a health breakfast for R25 a head. For details, tel: 028-514-3799.

Swellendam Backpackers Adventure Lodge is a colourful, vibey joint 1.5 kilometres east of town in Lichenstein Street. It's been owner-run by Steph for 12 years, and offers all sorts of activities and accommodation. They organise horse riding, hiking, a waterfall walk, nature reserve or national park trips, and even ones down to the coast to see the whales. Dinner options include steak or snoek braai. The dorm, sleeping 8–10, costs R90 per person; double en suites R350 per room; and cabins, sleeping 2–3, cost R200–R290, or camp in the large garden for R50 per person. Booking is essential, so call on tel: 028-514-2648 or check the website www.swellendambackpackers.co.za.

Swellendam Municipal Campsite is surprisingly attractive and well maintained. There's plenty of lawn and abundant trees, including old oaks. Take the main street heading east, fork to the left into Van Oudtshoorn Street, drive over the hill and down to the right into Glen Barry Road – and it's on your right. It also has thatched chalets, but check the facilities before booking in. Rates are R140 to camp, plus R25 for power; chalets for 4 people cost around R400, plus a bedding fee of R25 per person. For info, tel: 028-514-2705.

We have two favourite farmstays. If possible, don't miss spending a night at the 4-star **Jan Harmsgat Country House**, overlooked by the Langeberg about 22 kilometres north of Swellendam on the tarred R60. The 680-hectare farm, founded in 1723, is surrounded by olive, nut and citrus orchards, and has an interesting history. The main lounge and dining room is a 25-metre-long barn cellar that once belonged to Hermanus Steyn, who proclaimed the Independent Republic of Swellendam in 1795, and farmed wine here. You will dine on sublime food prepared by Judi's chef, Lena. Much of the fresh produce used is organically grown on the farm, and Brin is a member of La Confrérie des Chevaliers du Tastevin, so you can be assured of an excellent wine list. The guest rooms in old slave quarters are large and come with wonky 1-metre-thick walls, and small windows that add to the atmosphere. They adjoin a lounge and library, and the pool's nearby. Our voluminous suite was tucked beneath the thatch in the barn-cellar loft, and from our bed we looked straight through the door at the mountains. Guests are welcome to explore the farm and wander across the road to the dairy where Paul, the cheese-maker, produces his fabulous farm cheese. In fact, Paul's cheese is so good, he struggles to keep up with demand. Jan Harmsgat is an establishment that sets its own standard of professionalism and attention to detail. They're also accredited by Fair Trade in Tourism South Africa. Rates are R440–R1 030 per person, depending on room and season. To book, tel: 023-616-3407 or click on www.jhghouse.com.

Our other favourite is **Eenuurkop Guest Farm**. Drive 3.4 kilometres along the R60 towards Ashton, turn right and travel 1.2 kilometres along a good gravel road, where you'll be met by the owners, Jeremy and Tersia Puren. Their 110-hectare farm is situated in the rolling green foothills of the mountains beneath Eenuurkop, and they have 2 delightful guest cottages in a setting so inviting you could stay for a year! The cottages are styled in keeping with the history of the area (the floor tiles in the smaller cottage, which sleeps 2, are from an old church roof). The larger cottage sleeps 8 in 2 doubles, and 2 double-bunk beds, and has a loo with a stunning view. Self-catering rates are R600 for the small cottage, R800 for the larger cottage. An optional extra is to request breakfast ingredients, which are put in your fridge. To book, tel: 028-514-1442 or see the website at www. eenuurkop.co.za.

Eating out in Swellendam

This is a tricky one because there are so many great restaurants, some of which have been around for years and are synonymous with Swellendam, such as **The Old Gaol Restaurant**. It's housed in what was indeed the old jail, built in the mid-1700s, and Brin and Judi Rebstein of Jan Harmsgat Country House established the restaurant in 2001. Once profitable, they offered their staff a 30% equity shareholding and today the Old Gaol is a highly successful empowerment project born of a private-sector initiative. Their specialities include *roosterkoek* and

Throughout the Overberg, labourers' cottages such as this one dot the rolling landscape.

A bontebok stands in a patch of beige grass in the Bontebok National Park near Swellendam.

traditional *melktert* baked in a copper pan over coals, old-fashioned chicken pie, authentic Cape curries … the list is long, very long. Baking is done in the Ambagswerf of the Drostdy Museum, and you're welcome to watch. They make 'slow food' using original methods of preparation wherever possible. Try the *roosterkoek* with Jan Harmsgat cheese – it's excellent. Tables are in several rooms, and in a large courtyard that's part of the Drostdy Museum complex. Not surprisingly, they've won several prestigious awards. At the time of writing, the authorities were trying to force the partners' hands and move them out of these premises. However, they'll remain in the old jail for now and, whatever happens in the future, you can be assured they'll still be dishing up fabulous meals. Open 08h00–17h00 daily; dinner is served in high season (October–April) from 18h30 until late Tuesday–Saturday. To book, tel: 028-514-3847.

Roosje van de Kaap, at 5 Drostdy Street, is another Swellies institution. Owner, Elsabet, is internationally renowned for her fillet, which she sources and handpicks. It comes with porcini mushroom sauce made from fungi picked on the mountain slopes in the area. Then there's the chicken, deboned and marinated for 24 hours, then put into a wood-burning oven and served with a watercress sauce. The pizza and ostrich are just as good. Breakfast is served 08h00–10h00, dinner from 19h00 until late. For bookings, tel: 028-514-3001 or click on www.roosjevandekaap.com.

Mattsen's Restaurant, at 25 Swellengrebel Street, is a steak-eater's paradise. The owners, Alize and Herman, are finicky about their meat and have it aged in a special facility and then cut it to order. Steaks are wet-cured for 28 days, and the menu gives masses of info on cuts and preparations. There is a long list of cuts, sauces, specialities and sizes up to

750 grams! Your barman will undoubtedly be Cliffie, who's a Swellendam icon. He's been in the trade for decades and is known for his impeccable service. To book, tel: 028-514-2715.

Powell House Restaurant, at 113 Voortrek Street, is owner-run by Alan and Derrick, the attentive hosts, and Cheryl, who's a wizard in the kitchen. They have an interesting menu that includes a springbok carpaccio starter, and a signature dish of springbok in a prickly pear and juniper berry jus. Open for breakfast, lunch and dinner. For details, tel: 028-514-3243.

La Belle Alliance, at 1 Swellengrebel Street, is a restaurant and tea garden on the banks of the Koornland River, with tables indoors or beneath a canopy of trees. If you're a keen birder, there's a bird list of the week's sightings. See how many matches you can make between mouthfuls. Open daily 08h00–17h00 in holidays, otherwise 09h00–17h00.

For really good Cape Malay food, **Manna Heaven** in the main street is a small shop selling eat-in or takeaway fare. People come from far to eat Karen's roti and curry, vetkoek and mince, samoosas and spring rolls.

If you want to dine in an old water mill, **De Molen Pub & Bistro** is 5 kilometres from town on the R60 to Ashton. Roger and Jean Beaumont serve hearty bistro-type dishes in this really atmospheric building, that's a national monument, and will regale you with stories from behind the bar. Make sure to ask about their daily specials. Open 10h00–15h00 Tuesday–Sunday, and at night on booking. For more info, tel: 028-514-1695 or 076-294-2145.

There's no quaint pub in town, so if you just want to watch the passing traffic, sit on the stoep at **Full Stop** in the main street. Nearby is **The Goose & Bear**, which is not the English pub its name suggests but a place to quench the thirst none-the-less.

VILLIERSDORP

Villiersdorp lies in the northwest, tucked between the folds of the Riviersonderend (or Sonderend) mountains and the country's seventh-largest dam, Theewaterskloof Dam. It services the wine and fruit farms in the area and, at first glance, it's an ordinary modern-day town with an unassuming main street – but venture into the residential area and it's a whole different story. The lower part of town rests peacefully under several species of old trees, and grand old houses and quaint cottages neighbour more modern ones. Oaks are numerous: silky oaks, pin oaks, standard oaks and human okes.

Out and about in Villiersdorp

The **Tractor Museum** is a highlight. It's behind Kelkiewyn and, even if you're not into tractors, there are wonderful examples reflecting the progress made in farming machinery. Rows of gleaming vintages show off their bright colours, while a few still sport the grease, oil and soil of their toil. Articles proudly displayed report on a 2002 record-breaking event in which the greatest number of tractors (786) ploughed a field simultaneously. Get keys to the museum from the tourist office alongside.

Dale & Mel Elliott Art Gallery and Studios is just around the corner from the tractor museum and is well worth a visit. If you're keen to learn to paint, they've been in the art workshop and painting holiday business for over 25 years and have had over 2 000 people join their courses, many doing advanced training. Dale's completed over 15 000 paintings in the past 30 years, and has a very long list of impressive commissions and achievements to his name. His wife, Janny, runs the business, and they were recently joined by their son, Mel, who's also a painter. They also sell art supplies. For more details, tel: 028-840-2927 or click on www.daleelliott.co.za.

For a taste of rural life, drive out to **Elandskloof Valley** and **Kaaimansgat**.

The turnoff is about 1.5 kilometres out on the R43 to Worcester, and is signposted. The road winds ever deeper into the mountains through orchards into a hidden enclave where a farm named High Noon stands. Keep a lookout for gun-slinging cowboys. The area is popular with outdoors enthusiasts who do everything from cliff-jumping to kloofing here, but you can just take a slow drive and enjoy the scenery. The 2–3 rated **Kroonland 4x4 Trail** is out here and can be done in your own vehicle, but is not recommended in winter. It's 13 kilometres long through fabulous fynbos and valley scenery, and there's an overnight mountain campsite. The proprietors also offer a **Mountain & Flower Tour** on the back of a bakkie or in a 20-seater open vehicle. Reservations are essential, so tel: 028-840-1979.

Stattyn wine farm is also off the R43, and has a rather convoluted claim to fame with the same family living full time on the farm for 8 generations. If you arrange in advance, you can visit the mill and original farmhouse that dates back to 1777 and, if you're a group, book ahead for a light meal and vineyard tour. Open for wine tasting 09h00–17h00 weekdays and 10h00–13h00 Saturdays. On the other side of town is the **Theewater Sports and Yacht Club**, a huge waterside property with various facilities. Out of season, it's peaceful, but in summer holidays it's frenetic. You have to buy a temporary membership permit at the gate, and this allows you to use the facilities and campsite. There's a strict membership code, so this is the only way you'll get in. If the gate isn't manned, there's a radio

Villiersdorp's Tractor Museum displays well-preserved examples of farming machines.

at the guard's hut for visitors to call the office. The wooden clubhouse overlooks the water and is open on weekends and more frequently over holidays. Get your angling licence from the post office, or from the CapeNature office on the road from Grabouw. In quieter times, the bird watching can be good, and you should see lots of aquatic waders. The dam is a favourite place for windsurfing, sailing, and water-skiing, and you can fish for black bass and carp. The access fee is R20 per person per day, plus a R20 craft fee for canoes, windsurfers and kitesurfers, and R25 for boats. For further info, call Lise or Leon on tel: 028-840-1334 during office hours.

Golfers will find a 9-hole golf course at the **Theewaters Country Club** 7 kilometres along the R43 to Caledon, and if that's not enough of a leg stretch, get info from tourism on various hikes and places to mountain bike.

Overnight in Villiersdorp
Vredelust B&B and Self-Catering offers everything you could need – and

at a reasonable price. It's a little up the hill, in Van Riebeeck Street, and within walking distance of the town centre and restaurants. There are 4 small open-plan self-catering units that sleep 2, with an option for an extra bed for children, and a fully equipped kitchenette; plus 3 en-suite B&B rooms in the main house. Rates are from R200 per person sharing, with breakfast an additional R45 a head. Call Paddy Dall on tel: 028-840-1735 or 082-779-4794 or visit www.vredelust. com. **Misty Mountain** self-catering accommodation is further up the hill, in Gunter Street, and has 2 bachelor flats for 2 people each. Both have good views over the town, valley and mountains. Doubles cost R300–R350. For details, tel: 028-840-1306 or click on www.misty-mountain.co.za. There are also several upmarket B&Bs in town, such as **Die Kunshuis** (tel: 083-312-1476), but out of town our favourite is **Rouxwil Country House** (see page 138) and **Rusty Gate Farm**. The latter is a 200-hecatre mountain fynbos farm bordering the Riviersonderend Mountain Reserve and the hillsides here are thickly covered in proteas. There are 5 well-equipped cottages, each sleeping 4. There are several dams on the farm where you can fish for trophy-sized trout on a catch-and-release basis; and canoes and bikes are available for the use of guests. Part of a large warehouse has been converted into a games room with a pool table, dartboard, table soccer (when last did you see one of those?) and board games. The farm is 25 kilometres from both Villiersdorp and Greyton, and there's no cellphone reception, TV or radio. Pure bliss! Rates are seasonal, from

R700–R1 300 per cottage. For details, tel: 021-685-0901 or visit the website at www.rustygate.co.za.

Campers can head to the **Theewater Sports Club** on the dam. You don't need to make a reservation because it's an enormous campsite but, to keep noise pollution to a minimum, only 7 stands have electricity. There are a few lines of trees with tables and braai places. Sites cost R60 per night for a maximum of 6 people (R120 with electricity), plus R20 per person per day 'Public Access' fee. For details, tel: 028-840-1334.

Eating out in Villiersdorp

Laventelbos, at 28 Main Street, is in an atmospheric old house offering unpretentious home cooking and good value for money. It's run by Betsie Swart, who took over in November 2007 and is as cute as the décor. The menu features a good variety, from salads to snails to steaks, seafood and schnitzels. Every second Wednesday, there's a themed meal, e.g. Italian. Betsie's fillet is very popular and is locally sourced, as is the coffee she serves. The restaurant's usually full of fresh roses, thanks to the 600-odd bushes on the owners' farm. Open 08h00 until late Monday–Saturday, and 09h00–15h00 for Sunday lunch. **Die Ou Meul Restaurant**, at 39 Main Street, sells 17 different types of pizza or you can build your own. Tables are indoors or on the back patio, and there's a pub upstairs that's open in the evenings. Open 09h00–22h30 Tuesday–Saturday and 10h00–16h00 Sunday. **Kelkiewyn** at the wine shop has seating outside on the lawn or alongside the fireplace for chilly days. They serve light meals

and slow food, and Monday–Friday they have a 'meal of the day', such as curry and rice, pickled fish or chicken teriyaki. Book ahead for their Sunday buffet on tel: 028-840-1151. **Café de Gallerie** in the main street does breakfasts and lunches 08h00–17h00 Monday–Friday and Saturday mornings, with 'speciality dinners' on Friday nights. For info, tel: 028-840-1854. There's some hype about the new **Dagbreek Museum and Restaurant** that's the brainchild of 3 partners who have big plans for Villiersdorp. Open Thursday–Saturday for supper, and Saturday–Sunday for breakfast and lunch as well.

WITSAND AND PORT BEAUFORT

To a newcomer, it's not immediately evident that Port Beaufort and Witsand are two distinctly individual settlements situated at the mouth of the Breede River. Urban sprawl has merged them, but the former is where all the history lies.

The Barry family plays a major role in Port Beaufort's history, and the Barry descendants still live here today. Having fallen in love with a local girl and the Overberg region she lived in, Londoner Joseph Barry moved here in 1819. He secured the tender for transporting rice and grain by boat to Port Beaufort, and opened a small trading store in 1823. The business expanded, he moved to Swellendam, and his nephew took over. Misfortune saw the business go bankrupt in 1827, but Joseph forged ahead and by 1834 his firm, Barry & Nephews, was formed. So successful was this company that Port Beaufort was declared an open port in 1841, and by the end of the 1850s there were stores all over the region and branches in Cape Town and London. One of his descendants, Alfred John Barry, and his wife, Valerie, built The Lucky Strike Botel here in 1971. It's now the Breede River Lodge. Their second daughter, Lorraine, is a fifth-generation Barry and today runs Barry's Holiday Accommodation along with her husband.

Out and about in Witsand

Witsand claims to have the largest concentration of southern right whales on the South African coast between May and November. It's known as the Whale Nursery of South Africa, and each October an aerial survey is done by the Mammal Institute of South Africa. The 2008 count recorded the highest numbers ever, with 62 cow/calf pairs and 41 adults, totalling 165 whales. You can see the whales from the beach but the area is a conservancy so whale-watching boat trips are not allowed and boats are warned to be extremely cautious of colliding with whales.

The beaches at Witsand are those of clean white sands, and are safe for walking and swimming if you take the usual precautions, and if you have small children there are also the calmer waters of the mouth and river. The main swimming beach is around Hoonkers Restaurant, but be aware that there's a big hole here so don't go in deep. There's also a tidal pool in front of the coastal caravan park next to Dune Park, but it's difficult to access unless you walk along the beach. Winters are mild and on a windless day it's idyllic to walk eastwards for several kilometres along the beach.

Surfing is good here, and windsurfing, kitesurfing, kiteboarding and sailing are popular on the river, especially in summer when the wind picks up. You can canoe and do river cruises but water-skiing is not allowed.

The Breede River is one of the country's widest and deepest rivers, and the area around Port Beaufort and Witsand is part of the **Lower Breede River Conservancy** – an area from the mouth to a few kilometres past Malgas (35-plus kilometres) and the speed restriction is 16 kilometres per hour. There are numerous laws to be followed, and it's patrolled by professional rangers, so get their leaflet if you plan to take to the river (but remember that jetskis are strictly not allowed on the river).

Estuary fishing in the Breede River, with its tidal action reaching 60 kilometres upstream, is some of the best in the country, and the mouth is also regarded as a top location. Enthusiasts can also rock- and deep-sea fish, and fly-fishing is done either from the river's edge or the sand banks of the estuary.

Bird watching along the river is spectacular, with about 260 species to be seen (see Mudlark on page 180). Nature lovers should get the *Walks in Witsand* map from André or Lorraine at the reception for Barry's Holiday Accommodation. It details 8 walks, their duration and features, and one of the perks of staying with them is that they've done all these walks and can tell you exactly what they're like.

If golf's your thing and you're staying at **Barry's Holiday Accommodation**, owner André Martin does golf tours to

South Africa's national flower, the protea, in full spring bloom above the Breede River.

the quaint 9-hole country courses of Heidelberg, Riversdale and Swellendam. He's a 'senior amateur provincial player', so he knows his stuff – call him on tel: 082-713-3354. **Westfield Holiday Farm**, just outside of Port Beaufort has a guided 4x4 nature trail. Call Guy or Lorraine Moodie on tel: 028-537-1911. **Ostrich Trails** has a new eco 4x4 trail and offers various other activities. Call Piet or Janet Uys on tel: 028-537-1942.

Overnight in Witsand

Barry's Holiday Accommodation is owner-run by Lorraine and André Martin and offers a variety of accredited houses, apartments, flats and B&Bs all over Witsand and Port Beaufort. They're an invaluable source of information on the area, and can accommodate groups of 2–12 people (children welcome). All properties are of a high standard, with some graded 3 stars. All requirements, from budget, through family, to up-market, are catered for; some properties have wheelchair access, and some allow pets. Their 3-star **Barrymore** is a 3-bedroom, 3-bathroom, first-floor apartment that has fantastic views of the Breede River, the mouth and sea beyond. They also offer a backpacker service, with dorm rooms for R120 per person, doubles for R270 and singles at R180. Rates for other accommodations start at R150 per person sharing, but depend on the number of people and season, for example. Contact Lorraine, who'll quote and send you a map showing the location of each property, on tel: 028-537-1717 or visit www.witsand.co.za. **Whale Watchers Inn B&B** is one street from the beach, and offers sea-facing rooms from R320 per person, and non-sea-facing from R280. They also have self-catering units, and a garden cottage, and prices vary depending on number of people – for details, tel: 028-537-1825 or click on www.whalewatchersinn.com. **The Breede River Lodge** is on the river mouth and has a private harbour. It provides 4-star self-catering accommodation, as well as a 3-star hotel. For more info, tel: 028-537-1631 or visit www.breederiverlodge.co.za. The **Witsand Caravan Park** is run by Tollie and Twinkle (seriously, those are their names). It's small and, although not on the seaside, is within walking distance of the beach. A few trees shelter electrified sites. There is a strict rule of no quad bikes or pets. Rates are R135–R180 for a maximum of 6 people, depending on the season. For details, tel: 028-537-1627.

If you want to stay on a farm in the area, the **Waterkloof Guest House** lies on the R324, about 18 kilometres from Malgas and 15 kilometres from Witsand. It's a 1 700-hectare working farm, said to be one of the finest commercial farms in the district, and is owned by Hannes and Christine Uys, who have a 4-star full-board guesthouse. The farm has been in the Uys family for 7 generations, and today Hannes farms with merino sheep, Nguni cattle and a couple of thousand ostriches. Guests are invited to accompany him on a guided tour of the farm and, in season, you can watch ostriches breeding, and help collect eggs. Christine serves traditional South African meals, such as *bobotie* (with ostrich mince), and they enjoy a braai with their guests. You may be served deer, which they farm and believe is best of all their home-grown produce. B&B rates are from R300–R420, and dinner around R180 a head (including wine). Their renovated self-catering cottage is a few kilometres from the house. It was built by Hannes' great-great-grandfather, and has 2 bedrooms and a large front stoep with fabulous views over the fields. Rates, including a light breakfast, are R250–R350 per person. For details, tel: 028-722-1811 or 083-270-2348 or click on www.waterkloofguesthouse.co.za.

Eating out in Witsand

The Whalers' Grill, at the Sands Centre, is getting a good name among the locals. They're open 10h30–21h00 and serve breakfast, light eats, pizzas, salads and grills. The fully licensed bar is open later at night but closed during peak restaurant hours (18h00–21h00) to ensure diners have a quiet meal. Manager-chef Stephen makes great pizza and has a special every Thursday

> ## The currents around
> Witsand are strong, particularly at spring tide, and the wind on the river can make the waters dangerously rough. Craft have been swamped and passengers drowned. Be aware of weather reports and tides, and carry the compulsory safety equipment.

The small boat harbour on the Breede River at Port Beaufort.

night (his ribs are very popular). After the restaurant's busy hours, the venue is used for dancing by the younger crowd. **Di Mond** is across the way from Whalers' and offers fish and chips, and other meals. They do takeaways, and their curry vetkoek made on Fridays is a hit. Open daily from 09h00, and closing time depends on the season. At the Breede River Lodge, **The Fisherman's Pub** is open 11h00–22h00, and serves pub lunches until 16h00. The lodge's **Estuary Restaurant** does breakfasts, light lunches and has an à la carte evening menu that leans towards locally caught fish. According to the locals, the Sunday carvery is good value for money, so book in advance.

WOLVENGAT

This tiny pinpoint on the map really is a case of 'blink and you'll miss it'. We would have driven straight through if we'd not spotted the cement statues of pilgrims in flowing robes, staffs in hand, standing deep in conversation in a garden. By the time you visit Wolvengat, the pilgrims may be adorning a path up a koppie somewhere near Swellendam. Pilgrims or not, pop into **De Roubaix Gallery** and have a chat with Wim, who created these statues, and his wife Tina, who's also an artist. Much of Wim's work has a unique style inspired by the rock art of the San in the Drakensberg; and he's deviated from the standard rectangular canvas, preferring circular creations set in frames he makes himself. Call them on tel: 028-482-1773. Another artist you may want to visit is **Kali Griffin**, who does cloth painting and makes cheeses. Call Kali on tel: 028-482-1949.

The only place to buy supplies or fuel in the tiny hamlet of Wolvengat is at Jenny's Store.

Index

Other titles in this series...